WITHDRAWN
UTSA LIBRARIES

Archival Information
How to Find It, How to Use It

Archival Information
How to Find It, How to Use It

Edited by
Steven Fisher

GREENWOOD PRESS
Westport, Connecticut • London

Library of Congress Cataloging-in-Publication Data

Archival Information / edited by Steven Fisher.
       p. cm.— (How to find it, how to use it)
  Includes bibliographical references and index.
  ISBN 1-57356-389-7 (alk. paper)
  1. Archives—United States—Handbooks, manuals, etc.
I. Fisher, Steven, 1951–
II. Series
CD3021.A38   2004
027.073—dc22   2003060051

British Library Cataloguing in Publication Data is available.

Copyright © 2004 by Steven Fisher

All rights reserved. No portion of this book may be
reproduced, by any process or technique, without the
express written consent of the publisher.

Library of Congress Catalog Card Number: 2003060051

ISBN: 1–57356–389–7

First published in 2004

Greenwood Press, 88 Post Road West, Westport, CT 06881
An imprint of Greenwood Publishing Group, Inc.
www.greenwood.com

Printed in the United States of America

∞™

The paper used in this book complies with the
Permanent Paper Standard issued by the National
Information Standards Organization (Z39.48–1984).

10 9 8 7 6 5 4 3 2 1

Library
University of Texas
at San Antonio

For Navis, Paul, and Barbara

Contents

Introduction

While much has been written about archives and archival collections, the vast majority consists of professional literature aimed at the archival community itself. What remains tends to focus on specific collections, the archives of a particular subject, or a particular collecting institution. This book is aimed at the general researcher who finds the need to conduct archival research. The book is divided into chapters covering popular research subject areas written by an archival authority for that particular field of study. The best sources for that particular subject are covered, as are the major libraries, museums, and historical societies collecting in that field.

THE DIGITAL AGE

"It's all on the Internet" is an expression one hears quite often these days, mostly from high school students and college undergraduates. The Internet has made finding information on a wide range of topics faster and easier than ever before. Unfortunately, not all information is on the Internet, and some never will be. In no area of research is this more true than in the area of unique primary sources.

The Internet has been of great assistance in allowing archival repositories to share more information about their holdings than ever before. The majority of the larger archives now have their own Web presence, giving researchers contact information, hours of service, and descriptions of collections. Few, however, have had the time or means necessary to digitize the majority of their collections. This is understandable when one considers that digitization is labor-intensive and that collections may run into thousands of pages. Most collections that have been digitized have been done so via grant dollars, rather than general operating funds.

LIBRARIES AND ARCHIVES

Most of us grow up using libraries. The local public library is familiar in communities large and small, urban and rural. Many of us first use libraries as children in the Juvenile section, and later we browse the current best sellers, find a how-to book, or research a particular topic from encyclopedias and other popular reference sources. For those familiar with using libraries as a source of information, finding and using archival information for the first time may be a challenge. Most library materials are published materials, also known as secondary sources, while most archival material is unique, referred to as primary sources. Library materials are usually duplicated in other libraries, while archival material is not. Library material, if lost, is usually replaceable. Archival material, because it is unique, is usually not replaceable.

While we are free to browse through most library material, archival material is kept in secured areas away from the public and usually may not be browsed. Archival information may sometimes be found in public libraries, but more often it is located in governmental agencies, historical societies, museums, or academic libraries. Archival material originating from one source may be scattered throughout the United States or around the world. Consider the case of novelist James Michener. A prolific writer, Michener produced dozens of works that sold millions of copies. To research his novels he traveled extensively and often left his research material wherever he had done the research. Hence Michener papers may be found at the Library of Congress, Swarthmore College, the University of Alaska, the University of Hawaii, the University of Miami Florida, the University of Northern Colorado, the University of Pennsylvania, and the University of Texas. For someone doing research on Michener, this presents a definite challenge. Michener is an extreme example, but he illustrates the fugitive nature of archival material.

It follows that because archival information is unique, it tends to be found in only one physical location. Information about a particular library's holdings was traditionally found in a paper card catalog and now is found in the online public access catalog (PAC), and national databases document the vast majority of printed material. Guides and indexes to archival information, on the other hand, are usually unpublished or available only in-house and may be difficult to locate. Archives often operate with smaller staffs and shorter hours than do libraries, or by appointment only.

WHAT ARE ARCHIVES?

To understand archives one must first understand records. Simply put, a record is any document that contains information. Archives are those records that have been determined to be of enduring value, perhaps only five percent of all created records. This enduring value may be based upon historical, legal, or administrative factors. Like published material, archival material comes in a variety of formats. The most common format is still paper (despite the digital revolution), but archives can also be photographs, film, videocassettes, or computer disks. The term archives may itself be confusing because it refers not only to records of enduring value but also may refer to a specific department within a larger institution. ("That is located in the Archives.")

There are several types of archives. An institutional archives is one that collects only material generated in-house, such as a corporate archives. A collecting archives collects material based on a subject or theme, such as a military archives. Many archives are a combination of these two types.

ARCHIVAL TERMINOLOGY

Like most professionals, archivists have a select vocabulary to describe various functions. It is helpful for the researcher to have a basic understanding of some of the terms commonly used by archivists.

Accession: an acquisition, a new collection coming into the archives. To accession a collection means to take legal and physical custody.
Processing: the act of arranging and describing a collection to make it usable for researchers. Arranging and describing collections are two of the primary responsibilities of archivists.
Finding Aid: a guide, an index, or an inventory of a collection, usually describing it at a file folder level. Finding aids may or may not be published.

CONTACTING THE ARCHIVES

Before contacting an archival institution, the researcher must first determine if it is in fact archival material that is really needed. It is best to fully exhaust all secondary sources in your subject area before turning to primary materials. This serves two purposes. First of all, the researcher may find that the needed information is available in secondary sources and archival research is unnecessary.

Secondly, a familiarity with published materials in a given subject area makes the use of archival materials much easier. If the researcher is aware of key names and dates, less time must be spent navigating entire archival collections. Information about a particular research subject may be found in published books, periodicals, and newspapers, as well as Web sites. Checking bibliographies will lead to further published sources.

If the researcher finds that archival material will be needed, the next step is locating primary sources. Much of this book will be devoted to providing guidance on finding the location of archival material on a wide range of subjects. Once material has been located, the researcher may request a copy of a finding aid to the particular collection if one is not available online. Once the finding aid is reviewed, the next decision for the researcher is whether an actual trip to the archives is necessary. It is possible that the staff of a particular repository may be able to answer simple requests for information by mail, e-mail, fax, or phone. Some material may be available on microfilm, through interlibrary loan, or may be photocopied and mailed by archives staff if the quantity is reasonable.

Some archives set a time limit, perhaps fifteen minutes to a half-hour, that they will research a particular question for free. Questions taking longer than that may incur a staff fee or the researcher may be referred to an independent fee-based researcher for help. Many archives maintain lists of independent researchers who perform this service. Independent researchers may also be utilized if the remote location of the archives makes a trip impractical.

If the researcher is able to make a trip to the archives, it is always best to first phone or write ahead. As previously mentioned, archives often have irregular hours and small staffs. Many archives are open weekdays only and rarely in the evening, though there are exceptions. Fortunately, technology has made archival institutions more accessible. Many archives may be contacted not only by phone or mail, but also by fax or e-mail. This book contains contact information for a large number of archival repositories. Making an appointment ahead of time not only assures access but also allows staff to retrieve any materials that may be stored off-site if necessary.

ARCHIVAL ETIQUETTE

When visiting an archives, the researcher will be presented with a list of rules and regulations that may seem alien to those only familiar with the more traditional library setting. The researcher will probably be asked to fill out a user form with his or her name, address, phone number, the purpose of the visit, and material requested. A driver's license or other form of identification may be requested. While this may seem to the uninitiated an unnecessary invasion of privacy, it is simply standard practice. If an item is later missing or damaged, it is useful for archives staff to know who last used it. Information forms are also used for statistical purposes, tracking the time of day when collections are most heavily used, or what types of materials are being requested most frequently. This will help the archives staff in better serving future users.

While in a typical library browsing is the norm, archival material is usually closed-access and must be retrieved by staff. Material may not leave the area, and researchers will usually find that they are watched while using archival material. This should not be taken as a personal affront, as it is standard practice to ensure the preservation of unique materials.

RULES AND REGULATIONS

Besides filling out a form, the researcher will often be asked to read a copy of local guidelines for the use of archival material. Typical rules and regulations may include:

No coats, briefcases, or backpacks at the reading table. This is a security measure to prevent theft of manuscript material. You may usually check these items with the staff when entering the reading room area.
No pens—pencil only. This is to prevent damage to the materials.
No hand-held scanners. This serves two purposes. It prevents any potential damage to materials and also prevents extensive copying that may violate copyright.

PHOTOCOPYING

Photocopying is permitted in most archival institutions, within limits and depending upon the particular restrictions of the collection. Archives staff will usually perform the copying, and for this reason photocopy charges may be expensive—fifty cents to one dollar is not uncommon. Some collections may be restricted from copying, because the collection is fragile or restricted in some way.

COPYRIGHT

Finding archival material is one thing; being able to use it is another. The user of archival material must be especially aware of copyright law. It is a common misunderstanding that only published works are covered under copyright law, but this is not the case. The current copyright law of the United States, known as Title 17, U.S. Code, took effect on January 1, 1978. It protects both published and unpublished material. Copyright is the right given to an author or creator to:

1. Reproduce.
2. Prepare derivative works based upon the original work.
3. Distribute copies by sale, lease, or rent.
4. Publicly perform (music, drama, dance, etc.).
5. Display the work.

Copyright law, however, does not apply to everything. Some things are not protected. These include:

1. Titles
2. Names
3. Short phrases
4. Slogans
5. Ideas
6. Procedures
7. Methods
8. Systems and processes
9. Concepts

The concept of *fair use* also limits copyright. Fair use allows for the use of copyrighted material for:

1. Criticism
2. Comment
3. News reporting
4. Teaching
5. Scholarship or research
6. Preservation

Up until the passage of new copyright legislation in 1976, unpublished material was not subject to the same copyright protection as published material was unless it was registered in the copyright office. This is no longer the case. Material is now considered to be subject to copyright when it is "fixed" by writing, filming, creating a work of art, and so on. Web pages are covered by copyright. Copyright remains in force for the life of the author plus seventy years.

When thinking of copyright in terms of archival material, it is important to always keep in mind that physical ownership and intellectual ownership are two separate things. Today, when a collection is acquired by an archival repository, copyright is usually transferred along with the physical custody of the material; however, this was not always the case in the past, and many archivists now spend much time and effort trying to track down individuals who donated material long ago to acquire copyright. Unless the deed of gift specifically transferred copyright to the archives, it remains with the donor. This is not so much an issue with institutional archives, such as corporate archives that mainly collect material generated in-house, but it is an issue for collecting repositories, such historical societies. Archival material generated by governmental agencies is usually not subject to copyright and may be freely used. Photographs may be especially tricky, because there is the issue not only of the rights of the photographer but also of the persons photographed, who may have to give permission for photos to be used. Photographs of public figures, such as politicians or entertainers, are exempted from this rule.

Many collection level descriptions of collections and finding aids to particular collections will describe copyright status, but not always. The archivist will discuss with the researcher any issues of copyright that may apply to the collection being requested. Copyright may be waived by the archives or by the original donor if it was not waived at the time the collection was donated to the institution. How the collection is to be used is the critical factor.

FEES

If the researcher seeks material that is to be used for a commercial publication or for profit, there may be a use fee charged by the archives. These fees usually pertain to photographs or works of art, and are often referred to as commercial service fees. Whether the reproduction is for a book, magazine, newspaper, poster, postcard, videotape, or motion picture, fees are usually based on the number of copies being produced. For example, fees may be larger for mass-market book publication than they would be for smaller academic press runs. Fees are also larger for commercially produced, national film or television projects than they would be for smaller local productions. Typically these fees range from $10 to $150.

For an excellent introduction to archives and archival procedures, visit the National Archives of Canada Web site at http://www.archives.ca/04/ 0416_e.html.

Though Canadian in origin, the information given applies to researchers of material found in any country.

CHAPTER 1
American Governmental Archives

Faye Phillips

Governmental records in the United States of America are created at four levels: the national/federal, the state, the county, and the municipal/city. Of the millions of records created each year by these governments, approximately one-third are deemed archival. These archival records are acquired by, preserved, and made accessible to the public by archival institutions administered by agencies of the four levels of government. A brief review of the holdings of federal, state, and local government archives, as well as contact information, is included in this chapter. Some governmental and agencies records have been acquired over time by nongovernment archives. These are not discussed in this chapter.

NATIONAL ARCHIVES AND RECORDS ADMINISTRATION

The National Archives and Records Administration (NARA) of the United States was formed in 1934 for the purpose of appraising, arranging and describing, making available for research, and preserving the records of the agencies of the U.S. government from its inception to the present.

NARA's published vision and mission statements are:

Vision: The National Archives is not a dusty hoard of ancient history. It is a public trust on which our democracy depends. It enables people to inspect for themselves the record of what government has done. It enables officials and agencies to review their actions and helps citizens hold them accountable. It ensures continuing access to essential evidence that documents: the rights of American citizens, the actions of federal officials, and the national experience. To be effective, we at NARA must do the following: deter-

mine what evidence is essential for such documentation; ensure that government creates such evidence; make it easy for users to access that evidence regardless of where it is, where they are, for as long as needed; find technologies, techniques, and partners world-wide that can help improve service and hold down cost; and help staff members continuously expand their capability to make the changes necessary to realize the vision. **Mission:** NARA ensures, for the citizen and the public servant, for the President and for the Congress and the Courts, ready access to essential evidence. http://www.archives.gov/about_us/vision_mission_values.html

NARA contains the government records of federal agencies, Congress, federal courts, executive agencies, and presidential offices. These records are housed in a number of facilities throughout the country. The historic National Archives Building at 700 Pennsylvania Avenue NW in downtown Washington, D.C., (between Seventh Street and Ninth Street) is the home to the Rotunda Exhibit Hall, which contains the Charters of Freedom: the original manuscript copies of the Declaration of Independence, 1776, and the United States Constitution, 1787. See http://www.archives.gov/exhibit_hall/charters_of_freedom/declaration/declaration.html for digital images of the Charters of Freedom.

Materials Available at NARA Locations

At the National Archives Building in Washington, D.C., researchers can gain access to the archival records of the U.S. Congress through the Legislative Archives Center. See also Robert W. Coren, et al., *Guide to the Records of the United States Senate at the National Archives 1789–1989,* Washington, D.C.:

United States Senate, 1989. Also see Charles E. Schamel, et al., *Guide to the Records of the United States House of Representatives at the National Archives, 1789–1989,* Washington, D.C.: United States House of Representatives, 1989. The papers of members of the Senate and the House of Representatives are by tradition considered personal papers. Therefore, these papers may be deposited in or given to libraries or archives in the members' home states or even disposed of if the member so chooses. There are no federal laws governing the disposition of the papers and the records of members of Congress. See Karen Dawley Paul, *Guide to the Research Collections of Former United States Senators, 1789–1995,* Washington, D.C.: Government Printing Office, 1995; and *Guide to the Research Collections of Former Members of the United States House of Representatives, 1789–1987,* Washington, D.C.: Government Printing Office, 1988. Many types of genealogical information may also be accessed at this location, including census microfilm from 1790 through 1930. See also the National Archival Information Locator (NAIL) database http://www.archives.gov/research_room/nail/ of selected records descriptions and digital copies, and Robert B. Matchette with Anne B. Eakes, et al., *Guide to Federal Records in the National Archives of the United States,* Washington, D.C.: NARA, 1995 (this guide is available at most public libraries). Archival records of federal and executive agencies and federal courts may be accessed at the National Archives and Records Administration Archives II: National Archives at College Park, 8601 Adelphi Road, College Park, MD 20740-6001, located near the University of Maryland's College Park campus. Through appraisal and records scheduling, the National Archives determines which federal records will be permanently held in NARA. Records that are determined to be permanently valuable are then arranged and described through the standard procedures of written records inventories and guides. Many of the inventories and guides can be purchased in print or are available on NARA's Web site http://www.archives.gov/. Also on the Web site, see the *Guide to Federal Records in the National Archives,* which describes records in NARA at the records group level. This resource provides the broadest view of the organization of federal records in NARA and includes federal records housed in facilities nationwide http://www.archives.gov/research_room/federal_records_guide/. The National Archival Information Locator http://www.archives.gov/research_room/nail/

is a prototype database that contains information about NARA's holdings across the country. Researchers use NAIL to search archival descriptions for keywords or topics, and then to retrieve digital copies of selected textual documents, photographs, maps, and sound recordings. Although numerous and growing continually, the records described and/or reproduced in NAIL represent only a limited portion of NARA's vast holdings. NAIL also contains descriptions of NARA's guides to microfilm and lists locations where the microfilm can be found. Each description indicates all NARA units that have copies of a microfilm publication in part or in full.

As part of its records management program, NARA operates 19 records centers where users can access the archival records of federal agencies. Records scheduled as non-permanent that will be destroyed at a determined date can also be accessed at records centers. These are referred to as records center holdings. Materials may also be obtained through the Freedom of Information Act (FOIA) http://www.archives.gov/research_room/foia_reading_room/foia_reading_room.html. Records centers all have research rooms where users can view paper records and microfilm. Contact the records centers through their online sites or by telephone, fax, or U.S. mail. Their current addresses and contact information are:

Alaska

NARA's Pacific Alaska Region
654 West Third Avenue
Anchorage, Alaska 99501-2145
http://www.archives.gov/facilities/ak/anchorage.html
alaska.archives@nara.gov
907-271-2443
Fax: 907-271-2442

Archival holdings from federal agencies and courts in Alaska and microfilm.

California

Laguna Niguel, NARA's Pacific Region
24000 Avila Road, First Floor-East Entrance
Laguna Niguel, California 92677-3497
http://www.archives.gov/facilities/ca/laguna_niguel.html
laguna.archives@nara.gov
Fax: 949-360-2624

Archival, microfilm (call 949-360-2641), and records center holdings (call 949-360-2628) from federal agencies and courts in Arizona; southern California; and Clark County, Nevada, as well as records of the Nevada District Court, Las Vegas, 1954–1968.

California

NARA's Pacific Region (San Francisco)
1000 Commodore Drive
San Bruno, California 94066-2350
http://www.archives.gov/facilities/ca/san_francisco.html
sanbruno.archives@nara.gov
Fax: 650-876-9233

Archival, microfilm (call 650-876-9009), and records center (call 650-876-9001) holdings from federal agencies and courts in northern California, Hawaii, Nevada (except Clark County), the Pacific Trust Territories, and American Samoa.

Colorado

NARA's Rocky Mountain Region
Building 48, Denver Federal Center
West 6th Avenue and Kipling Street
Denver, Colorado 80225
P.O. Box 25307
Denver, Colorado 80225-0307
http://www.archives.gov/facilities/co/denver.html
denver.archives@nara.gov
303-236-0804
Fax: 303-236-9297

Archival and records center holdings from federal agencies and courts in Colorado, Montana, New Mexico, North Dakota, South Dakota, Utah, and Wyoming. Call 303-236-0817 for microfilm holdings.

Georgia

NARA's Southeast Region
1557 St. Joseph Avenue
East Point, Georgia 30344-2593
http://www.archives.gov/facilities/ga/atlanta.html
atlanta.center@nara.gov
404-763-7474 or 404-763-7383
Fax: 404-763-7815 or 404-763-7967

Archival, microfilm, and records center holdings from federal agencies and courts in Alabama, Florida, Georgia, Kentucky, Mississippi, North Carolina, South Carolina, and Tennessee.

Illinois

NARA's Great Lakes Region
7358 South Pulaski Road
Chicago, Illinois 60629-5898
http://www.archives.gov/facilities/il/chicago.html
chicago.archives@nara.gov

773-581-7816
Fax: 312-353-1294

Archival holdings from federal agencies and courts in Illinois, Indiana, Michigan, Minnesota, Ohio, and Wisconsin. Records center holdings from federal agencies in Illinois, Minnesota, and Wisconsin, and from federal courts in Illinois, Indiana, Michigan, Minnesota, Ohio, and Wisconsin. Microfilm holdings.

Maryland

Washington National Records Center
4205 Suitland Road
Suitland, Maryland 20746-8001
http://www.archives.gov/facilities/md/suitland.html
suitland.center@nara.gov
301-457-7000
Fax: 301-457-7117

Records center holdings for federal agency headquarters offices in the District of Columbia, Maryland, and Virginia; federal agency field offices in Maryland, Virginia, and West Virginia; federal courts in the District of Columbia; and U.S. armed forces worldwide.

Massachusetts

NARA's Northeast Region (Boston)
380 Trapelo Road
Waltham, Massachusetts 02452-6399
http://www.archives.gov/facilities/ma/boston.html
waltham.center@nara.gov
781-647-8104
Fax: 781-647-8088

Archival and records center (call 781-647-8108) holdings from federal agencies and courts in Connecticut, Maine, Massachusetts, New Hampshire, Rhode Island, and Vermont. Call 781-647-8100 for microfilm holdings.

Massachusetts

NARA's Northeast Region (Pittsfield)
10 Conte Drive
Pittsfield, Massachusetts 01201-8230
http://www.archives.gov/facilities/ma/pittsfield.html
archives@pittsfield.nara.gov
413-445-6885, ext. 14
Fax: 413-445-7599

Records center holdings from selected federal agencies nationwide. For microfilm holdings, call 413-445-6885, ext. 24.

Missouri

NARA's Central Plains Region (Kansas City)
2312 East Bannister Road
Kansas City, Missouri 64131-3011
http://www.archives.gov/facilities/mo/kansas_city.html
kansascity.archives@nara.gov
816-926-6272
Fax: 816-926-6982

Archival, microfilm, and records center holdings from federal agencies and courts in Iowa, Kansas, Missouri, and Nebraska.

Missouri

NARA's Central Plains Region (Lee's Summit)
200 Space Center Drive
Lee's Summit, Missouri 64064-1182
http://www.archives.gov/facilities/mo/lees_summit.html
kansascitycave.center@nara.gov
816-478-7079
Fax: 816-478-7625

Maintains retired records from federal agencies and courts in New Jersey, New York, Puerto Rico, and the U.S. Virgin Islands. (NOTE: The New York NARA Northeast Region Records Center in New York City also holds records from New Jersey, New York, Puerto Rico, and the U.S. Virgin Islands.) Also holds most Department of Veterans Affairs offices nationwide.

Missouri

NARA's National Personnel Records Center
Civilian Personnel Records
111 Winnebago Street
St. Louis, Missouri 63118-4199
http://www.archives.gov/facilities/mo/st_louis/civilian
_personnel_records.html
cpr.center@nara.gov
Fax: 314-538-5719

Civilian personnel records from federal agencies nationwide; selected military dependent medical records. (Telephone requests not accepted.)

Missouri

NARA's National Personnel Records Center
Military Personnel Records
9700 Page Avenue
St. Louis, Missouri 63132-5100
http://www.archives.gov/facilities/mo/st_louis/military
_personnel_records.html
MPR.center@nara.gov
Fax: 314-538-4175

Military personnel records and military and retired military medical records from all services; selected dependent medical records, morning reports, and rosters. World War II Philippine army and guerilla records were formerly held by the Army Reserve Personnel Command. During World War II, some parts of the Philippine Commonwealth Army were made a part of the United States Army Forces Far East. (Telephone requests not accepted.)

New York

NARA's Northeast Region (New York City)
201 Varick Street
New York, New York 10014-4811
http://www.archives.gov/facilities/ny/new_york_city.html
newyork.archives@nara.gov
212-337-1300
Fax: 212-337-1306

Archival and microfilm holdings from federal agencies and courts in New Jersey, New York, Puerto Rico, and the U.S. Virgin Islands. (NOTE: The Missouri NARA Central Plains Region Records Center in Lee's Summit, MO, also holds records from New Jersey, New York, Puerto Rico, and the U.S. Virgin Islands.)

Ohio

NARA's Great Lakes Region (Dayton)
3150 Springboro Road
Dayton, Ohio 45439-1883
http://www.archives.gov/facilities/oh/dayton.html
dayton.center@nara.gov
937-225-2852
Fax: 937-225-7236

Records center holdings from federal agencies in Indiana, Michigan, and Ohio; federal bankruptcy court records from Ohio since 1991/92; Defense Finance Accounting System records nationwide and from Germany and Korea; and Internal Revenue Service records from selected sites nationwide.

Pennsylvania

NARA's Mid Atlantic Region (Center City Philadelphia)
900 Market Street
Philadelphia, Pennsylvania 19107-4292
http://www.archives.gov/facilities/pa/philadelphia
_center_city.html
philadelphia.archives@nara.gov
215-597-9770
Fax: 215-597-2303

Archival and microfilm holdings from federal agencies and courts in Delaware, Maryland, Pennsylvania, Virginia, and West Virginia. (NOTE: For records center holdings from these states contact the Northeast Philadelphia center.)

Pennsylvania

NARA's Mid Atlantic Region (Northeast Philadelphia)
14700 Townsend Road
Philadelphia, Pennsylvania 19154-1096
http://www.archives.gov/facilities/pa/philadelphia
_northeast.html
center@philfrc.nara.gov
215-671-9027 ext. 105
Fax: 215-671-8001

Records center holdings from federal agencies in Delaware and Pennsylvania and federal courts in Delaware, Maryland, Pennsylvania, Virginia, and West Virginia. (NOTE: For archival and microfilm holdings from these states, contact the Center City Philadelphia Center.)

Texas

NARA's Southwest Region
501 West Felix Street, Building 1
Fort Worth, Texas 76115-3405
P.O. Box 6216
Fort Worth, Texas 76115-0216
http://www.archives.gov/facilities/tx/fort_worth.html
ftworth.archives@nara.gov
817-334-5525
Fax: 817-334-5621

Archival, microfilm, and records center (call 817-334-5515) holdings from federal agencies and courts in Arkansas, Louisiana, Oklahoma, and Texas.

Washington (State)

NARA's Pacific Alaska Region (Seattle)
6125 Sand Point Way NE
Seattle, Washington 98115-7999
http://www.archives.gov/facilities/wa/seattle.html
seattle.archives@nara.gov
206-526-6501
Fax: 206-526-6575

Archival holdings from federal agencies and courts in Idaho, Oregon, and Washington State. Records center holdings for federal agencies and courts in the same states and Alaska. Microfilm holdings.

Presidential libraries are another division of the National Archives and Records Administration. These nine libraries are located in various parts of the United States, usually near the birthplaces or homes of the former presidents, or near the universities they attended. Facilities including museums, libraries, archival storage areas, and research rooms are constructed with private funds. A staff composed of NARA employees is responsible for arranging, describing, and making the records available. The records contained in the facilities are mainly government records. Through the Presidential Record Act of 1972, Congress determined that all records and papers created by a president during his term in office would remain the property of the U.S. government and would be held and preserved by NARA. However, the law provides a period of 12 years from the end of the presidential term until the records must be made fully accessible by NARA. During those 12 years, copies of materials may only be obtained by individuals through the Freedom of Information Act http://www.archives.gov/research_room/foia_reading_room/foia_reading_room.html. Before the Presidential Records Act of 1972, the records and papers of the presidents were traditionally considered personal papers. This tradition allowed presidents and their families to determine where these materials would be housed and maintained. Some presidential papers can be found in the Library of Congress in Washington, D.C. Other materials contained at presidential libraries include the papers of the vice presidents, the first ladies, other family members, members of the cabinet, presidential staff and aides, and campaign staff, and volunteers. Some of the records and papers of these various individuals may be federal records, while others are personal papers.

The locations and addresses of the presidential libraries are:

George Bush Library
George Bush Drive West
College Station, TX 77845
http://bushlibrary.tamu.edu/
979-260-9554
Fax: 979-260-9557
bush.library@nara.gov

Jimmy Carter Library
441 Freedom Parkway
Atlanta, GA 30307-1498
http://www.jimmycarterlibrary.org/
404-331-3942
Fax: 404-730-2215
carter.library@nara.gov

William J. Clinton Presidential Materials Project
1000 LaHarpe Boulevard
Little Rock, AR 72201
http://clinton.archives.gov/
501-244-9756
Fax: 501-244-9764
Clinton@nara.gov

Dwight D. Eisenhower Library
200 SE 4th Street
Abilene, KS 67410-2900
http://www.eisenhower.utexas.edu/
785-263-4751
Fax: 785-263-4218
eisenhower.library@nara.gov

Gerald R. Ford Library
1000 Beal Avenue
Ann Arbor, MI 48109-2114
http://www.ford.utexas.edu/
734-741-2218
Fax: 734-741-2341
http://www.ford.utexas.edu/email.htm

Gerald R. Ford Museum
303 Pearl Street NW
Grand Rapids, MI 49504-5353
http://www.ford.utexas.edu/
616-451-9263
Fax: 616-451-9570
http://www.ford.utexas.edu/email.htm

Herbert Hoover Library
210 Parkside Drive
P.O. Box 488
West Branch, IA 52358-0488
http://hoover.nara.gov/
319-643-5301
Fax: 319-643-5825
hoover.library@nara.gov

Lyndon B. Johnson Library
2313 Red River Street
Austin, TX 78705-5702
http://www.lbjlib.utexas.edu/
512-916-5137
Fax: 512-916-5171
johnson.library@nara.gov

John F. Kennedy Library
Columbia Point, Boston, MA 02125-3398
http://www.jfklibrary.org/
617-929-4500
Fax: 617-929-4538
kennedy.library@nara.gov

Nixon Presidential Materials Staff
National Archives at College Park
8601 Adelphi Road
College Park, MD 20740-6001
http://www.archives.gov/nixon/index.html
301-713-6950
Fax: 301-713-6916
nixon@nara.gov

Ronald Reagan Library
40 Presidential Drive
Simi Valley, CA 93065-0600
http://www.reagan.utexas.edu/
800-410-8354
Fax: 805-522-9621
reagan.library@nara.gov

Franklin D. Roosevelt Library
4079 Albany Post Road
Hyde Park, NY 12538-1999
http://www.fdrlibrary.marist.edu/
845-229-8114
Fax: 845-229-0872
roosevelt.library@nara.gov

Harry S. Truman Library
500 West U.S. Highway 24
Independence, MO 64050-1798
http://www.trumanlibrary.org/
816-833-1400
Fax: 816-833-4368
truman.library@nara.gov

NON-NARA FEDERAL ARCHIVES

Some federal agencies maintain their own archival records, but access to these records varies. It is best to contact the agency archives to determine whether they will assist researchers. If the agency archives are not open to the public, materials may be obtained through the Freedom of Information Act (FOIA) http://www.archives.gov/research_room/foia_reading_room/foia_reading_room.html.

Some examples of agency archives are: the Federal Reserve Board, the Kennedy Space Center, the NASA Glen Research Center, Los Alamos National Laboratory, the National Agricultural Library, the National Library of Medicine, the National Park Service, National Public Radio, the Naval Research Center, the Smithsonian Institution, the United States Capitol Office of the Architect, the U.S. Geological Survey, the U.S. Corps of Engineers, the U.S. Department of Justice, the U.S. Environmental Protection Agency, the

U.S. Mint, and the U.S. Patent and Trademark Office. A separate guide to all agency archives does not exist, but information on some of them can be found in standard guides. NARA can answer questions regarding federal agency archives and can put researchers in touch with staff at the agency archives. NARA's Web site also includes information about agency archives.

STATE ARCHIVES

Each of the 50 states in the United States has an agency that serves the function of the state archives. Each has a mission similar to that of the National Archives and Records Administration: to appraise and provide records schedules, accession, arrange and describe, preserve and make available for research the records of the state government and state agencies. Some state archives also collect, preserve, and make available the papers of private individuals and families. The locations, contact information, publications, and descriptions of content of the state archives follows.

Alabama Department of Archives and History
P.O. Box 300100
624 Washington Ave.
Montgomery, AL 36130-0100
http://www.archives.state.al.us/
334-242-4435
Fax. 334-240-3433

The Web site gives a link for each county and shows what local records are held for each county. Records include official archives of the Territory and State of Alabama; county records; private manuscript collections of Alabamians beginning with the eighteenth century; military records and soldiers' correspondence from all wars in which Alabamians have participated; and compilations of correspondence and other material of genealogical interest.

Alaska State Archives
P.O. Box 110571
141 Willoughby Avenue
Juneau, AK 99811-1720
http://www.archives.state.ak.us/
archives@eed.state.ak.us
907-465-2270
Fax: 907-465-2465

The Archives Section identifies, preserves, and makes available for research the public records of the state, including those of the state and territorial governments of Alaska.

Arizona State Archives
1700 West Washington, Room 200
Phoenix, AZ 85007
http://www.lib.az.us/archives/
602-542-4035
Fax: 602-542-4402

Agency records include those from boards, commissions, and departments, as well as executive, legislative, and judicial branches and date from 1863 to the early 1990s. Local records include those from county and city governments and date from 1863 to the 1940s. The Archives currently holds 143 record groups. The Web site gives information regarding local government records holdings through an interactive map. Each county in Arizona is represented.

Arkansas History Commission
One Capitol Mall
Little Rock, AR 72201
http://www.ark-ives.com/
501-682-6900
Fax: 501-682-1364

The records as a whole span Arkansas's history from its territorial days to the late twentieth century. Agencies holdings include those from the Bank Department, Attorney General's office, Soil Conservation District, State Council of Defense, Railroad Commission, Correction Department, and State Hospital. There are letter books of correspondence of nineteenth-century governors, ledgers of trademarks and labels, notaries public, Highway Commission audits, and records from the treasurer's office and the auditor's office. This material may be accessed through the card catalog, inventories, and finding aids. Selected records from 1797–1950 are available from all Arkansas counties. These records include marriage licenses; deeds; circuit and chancery court records; tax records (both personal property and real estate); probate records (wills, guardianships, executors, and letters of administration); and some naturalization records.

California State Archives
1020 O Street
Sacramento, CA 95814
http://www.ss.ca.gov/archives/archives_e.htm
916-653-8099
Fax: 916-653-7134

The collections document the broad scope of California government and its impact on the people of the state. Over 65,000 cubic feet of records of all types are represented, including millions of documents and bound volumes. Finding aids that describe California State Archives' collections are available via the California Digital Library's Online Archive Web site. Additional descriptive information can also be obtained through the Research Libraries Information Network (RLIN) http://www.rlg.org/rlin.html. Collections include California Constitutions, Spanish and Mexican Land Grants, Family History Resources, Legislative Materials, Robert F. Kennedy Assassination Investigation, California Governors, Supreme and Appellate Courts, Elections and Political Campaigns, State Agencies, and Constitutional Officers.

Colorado State Archives
1313 Sherman Street, Room 1B-20
Denver, CO 80203
http://www.archives.state.co.us/
303-866-2358 or 303-866-2390, in Colorado toll-free at
1-800-305-3442
Fax: 303-866-2257

The Colorado State Archives is the legal repository for selected historical and contemporary records and information generated by state and local governments in Colorado. The record holding listings identify government records that are currently available for research. Available resources include records from the Department of Agriculture, Department of Corrections, Department of Education, the court and judicial system, Colorado governors, Civilian Conservation Corps, Governor's Council of Defense—WW I and II, and Colorado Children's Home. Also available are legislative history resources, business incorporation records, military records, school records, federal census, Colorado tourism files, historic mine report files, railroad records, and the Index to Water Decrees (1899–1926).

Connecticut State Archives
Connecticut State Library
231 Capitol Avenue
Hartford, CT 06106
http://www.cslib.org/archives.htm
860-757-6595
Fax: 860-757-6521

Records from and/or about the following offices: governors; Judicial Department (Supreme Court, Superior Courts, probate courts, and predecessor courts); the General Assembly (leaders, committees, special task forces, commissions, and subcommittees); elected state officials; military units and the Adjutant General of the Connecticut National Guard; and all other state agencies (including defunct bureaus, divisions, departments, or predecessor agencies). The State Archives supports retention of local government archival records in the locality of origin but shall accept such records when offered if they have enduring informational value and otherwise would be destroyed.

Delaware Public Archives
Hall of Records
121 Duke of York Street
Dover, DE 19901
http://www.state.de.us/sos/dpa/index.htm
302-744-5000
Fax: 302-739-2578

The Delaware Public Archives identifies, collects, and preserves public records of enduring historical and evidential value to ensure access to public records for present and future generations of Delawareans and to promote the availability and use of public records. Collections include agency histories, vital records (births, marriages, and deaths), census records, Civil War records, naturalization records, and probate records. An online guide to the collections is available at http://www.state.de.us/sos/dpa/collections/guideintro.htm.

Florida State Archives
R.A. Gray Building
500 South Bronough Street
Tallahassee, Florida 32399-0250
http://dlis.dos.state.fl.us/barm/fsa.html
barm@mail.dos.state.fl.us
850-245-6700

The core collection is approximately 30,000 cubic feet of records documenting the activities of Florida's territorial and state governments from 1821 to the present. Included are gubernatorial records, legislative acts and committee records, Supreme Court case files, military records, and the records of cabinet officers and their departments. The Archives maintains a small collection of original public records generated by local government agencies throughout the state. Probate, tax, voting, and commission records of different city, town, and county agencies are among the materials kept in the Local Government Records Collection, as well as microfilmed county tax, deed, marriage, probate, and some birth and naturalization records.

Georgia Department of Archives and History
330 Capitol Avenue, S.E.
Atlanta, GA 30334
http://www.sos.state.ga.us/archives/
404-656-2358
Fax: 404-657-8427

Primarily official state government records and a significant collection of local government records (110,000 cubic feet). The Archives enters descriptions of these records into RLIN (Research Libraries Information Network http://www.rlg.org/rlin.html). The microfilm library contains nearly 30,000 reels of Georgia governmental records, selected U.S. records, Georgia county records, tax digests, a few municipal records, and 1.5 million land grants and plats from 1755 to 1909. Other important collections include the federal census schedules; Georgia Confederate Service and Pension Records; and Colonial, Headright, and Land Lottery records. By law, city and county boundary changes, as well as city annexations, are filed with the secretary of state's office in the archives department. In addition, holdings include the state's original Surveyor General collection, which includes over 10,000 county and state maps.

Hawaii State Archives
Historical Records Branch
Kekauluohi Building, Iolani Palace Grounds
Honolulu, HI 96813
http://www.state.hi.us/dags/archives/welcome.html
808-586-0329
Fax: 808-586-0330

The primary government records cover the period from the monarchy to the current legislative session, with a total of over 10,000 cubic feet of material. The largest groups of government records include minutes, correspondence, reports, plans, registers, certificates, and ledgers documenting activities of the executive branch agencies from 1840 to the present. Bills, committee reports, journals, testimonies, petitions, messages, communications, and minutes of the legislative branch from 1840 to the present. Judiciary Records including nineteenth- and early twentieth-century probate, divorce, criminal, civil, equity, law and admiralty case files, minute books, and wills from 1847 to ca. 1916. Governor's records include correspondence, speeches, press releases, reports, and proclamations of the chief executive of the territory and the state from 1900 to 1990. Access is through Hawaii Voyager (online catalog) http://statearchives.lib.hawaii.edu/.

Idaho State Archives
Idaho State Historical Society
450 N. Fourth St.
Boise, ID 83702
http://www2.state.id.us/ishs/Lib%26Arch.html
208-334-2620
Fax: 208-334-2626

The Idaho State Historical Society serves as the state archives and holds a variety of public records created by state and local governments, such as state agencies, counties, and cities. The collection includes territorial records; papers from most governors; selected vital, financial, and court records; and a variety of other materials. Microfilm materials include Idaho Death Index and Certificates, 1911–1932; a substantial portion of U.S. Census records; newspapers; and selected Idaho county records (1864–1920), such as vital records, court records, and deeds.

Illinois State Archives
Office of the Secretary of State
Norton Building, Capitol Complex
Springfield, IL 62756
http://www.sos.state.il.us/departments/archives/archives.html
217-782-4682
Fax: 217-524-3930

The Illinois State Archives serves by law as the depository of public records of Illinois state and local governmental agencies that possess permanent administrative, legal, or historical research value. Its collections do not include manuscript, newspaper, or other nonofficial sources. All three branches of state government are represented in 2,443 record series arranged under 191 different offices, departments, divisions, institutions, boards, the legislature, the supreme court, and several federal agencies whose records were transferred officially to the state of Illinois. The Archives' holdings of state and related federal records are described in *Descriptive Inventory of the Archives of the State of Illinois,* Second Edition (1997). To search this inventory online see http://www.sos.state.il.us/departments/archives/di/toc.htm.

Indiana State Archives
6440 E. 30th St.
Indianapolis, IN 46219
http://www.state.in.us/icpr/webfile/archives/homepage.html
317-591-5222

To search the Indiana State Archives Collections Database see http://www.state.in.us/icpr/webfile/INDWEB/FRAME.HTM. The Indiana State Archives is the official repository of Indiana government records of permanent historical and legal significance. It principally contains records generated by state government and state agencies, but also holds a major collection of county and local government records. Records of the executive, legislative, and judicial branches begin in the 1790s and include papers of every governor; bills, acts, and reports of the General Assembly; and proceedings of both the supreme and appellate courts. The lives of Indiana citizens are recorded in the many ways they intersect with government, including military service, naturalization procedures, the state land office, and state institutions.

Iowa State Archives
State Historical Society of Iowa
600 East Locust
Des Moines, IA 50319
http://www.iowahistory.org/archives/index.html
515-281-6200
Fax: 515-282-0502

The State Archives in Des Moines contains records created by state offices and agencies that have been determined to have permanent historical value. With the exception of a few confidential records series, the State Archives is open for public use. Among the materials in this collection are the Secretary of State Land Office's original land survey notes and plats of the state; Adjutant General's records of Iowa units serving in the Civil War and the Spanish-American War; Supreme Court records; and Iowa governors' papers. Microfilm of some State Archives records are available in Des Moines and Iowa City.

Kansas State Historical Society
Kansas History Center
6425 SW Sixth Avenue
Topeka, KS 66615-1099
http://www.kshs.org/archives/index.htm
785-272-8681, ext. 202
Fax: 785-272-8682

State archives holdings include the inactive, unpublished records of state government with enduring value. The state archives also collects local records from Kansas counties and towns and is filming local government records. Finding aids are available for some record series, and an electronic, searchable inventory of archives holdings to the "series" level is online in the Archives only. Public access to some archives holdings is restricted because of state or federal statutes or administrative regulations that prohibit or limit their disclosure. Major record series include territorial records, 1854–1861; Executive Department, 1854–1861; Legislature, 1855–1861; U.S. District Court, 1854–1861; U.S. Surveyor General of Kansas and Nebraska, 1833–1876; and Adjutant General records about Kansas Civil War volunteer regiments and militia or national guard units prior to World War I, selective service records, enrollments of veterans

living in Kansas in 1883, 1889, and 1930, national guard unit histories, correspondence of the adjutant general, and miscellaneous documents. Microfilm is available through interlibrary loan. For other state records from 1861 to the present, visit the Web site.

Kentucky Department for Libraries and Archives
P.O. Box 537
300 Coffee Tree Road, off State Highway 676
Frankfort, Kentucky 40602
http://www.kdla.net/arch/arch.htm
502-564-8300, ext. 252
Fax: 502-564-5773

The Kentucky State Archives is the central repository for the permanent public records of Kentucky state government and many of the Commonwealth's local governments and judicial offices. Private materials are not collected. *A Guide to the Holdings of the Kentucky State Archives* contains information on the scope, content, and organization of state and local government records holdings. Also available is the *Catalog of Kentucky State Archives Holdings,* with over 10,000 descriptions of records series and histories of many of the government agencies that created the records. These are indexed by title, by name of creating agency, by topic, and by record type, searchable using both words and phrases http://cuadranew.kdla.net/marcat.htm.

Louisiana State Archives
P.O. Box 94125
3851 Essen Lane
Baton Rouge, LA 70821-9125
http://www.sec.state.la.us/archives/archives/archives-index.htm
225-922-1208
Fax: 225-922-0433

The Louisiana State Archives maintains the following vital records: Orleans Parish birth records from 1790–1900; Orleans Parish marriage records from 1870–1950; Orleans Parish death records from 1804–1950; and statewide death records from 1911–1950. All marriage records outside of Orleans Parish are maintained by the clerk of court in the parish where the marriage license was purchased. Records are available from the following agencies or departments: Attorney General, Education, Environmental Affairs, Health and Human Resources, Public Safety, Supreme Court, and Treasurer. Other state records include colonial documents, economic development documents, legislative records, and military records. The earliest parish records on deposit date from the

Spanish colonial period with the largest collection being from the southwestern portion of the state called the Opelousas Post. The records contained within the collection begin in 1764 and continue into the mid-1800s; however, only records from 1764 to 1803 are indexed. Colonial records from the Avoyelles Post dating from 1782 to 1803 are also available.

Maine State Archives
84 State House Station
Augusta, ME 04333-0084
http://www.state.me.us/sos/arc/research/homepage.htm
207-287-5795
Fax: 207-287-5739

The permanently valuable records of state government available in the Archives include bills introduced in the Legislature; Governor's Executive Orders; election returns; deeds to and from the State of Maine; maps from the Land Office; vital statistics; federal census records from Maine up to 1920; county court records dating back to the 1600s; military records through World War I; Attorney General and State Supreme Court opinions; Marriage Index (1892–1967, 1976–1996); Death Index (1960 to 1996); and Partial Index to Court Records for Kennebec County 1799–1804, Washington County 1839–1845, and York County 1695–1760. The Archives provides publications in paper and electronic formats for the agencies of State Government, 1820–1971, and other guides such as Black House Papers—A Guide to Certain Microfilmed Land Records; Counties, Cities, Towns and Plantations of Maine; Dubros Times: Depositions of Revolutionary War Veterans; Land and Forests; and Maine and the Nation: A Select Bibliography. The Maine Legislative Index: 1820–1825, 1826–1830, 1831–1835, contains titles of all bills, acts, or resolves, whether they passed or not, indexed by keyword (an electronic version for 1820–1855 is available). Maine Town Microfilm List: Town and Vital Records, and Census Reports, is also in an electronic version (see the Web site).

Maryland State Archives
350 Rowe Boulevard
Annapolis, MD 21401
http://www.mdarchives.state.md.us/
410-260-6400
Fax: 410-974-2525, in Maryland toll-free at 800-235-4045

The Web site provides a "Guide to Government Records" and includes the Combined Records Series List, a comprehensive listing of all series titles of government records at the Maryland State Archives.

Under each series title are listed the agency, date span, and series number. State agency histories and series descriptions are provided where available. Four other lists included in the "Guide" provide more detailed information. The County Agency Series, the Municipal Agency Series, and the State Agency Series are listings of accessioned series from those jurisdictions. Each lists agencies, series, date spans, and series numbers and includes original records, records on microfilm, and records on electronic media. The Transferred State & Local Series is a listing of series transferred to the Maryland State Archives which have not been fully described through archival accessioning procedures. Under each jurisdiction (county, municipality, state agency) are listed agencies, series, date spans, series numbers, original records, and microfilm. All adoptions occurring after May 31, 1947 are sealed and can be opened only with a court order. Most adoptions prior to June 1, 1947 are open and available to anyone. The Archives has birth records for the 23 counties from 1898–1978 and for Baltimore City from 1875–1978. Death records are available for Maryland's 23 counties from 1898–1987 and for Baltimore City from 1875–1987. The Archives has marriage records from most local jurisdictions prior to 1914. After that date there are both statewide and local records, many of which can be found at the Archives.

Massachusetts Archives at Columbia Point
220 Morrissey Blvd.
Boston, MA 02125
archives@sec.state.ma.us
617-727-2816
Fax: 617-288-8429

Holdings include colonial charters, treaties, compacts, and agreements with Indian tribes and with other states; proceedings of state constitutional conventions; and state legal codes. Legislative records include files from 1629 to the present; enacted statutes and resolves, as well as legislation not enacted; House and Senate dockets, roll calls, and journals; and committee and legislative commission hearing and background files. State secretary records include administrative files; initiative and referendum petitions; state and national election returns; state regulation files and register; lobbyist registrations; municipal home rule charters and acceptances of local option statutes; notices of appointment, lists, and qualifications (oaths of office) of state and local officials; census registers and returns; and returns of town vital records (1841–1905; indexes to 1971). Executive records include: Governor (1802–present), Council, Administration and Finance, Consumer Affairs and Business Regulation, Economic Development and Manpower Affairs/Labor, Education, Environmental Affairs, Health and Human Services, Public Safety/Adjutant General, Transportation and Construction, Treasurer records, Troy and Greenfield and other railroad financial records, Attorney General records, and State Ethics Commission designation lists. Court records include: Supreme Judicial Court and predecessors, Superior and district courts by county, and probate and naturalization records. Also available are special colonial and early state materials to 1800; transcripts of the Archives of the Plymouth Colony, 1620–1691, relating to Indian affairs, including military, trading, and census records; and nineteenth-century records of the Guardians of Indians. Witchcraft records include depositions, examinations, warrants, and other court documents.

Michigan State Archives of Michigan
717 West Allegan Street
P.O. Box 30740
Lansing, MI 48909-8240
http://www.sos.state.mi.us/history/archive/index.html
517-373-1408
Fax: 517-241-1658

More than 80 million state and local government records and private papers dating back to 1797, 300,000 photographs and 500,000 maps, plus films and audiotapes are available for public research. Records in the State Archives are particularly useful for tracing genealogy; legislative history/intent; land surveys; military service; and governmental policy on mental health, public health, education, labor, welfare, and corrections. Archives handout sheets identify all records in its holdings on specific subjects. As new records are received by the State Archives, these accessions are added to the handout sheets to keep the circulars up-to-date. These are listed on the Web site along with indexes to naturalization records.

Minnesota State Archives
345 Kellogg Blvd. W.
St. Paul, MN 55102-1906
archives@mnhs.org
http://www.mnhs.org/preserve/records/index.html
651-297-4502
Fax: 651-296-9961

The State Archives identifies, collects, and preserves the historically valuable records of almost 4,000 units of state and local government in Minnesota from the territorial period to the present day. Materials preserved in the State Archives come from the executive branch of state government, including the constitutional officers and state departments, boards, and commissions; the legislative branch, including the Minnesota legislature and its committees, commissions, and officers; and the judicial branch, including the supreme and appellate courts, 87 district courts, and antecedent probate, municipal, and justice of the peace courts. Local government records include material from Minnesota counties, cities, school districts, townships, and regional government organizations. Records include correspondence, reports, minutes, memoranda, published records, maps, photographs, architectural drawings, microfilm, sound recordings, ephemera, and videotapes. Available online are informational leaflets on various records from townships, school districts, county superintendents of schools, municipalities, law enforcement agencies, county auditors, public libraries, public health care facilities, historic preservation commissions, watershed districts, and soil and water conservation districts. The starting point for searching the archives collections is the online catalog (PALS).

Mississippi Department of Archives and History
P.O. Box 571
100 South State Street
Jackson, MS 39205-0571
http://www.mdah.state.ms.us/
601-359-6876
Fax: 601-359-6964

The Mississippi Department of Archives and History collection documents the area known today as Mississippi from prehistory through contemporary times and includes 29,000 cubic feet of records of all type, such as government documents, bound volumes, maps and drawings, photographs, oral histories, and video and audiotapes. Holdings include records that document Mississippi's colonial periods—French, Spanish, and English. Mississippi territorial records illustrate the development of American democracy on the frontier. State records are organized into 2,400 series, including legislative records, governors' papers, court documents, and state agency records. In 1998 the records of the State Sovereignty Commission were made available. The Mississippi State Sovereignty Commission was formed in 1956, two years after the U.S. Supreme Court outlawed legally imposed racial segregation in public schools. The organization became a notorious watchdog agency for maintaining racial segregation in Mississippi (see Yasuhiro Katagiri, *The Mississippi State Sovereignty Commission,*

University Press of Mississippi, 2001). Commission records can be viewed in electronic format in the Search Room and will soon be on the Web site. Copies of records can be requested. The Name Index Search and the Folder Title List (both online) expedite research online.

Missouri State Archives
State Capitol, Room 208
600 W. Main Street
P.O. Box 1767
Jefferson City, MO 65102
http://www.sos.state.mo.us/archives/
archref@mail.sos.state.mo.us
573-751-3280
Fax: 573-526-4903

More than 120 million pages; 100,000 photographs; 12,500 books; 55,000 rolls of microfilm; and 176,000 microfiche documents comprise the collection. These records include Missouri's history under French and Spanish colonial rule, as a U.S. territory, and during early statehood; Journals of the House and Senate; supreme court case files; state agency records; state government publications; local records inventory database (a searchable online database of the inventories of local government records); and federal census schedules for Missouri from 1830–1920. Online indexes exist for military records of Missourians from the War of 1812 through World War I, county records on microfilm, and birth and death records.

Montana Historical Society
P.O. Box 201201
225 N. Roberts
Helena, MT 59620-1201
http://www.montanahistoricalsociety.com/departments/archives/
406-444-7482
Fax: 406-444-2694

The Montana Historical Society was the unofficial archives of Montana state government from 1865 to 1969, when it became the official state archives. In addition to the records of executive branch agencies and elected officials, the State Archives includes records of legislative sessions. Minutes of legislative committees are available, including audiotape recordings of committee meetings from 1995 to the present. Unfortunately, the legislature did not consistently keep committee minutes until the 1960s, although scattered material can be found even in the records of the earliest legislative assemblies. Local governments are encouraged to find repositories for their archival records in their locality; however, if such a repository cannot be found, the records may be deposited with the Montana Historical Society. Currently, the local government records' strongest areas are marriage records and naturalization records from the district court clerk's office and school census records submitted to the Office of Public Instruction by the County Superintendent of Schools. Since the Montana Historical Society is in Lewis and Clark County, it has become the local repository for that county's records.

Nebraska State Historical Society
Box 82554
1500 R Street
Lincoln, NE 68501
http://www.nebraskahistory.org/
402-471-4785
Fax: 402-471-8922

In 1905 the Nebraska legislature designated the Historical Society as official custodian of all state and local public records of historical value. The Society received the designation of state archives in 1969. The archives stores about 20,000 cubic feet of paper records and close to 50,000 rolls of microfilm. The records date from 1854 to the present and are available for research in the Library/Archives reference room. The archives, in conjunction with the Records Management Division and each agency, ensures that the important records of state government are identified and kept safely for posterity. Practically every state agency or commission dating from 1854 to the present is represented in the holdings. The state archives section works closely with county government in the state. Marriages and divorces, taxes, elections, civil and criminal suits, naturalization proceedings, property ownership, county board decisions, and education all have impact and occur at the county level. The Archives has records from many of the counties either on microfilm or in original paper form. These provide evidence for county residents about taxes paid, social security or insurance entitlements for a spouse, property ownership, local ordinances, and many other situations. Efforts to inform local officials of the importance of their records have resulted in the acquisition of many records by the archives as well.

Nevada State Library and Archives
100 North Stewart Street
Carson City, NV 89701-4285
http://dmla.clan.lib.nv.us/docs/nsla/
775-684-3360, in Nevada toll-free at 1-800-922-2880
Fax: 775-684-3330

The State Archives program preserves the records that document the history of Nevada state government dating back to 1851. It has custody of the historical records of the territory and state as defined in state statute, representing the three branches of government. There are more than 10,000 cubic feet of territorial and state government records and over 10,000 images of Nevada people and places, providing visual information that complements the Archives' documentation of Nevada history. The Archives keeps records arranged by the government office that created or received them in its course of business. Holdings include records from Carson County and Utah and Nevada Territories; Nevada Territorial Records; state officials; executive branch agencies; licensing and regulatory boards and commissions; special boards and commissions; Supreme Court records; Governors; Lieutenant Governors; Secretaries of State; Controllers; Treasurers; Attorneys General; and Surveyors General. Online guides are available on the Web site.

New Hampshire
Division of Records Management and Archives
71 South Fruit Street
Concord, NH 03301
http://www.state.nh.us/state/
603-271-2236
Fax: 603-271-2272

The Division of Records Management and Archives, an agency under the administration of the Secretary of State, houses several million archival items and more than 40,000 cubic feet of current public records created by 200 state government agencies. Holdings include Executive Records: Governors' messages and letters, Executive Council correspondence and minutes; Journals of House and Senate and Petitions and Acts; Secretary of State records: Corporations, Railroads, Elections, and Miscellaneous; Secretary of the Treasury records; Court records: Superior Court, Court of Common Pleas, County Courts, and General Court Records from 1680 to the present; Provincial probate records; Provincial land records; Town records: Municipal Records, Road and Highway layouts; Land Surveyors' records; Architectural drawings; Military records: Revolutionary War Rolls, Civil War Papers, and Militia. Research aids include the Guide to the New Hampshire State Archives http://www.state.nh.us/state/guide.html. Inventories and indexes to individual collections are available in the research area, and some are available online.

New Jersey State Archives
Division of Archives and Records Management, Department of State
185 West State Street CN307
Trenton, NJ 08625-0307
609-292-6260
Fax: 609-396-2454

The division includes state government record groups. Also accepts county and municipal records and, selectively, materials relating to New Jersey history. Holdings include the official archives of the State of New Jersey, including record groups relating to the executive, legislative, and judicial activities of the government, and some county and municipal records. Major groups include military records from the colonial period to World War I; judicial records, 1681–1865; state censuses, 1855–1915; records of the governors, 1878–1974; and colonial deeds and wills to 1900. Land, marriage, probate, and other records for most counties to 1900 are available on microfilm. These are supplemented by a small manuscript collection dealing with New Jersey history.

New Mexico State Records Center and Archives
Archives and Historical Services Division
404 Montezuma
Santa Fe, NM 87503
http://www.nmcpr.state.nm.us/archives/archives_hm.htm
archives@rain.state.nm.us
505-476-7908
Fax: 505-476-7909

The State Archives is mandated by law to collect, preserve, and make available to the public and all branches of government permanent public records, historical manuscripts, photographs, and other materials that contribute to the understanding of New Mexico history. All records are open for use except those specifically restricted by law. The Division offers reference assistance on-site, by telephone, mail, or e-mail. Online finding aids that describe collections are available through this Web site and through the Online Archives of New Mexico Web site at http://www. elibrary.unm.edu/oanm/. Holdings include public records containing historical, legal, financial, and administrative information relating to New Mexico. Included are the Spanish and Mexican archives (1621–1846), consisting of official records of governing agencies and administrators, correspondence, decrees, ordinances, military records, and papers relating to church matters; records of the territorial government, 1850–1912; District Court Records; the official papers of governors and elected officials; state agency records; legislative journals and bills; and county records 1850–1912. Private papers and collections relating to New Mexico history are also acquired.

New York State Archives
Empire State Plaza
Albany, NY 12230
518-473-7091
Fax: 518-473-7058
http://www.archives.nysed.gov/
sarainfo@mail.nysed.gov

The New York State Archives has custody of legislative, judicial, and executive agency records, which include canals records; criminal trials, appeals, and pardons; electoral college; military service records; naturalization and related records; probate records; and vital records (birth, death, and marriage). Records Created by Individual State Agencies include those from the Department of Correctional Services; the Joint Legislative Committee to Investigate Seditious Activities; the New York House of Refuge; the New York State Factory Investigating Commission; the New York State Legislature; and the New York State War Council. Local records on microfilm date from 1650 to 1975, with the bulk in the 1800–1850 era and only a few after 1900. The geographical coverage of the records is uneven. Most are public records, especially those of towns. The nonpublic materials microfilmed include church registers and minutes, store ledgers, business and commercial records, and records from private educational institutions. The State Archives' online catalog, *Excelsior,* provides a fully searchable index to all of the records series preserved in the State Archives and includes the database of the New York State Historic Documents Inventory http://www.sara.nysed.gov/holding/opac.htm. A published *Guide to Records in the New York State Archives* contains information on the complete records holdings of the State Archives as of December 1991. There are separate parts for the executive, legislative, and judicial branches. The executive branch part contains an entry for each agency. The entry consists of two sections: an administrative summary of the agency and a list of agency records, if any, in the State Archives. The administrative summary provides a brief synopsis of the agency's functions and organizational history. Similarly, entries in the legislative branch part are organized by the two houses—the assembly and senate—with a separate subdivision for joint legislative commissions and committees. For the

judicial branch, entries are organized by the current major types of courts in the Unified Court System http://www.sara.nysed.gov/pubs/guideabs.htm.

North Carolina Division of Archives & History
4614 Mail Service Center
109 East Jones Street
Raleigh, NC 27699-4614
archives@ncmail.net
919-733-3952
Fax: 919-733-1354
http://www.ah.dcr.state.nc.us/sections/archives/arch/default.htm

Holdings include General Assembly Session Records, 1707–1974; Governor's Office Records, 1688–Present; Secretary of State's Office Records, 1663–1959; Literary Board, Board of Education, and Superintendent of Public Instruction's Records; Attorney General's Office Records; Auditor's Office Records; Treasurer's and Comptroller's Office Records, ca. 1731–Present; Adjutant General's Office Records; Supreme Court Records; and Court Records including Colonial Court, district, and district superior courts. Archives Information Circular #9, "North Carolina Courts of Law and Equity Prior to 1868," includes details of early courts. A more detailed account of North Carolina's courts is available in *North Carolina Research: Genealogy and Local History* by Helen Leary (1996). Varying quantities of records covering various dates are preserved for many other agencies of state: Administration; Agriculture; Commerce; Community Colleges; Correction; Crime Control and Public Safety; Cultural Resources; Elections; Emergency Relief Administration; Ethics; Governor's Office; Governors' Papers; Human Resources; Insurance; Justice; Labor; Natural Resources and Community Development; Revenue; Transportation; University of North Carolina System; and various boards, such as the Boards of Architecture, Dental Examiners, Medical Examiners, Nursing, and Pharmacy. A *Guide to Research Materials in the North Carolina State Archives: State Agency Records* is available for purchase.

North Dakota State Archives and Historical Research
State Historical Society of North Dakota
Heritage Center (located on the grounds of the State Capitol)
612 East Boulevard Avenue
Bismarck, ND 58505-0830
archives@state.nd.us
701-328-2668
Fax: 701-328-3710
Reference Desk: 701-328-2091

The State Archives and Historical Research Library division of the State Historical Society of North Dakota is the official state archives and acquires and preserves all types of research materials relating to North Dakota and the Northern Great Plains, including manuscript collections, books, periodicals, maps, newspapers, audio and video materials, and photographs. The State Archives are the official records of the state, territory, and political subdivisions preserved for research purposes. Inventories exist for many series of records. Cataloged library-archives holdings are included in the Online Dakota Information Network (ODIN). A listing of North Dakota Newspapers held by the State Historical Society is also available on this Web site, as is a Guide to Manuscript Collections. The Guide to the North Dakota State Archives, published in 1985, is out of print. A revised Guide is available in typescript form. Individual series of records are also cataloged through OCLC.

Ohio Historical Society
1982 Velma Avenue
Columbus, OH 43211
http://www.ohiohistory.org/resource/statearc/index.html, or
http://www.ohiohistory.org/resource/archlib/index.html
614-297-2350
Fax: 614-297-2352

The Ohio Historical Society Archives/Library is, by law, the archives for the State of Ohio and collects, preserves, and makes available to the public documents pertaining to the operation of state and local governments. Materials include the Online Death Index and Youngstown Center of Industry and Labor Archives/Library (online for 1913–1937). For guidelines for off-site reference requests, see http://www.ohiohistory.org/resource/archlib/refemail.html. The State Archives has digitized and made some historical materials available online through the Ohio Vital Information for Libraries (OVIL). Materials include: Projects War of 1812 Roster, Fundamental Documents, Newspaper Index, National Registry of Historic Places, African American Experience in Ohio 1850–1920, and United States President Rutherford B. Hayes Diary and Letters. Records Series Finding Aids (in print and online) are alphabetical by State of Ohio Agency from which the records originated and include records from the Adjutant General, Agricultural Research and Development Center, Attorney General, Auditor of State, State Bank, Budget and Management, Bureau of Employment Services, Environmental Protection Agency, General Assembly, Governor, Ohio High Speed Rail Authority, Industrial Commission and Bureau of Workers' Compensation, State Library, Lieutenant Governor, Ohio Veteran's Children's Home, Ohio Veteran's Home, Public Utilities Commission, Board of Regents, Secretary of State, Treasurer of State; and the departments of Administrative Services, Agriculture, Commerce, Development, Education, Health, Highway Safety, Human Services, Industrial Relations, Insurance, Liquor Control, Mental Health, Mental Retardation and Developmental Disabilities, Natural Resources, Rehabilitation and Correction, Taxation, Transportation, and Youth Services.

Oklahoma State Archives
200 N.E. 18th Street
Oklahoma City, OK 73105
http://www.odl.state.ok.us/oar/
405-522-3579, toll-free 1-800-522-8116
Fax: 405-525-7804

Holdings include records of most state agencies and constitutional officers (i.e. those in the executive branch, such as the governor, lieutenant governor, and secretary of state). Among the records of the executive, legislative, and judicial branches are official papers of the governor's office; house and senate bills, joint resolutions, and concurrent resolutions; supreme court case files; secretary of state articles of incorporation; and General Land Office survey records and public land survey corner remonumentation filings. Collections with access through the Web site include the Index to Oklahoma's Confederate Pension Records (downloadable as an Adobe Acrobat PDF file), historical maps, index to aerial photographs, papers of the Territorial Governors, papers of Oklahoma's Governors, and Surveyors' Field Notes.

Oregon State Archives
800 Summer Street, N.E.
Salem, OR 97310
http://arcweb.sos.state.or.us/
503-373-0701
Fax: 503-373-0953

Guides for documenting state agency records held by the Archives can be searched online at the Web site. Components include agency history, scope and content notes, record series descriptions, image slide show, and Web links. The guides cover several agencies, including the departments of Agriculture, 1868–1996; Fish and Wildlife, 1901–1987; Forestry 1904–1998; the State Planning Board, 1860–1939; the

Division of State Lands, 1859–1989; and the Water Resources Department, 1852–1991. Online guides document county records held by the Oregon State Archives, all 36 Oregon counties, and other repositories. The inventory for each county is arranged alphabetically by series title. Because the organization of offices and their functions, the contents of the records, or the format of records may vary from county to county, notes have been included where necessary to indicate these differences. In appropriate cases, links are provided to the Genealogical Information Locator search page, which typically includes records such as probate case files, divorces, and censuses. The Oregon State Archives also holds the records of Territorial and State Governors and Legislative records. The Web site provides searchable descriptions and container listings of these records.

Pennsylvania Historical and Museum Commission
P.O. Box 1026
350 North Street
Harrisburg, PA 17108-1026
http://www.phmc.state.pa.us/bah/dam/overview.htm?
secid=31/
717-783-3281
Fax: 717-705-0482

Though primarily known as the official custodian of the permanently valuable records (Record Groups) of state government and its political subdivisions, the Archives is also, to a lesser extent, a repository for papers (Manuscript Groups) and records of individuals and families, businesses, and organizations that have statewide historical significance. Included among the holdings of the Pennsylvania State Archives are more than 195 million pages of documents and manuscripts; 20,000 reels of microfilm containing some 22 million images of county deeds, wills, mortgages, estate papers, and assessment books. For more information about the Pennsylvania State Archives, please refer to the *Pennsylvania Heritage* magazine article "A Treasure Trove of Historical Records: The Pennsylvania State Archives" by Sharon Hernes Silverman http://www.phmc.state.pa.us/bah/archives/overview. htm. Records are arranged and listed by series within record groups. Though most of the records groups correspond to Executive Branch department-level agencies of State Government, groups were also created to describe the archives of the Provincial and Revolutionary governments, the General Assembly, Supreme and Superior Courts, and County and Municipal governments. The record series are listed under the agency of origin or under the governmental unit which may have inherited the records and functions of a predecessor agency. Records are often further classified by subgroups that correspond to administrative units of the agency or defunct departments or commissions whose records and functions were transferred to that agency. For purposes of administrative control, local public records transferred to the State Archives are accessioned into three record groups: Record Group 47, Records of County Governments; Record Group 48, Records of Municipal Governments; and Record Group 55, Records of School Districts. The records of numerous state departments and agencies are available on microfilm. The Pennsylvania State Archives is an Affiliated Archives of the National Archives and Records Administration, which allows them to hold federal records. Records of the National Archives of the United States, which are deposited at the State Archives on permanent loan, are maintained and described in accordance with designations established by the National Archives and Records Administration. The affiliated archives records currently available for research at the Pennsylvania State Archives are Records of Brevet General John Frederick Hartranft as Special Provost Marshal for the Trial and Execution of the Assassins of President Lincoln: National Archives, Record Group 393, U.S. Army Continental Commands, 1821–1920 http://www.phmc.state.pa.us/bah/dam/aa/rg393.htm.

Rhode Island State Archives
337 Westminster Street
Providence, RI 02903
mailto:reference@archives.state.ri.us
401-222-2353
Fax: 401-222-3199

The repository maintains the original statewide manuscript filings for birth and marriage for the period 1852–1898 and deaths 1853–1948. Alphabetical indices for these records include 1852–1900 (birth and marriage) and 1853–1945 (deaths). Additionally, there are original reported out-of-state deaths recordings for the period 1900–1948 (alphabetical index available) and records of delayed birth filings, 1846–1898 (index available). Aside from these original manuscripts, the archives also maintains an extensive collection of pre-1852 municipal vital record filings (microfilm copies) dating from the earliest recordings in Providence, Westerly, Portsmouth, and other cities and towns.

South Carolina Department of Archives and History
Box 11669
Capitol Station, 8301 Parklane Road
Columbia, SC 29223
http://www.state.sc.us/scdah/
803-896-6100
Fax: 803-896-6198

The South Carolina Archives is a collection of more than 300 years of historical documents recording the rich and diverse history of the people and government of South Carolina. The Archives contains almost all known public records of South Carolina before 1785 and nearly complete records of the state government to 1950, as well as many more recent records. Included are all pre-1860 documents of permanent value, either in original form or on microfilm, from all South Carolina counties. The department also has extensive collections of post-1860 manuscripts and microfilm records of South Carolina's 46 counties.

South Dakota State Historical Society
900 Governors Drive
Pierre, SD 57501-2217
http://www.sdhistory.org/archives.htm
Archref@state.sd.us
605-773-3804
Fax: 605-773-6041

As the official repository of state records, the State Archives maintains and preserves the documents produced by the executive, legislative, and judicial branches of South Dakota state government. Many counties, municipalities, and townships have transferred historical records to the State Archives. The Archives collection also includes copies of federal records, such as censuses, land records, and files of the Bureau of Indian Affairs. Records are filed by series according to the agency that created them and the date they were received. Most records are kept in whatever file arrangement that existed when they arrived. Information and finding aids to collections are available on the archive's Web site. The State Archives is a member of the South Dakota Library Network and many of its resources are listed in the online catalog, available in many libraries in the state, and on the Internet http://sdln.net/. The catalog lists books, newspapers, serials, and some of the government and manuscript collections. The State Archives publishes information about collections and activities through the State Historical Society's quarterly journal, *South Dakota History,* and its newsletters, *History Notes* and *Hoofprints.*

Tennessee State Library and Archives
403 Seventh Avenue, North
Nashville, TN 37243-0312
http://www.state.tn.us/sos/statelib/tslahome.htm
615-741-2764
Fax: 615-532-5315

Archives and manuscript collections at the Tennessee State Library and Archives generally fall within four categories: (1) Archives of the State of Tennessee, organized as Record Groups; (2) Manuscript Collections; (3) Governors' Papers; and (4) Microfilm Collections. For each category the Web site lists processed collections available in that category. Follow hyperlinked collection titles for access to finding aids. Record Groups are numbered consecutively, and most are available on microfilm. An alphabetical listing of available Record Group finding aids is searchable on the Web site. The Archives has papers of every Tennessee governor beginning with the first territorial governor. Most are available on microfilm, and the finding aids are available online. The Web site also lists all records of state departments, agencies, committees, commissions, boards, and the legislature with links to the appropriate finding aids as well as information on the dates covered, the size of the collection, and whether or not the records are available in the originals and/or on microfilm.

Texas State Library and Archives
Box 12927
Austin, TX 78711
http://www.tsl.state.tx.us/arc/
512-463-5467
Fax: 512-463-5430

Archival holdings representing the official history of state government date as far back as the Spanish colonial period and the Republic Era and document activities of all three branches of Texas government. The Archives Collection also includes books and journals, private manuscripts, photographs, and maps. Brief descriptions of finding aids are available in the Library Catalog of Texas State Agencies. See Processed State Records for a list of finding aids to the processed records of Texas state agencies. Available are searchable databases to the Map Collection, Republic Claims, Confederate Pension Applications, Adjutant General Service Records, and Confederate Indigent Families List. Records Available on Microfilm include: 1867 Voters' Registration; Election Registers; Executive Record Books; Nacogdoches Archives, which include a variety of records maintained by national, regional, and local officials—

both political and military—of the Mexican government from the mid-eighteenth into the early nineteenth century; and Texas Convict Record Ledgers and Indexes. For holdings of local records, an index of County Records on Microfilm is available online.

Utah State Archives
P.O. Box 141021
Salt Lake City, UT 84114
http://www.archives.state.ut.us/
research@das.state.ut.us
801-538-3012
Fax: 801-538-3354

The Archives does not collect personal manuscript materials, such as diaries. Government records include annual reports, meeting minutes, legislative bills, city ordinances, birth and death records, naturalization records, incorporation records, court and probate records, correspondence, publications, and other agency mission–related record series. The Web site gives a list of records in the Archives' permanent holdings that have been processed (arranged and described) for research use. Some have links to sample records for viewing. The online catalog http://archives.utah.gov/catbegin.htm contains both permanent and non-permanent records, but searches may be limited to only permanent records in the Archives' holdings. The catalog allows a more advanced search, which includes links to all the possible agency names, titles, or subjects in the catalog. Most records held by the Utah State Archives are not indexed. Some creating agencies may have indexed record series, but frequently these are found as an index at the beginning or end of an individual volume or as a separate record series. Such indexes are then available in paper or on microfilm. A few series are indexed electronically. The Web site lists holdings available for searching online.

Vermont State Archives
Redstone Building
26 Terrace Street, Drawer 09
Montpelier, VT 05609-1103
http://vermont-archives.org/
802-828-2363
Fax: 802-828-2496

Holdings of the Archives can be accessed through the online catalog ARCCAT http://www.state.vt.us/vhs/arccat/. The Web site also provides a searchable guide that has a summary of the holdings. New links to descriptions are added as often as possible. While most agency and department records are deposited with the Public Records Division, the Archives has some agency and department records, most notably records from Tourism and Marketing and its predecessors and photograph collections from several agencies and departments. The governors' records at the Archives contain interactions between the governor's office and state agencies and departments. Holdings include records of Attorneys General, boards and commissions, corporations, Elections, Governors, the Legislature, Lieutenant Governors, Municipal charters, public buildings/state property, Secretaries of State, and Surveyors. Also included are various records on the Vermont Constitution, proposals of amendment and referenda, 1777 to the present, and manuscript Vermont State Papers.

Virginia
Library of Virginia, Archival and Information Services Division
800 East Board Street
Richmond, VA 23219-8000
http://www.lva.lib.va.us/whatwedo/archives/index.htm
804-692-3888
Fax: 804-692-3556

The official repository for all state records, the archives also accepts public records from the counties and cities and a wide variety of manuscript materials. A comprehensive collection of published local history and genealogy supplements the archives' extensive collection of surviving state, county, and city records and other manuscript holdings. County and city circuit court records include original deeds, wills, order books, case files, and loose court papers dating from the 1600s through the 1940s. The archives provides access to the surviving records of Virginia's colonial and revolutionary-era governments, various constitutional conventions from 1776 to 1969, and the governor, legislature and state judiciary. There is also an extensive map collection focusing on Virginia. There is a catalog of state and local government records, military records, personal papers, family Bible records, genealogical notes and charts, church and cemetery records, business records, maps, and other archival and manuscript material. Some finding aids are available online at http://eaglc.vsla.edu/bible/virtua-basic.html. The State Archives also contains the records of the Colonial and Revolutionary governments, records of the various constitutional conventions, and records of independent state agencies http://www.lva.lib.va.us/whatwehave/gov/govhist.htm. Record series are divided into 18 broad categories according to their type and function. The categories are: Board of Supervisors Records Bonds/Commissions/Oaths; Business Records and Corporations/Partnerships; Census Records; Court Records; Election Records; Fiduciary Records; Free Negro and Slave Records; Justice of the Peace Records; Land Records; Marriage Records and Vital Statistics; Military and Pension Records; Organization Records; Road and Bridge Records; School Records; Tax and Fiscal Records; Wills; and Miscellaneous Records. The Library of Virginia houses both loose and microfilmed county and city records. For more information on the content of these records, consult the "Introduction to County and City Records" http://www.lva.lib.va.us/whatwehave/local/intro-county_city_recs.htm.

Washington Division of Archives and Records Management
1120 Washington Street SE
P.O. Box 40238
Olympia, WA 98504-0238
http://www.secstate.wa.gov/archives/
research@secstate.wa.gov
360-586-1492
Fax: 360-664-8814

The State Records Collections provide a vital account of public government in Washington State, beginning with the establishment of Washington Territory in 1853 and continuing to the present. Included among the collection are the papers of each governor, legislative records, court records, records from all state agencies, and all of the "official records" of the state, including governors' proclamations, executive orders, election results, and the laws as passed and signed. Historical records of local governments are collected, preserved, and made available at five regional branch archives. These records document county and city governments, special districts, and other local or regional state entities. The Main Archives branch is in Olympia. The following are regional branches: Northwest Region in Bellingham, Southwest Region in Olympia, Central Region in Ellensburg, Eastern Region in Cheney, and the Puget Sound Region in Bellevue. The Web site gives a link to each regional depository.

West Virginia Archives and History
The Cultural Center
1900 Kanawha Blvd. East
Charleston, WV 25305
http://www.wvculture.org/history/wvsamenu.html
304-558-0230, ext. 168
Fax: 304-558-2779

When West Virginia became a state, records for the counties remained within each county. Microfilm copies of original county records are available. All West Virginia counties are included; however, some county records are incomplete. Records include births and deaths (since 1853), marriages, wills, deeds, surveys, estate records, and some circuit court records. The only significant tax records available are land tax books and personal property tax records. The land records, originally maintained by the State Auditor's Office and prepared by county assessors, exist from the date of the counties' formations to the 1930s, and for almost one-half the state's counties through 1959. Personal property tax lists for select West Virginia counties through 1850 are available on microfilm. The original tax lists are retained at The Library of Virginia, 800 E. Broad St., Richmond, VA 23219. Some vital statistics, including death certificates (1917–1970) and delayed and regular birth certificates (c. 1880–1919) are available. Most West Virginia and Virginia census records are available on microfilm prepared by the National Archives. The census of Virginia, which includes those counties now in West Virginia, is available for the years 1790 and 1810–1860. Also available are the Virginia census for 1870 and slave schedules for 1850 and 1860. West Virginia census records include the years 1870, 1880, 1900, 1910, 1920, and the *1890 Special Census of Union Veterans and Widows*. Records of service in the colonial wars, the Revolutionary War, and the War of 1812 can be found in lists of pensioners and in printed sources. The records and index to West Virginia Union troops (1861–1865) are available on microfilm. Confederate records of Virginia and West Virginia, with index, are available on microfilm. Other records on microfilm include the veterans' burial file, containing information on servicemen interred in the state prior to 1936. Records from the Adjutant General's Office provide muster information on men in the National Guard from 1890 through World War I and other World War I enlistments. The Web site has online guides for County Court Records on Microfilm, Naturalization records, maps, newspapers on microfilm, and state government records.

Wisconsin Historical Society
816 State Street, Madison, WI 53706-1482
http://www.wisconsinhistory.org/archives/index.html
608-264-6460

Online access to catalog information on manuscripts and public records is available through the

Archives Computer Catalog (ArCat): http://www.wisconsinhistory.org/archives/arcat.html. Holdings include the records of the governor's office; records of state agencies that contain formal minutes of governing boards, committees, commissions, and task forces; legal opinions; administrative rulemaking and legislative files; policy records; selected case files; narrative and statistical reports; special study records; and selected visual, audio, graphic, cartographic, and electronic records. Available also are records of local governments, school districts, and courts, including County Board proceedings, Common Council proceedings, County and Municipal ordinances and resolutions, probate case files, wills, court case files (including criminal, civil, family, and divorce cases), naturalization records, school district and school board reports, tax rolls, and land deeds and grantor/grantee indexes. Pre-1907 birth, death, and marriage records are available in the Society Library and at Area Research Centers.

Wyoming Division of Cultural Resources
Barrett Building, 2301 Central
Cheyenne, WY 82002
http://wyoarchives.state.wy.us/index.htm
307-777-7013
Fax: 307-777-3543

This unit collects and manages public records from Wyoming state and local governments that have long-term administrative, legal, and historical value. Records are filed under the office of origin. The Archives also collects nongovernmental records of historical value concerning Wyoming and the western United States. The Web site lists Wyoming counties, State Governors, and Territorial Governors whose records are available for research at the Archives. The records from the Secretary of State's office include: administrative; Wyoming constitutional convention; legislative; election; appointments, commissions, oaths, and bonds; corporation and business records; and executive criminal filings.

LOCAL GOVERNMENT ARCHIVES

Within the states many cities and counties have established local government archives and records centers. Some examples of local government archives are: Bedford (MA) Municipal Archives; Burlington (MA) Town Archives; Cape May County Clerk's Office; East Baton Rouge (LA) Clerk of Court's Office; Circuit Court of Cook County (IL); City Archives and Records Division of Henderson, NV; City Archives of Philadelphia; City Archives of Boston; City Archives of Dallas; City Archives of Hollywood; City Archives of Portland; City Archives of Richmond; City Archives of Venice, Florida; Harris County Texas; Hershey (PA) Community Archives; Irving (TX) Public Library; King County (TX) Records and Archives; Mobile (AL) Municipal Archives; Montgomery (AL) City Archives; New York Department of Records; New Orleans Public Library, which houses the New Orleans City Archives; Office of the City Clerk (Nashua, NH); Philadelphia City Archives; Providence (RI) Archives; Salt Lake City Records Management and Archives; Seattle Municipal Archives; and Troup County (GA) Archives. Public libraries and local historical societies may also be the archival repository for the records of the local government in their town, municipality, city, or county. Some generalizations can be made about the types of materials these local government archives acquire, arrange and describe, and make available. Most are responsible for the records of the governing elected body of the city or county as well as the records of the office of mayor or city/county managers. These governing bodies may be titled county commissions, boards of commissioners, city councils, city commissioners, or aldermen. The records of such local government agencies include minutes of meetings, resolutions and ordinances presented and adopted, correspondence, suits, and financial materials. Other local government records that archives may maintain are the records of school boards, police departments, parks and recreation departments, libraries, and local grants and contracts records. County clerks of courts records are often sought by the general research public. Types of records held by Clerks of courts are suits, civil and criminal files; probate records; marriage prenuptial agreements and divorce settlements; and naturalization and immigration records. Within the court and probate records can be affidavits identifying familial relationships and the wills of deceased persons.

Locating local government records may be easy if a researcher is only interested in one locality, in which case a telephone call to the local public library or directory assistance for the area will possibly locate an archives. For researchers seeking information from many different localities, no one method serves to locate all local government archives. The American Association of State and Local History publishes a guide to *State and local historical agencies in the United States and Canada,* which gives detailed information about the holdings of local government archives. Also helpful are state archives, which may maintain links to local government archives on their Web sites and may be able to answer questions regarding local government archives and their locations within the state through U.S. mail. See the Society of American Archivists Web site http://www.archivists.org/. The National Association of Government Archives and Records Managers will answer limited inquiries about local government archives.

MORE INFORMATION

The majority of the information in this chapter was compiled from the Web sites of the represented archives and from archival guides. More information on American governmental records can be found in various guides that also contain descriptions of other types of nongovernment archival materials. The *National Inventory of Documentary Sources (NIDS),* published by Chadwyck Healy Inc., was issued in paper and microfiche from 1982 to 1991. Included in Parts 1 and 2 (published in paper) is information on federal records, the National Archives, presidential libraries, and the Smithsonian Institution. Parts 3 and 4 (published in microfiche) include information on holdings of state archives as well as some local government archives. Since 1992 NIDS has been issued on CD-ROM. *The National Inventory of Documentary Sources* may not be found in small public libraries, but can usually be found in college and university libraries, as well as large public libraries.

Although it has not been updated since 1988, the *Directory of Archives and Manuscript Repositories in the United States* (Oryx Press) is still a helpful guide to determining the location of various governmental archives and the types of materials they make available for research. Also helpful is the subscription electronic database *Archives USA,* either on CD-ROM or online, which begin in 1997. *Archives USA* can be found in research libraries and major university research libraries.

Useful Web sites for general information about repositories holding American governmental records are:

http://www.uidaho.edu/special-collections/Other. Repositories.html. The Special Collections Department of the University of Idaho maintains an up-to-date geographical listing of government and nongovernment archives in the United States and Canada.

http://www.columbia.edu/cu/lweb/eguides/speccol. html. This is a selective guide to finding archives and manuscript collections and includes a list of national archives and libraries, college and university collections, and historical society archives.

http://www.archives.gov/. National Archives and Records Administration's Web site gives extensive and current information about the various departments of NARA, plus contact information and research procedures. The Web site also gives links to other agencies.

CHAPTER 2
Genealogical Archives

Russell P. Baker

The term *genealogical archives,* as used in the United States, has several different meanings. It can refer to an archival institution, such as the Maryland State Archives in Annapolis, Maryland, that collects and maintains the kinds of historic manuscripts, public records, publications, microfilm, and other materials that are the principal sources of information for genealogists and family historians. It also refers to a large collection of genealogical material housed in an institution such as the Genealogical Research Library of the National Society of the Daughters of the American Revolution in Washington, D.C. In fact, records of potential interest to genealogists can be found in almost any facility that houses historic records, be it a state archive, a local historical society, a public or private library, or the basement of a local courthouse. Genealogical archives, unlike more traditional archives that concentrate upon one or two major political, economic, religious, or cultural figures, groups, or events, are much more broadly focused in what they acquire. Genealogical records contain the information one needs to retell the lives of the quintessential American everyman and everywoman, regardless of their class, culture, or religion. They chronicle the seemingly mundane everyday activities and family interconnections that form the grist for the genealogist's mill. However, because genealogy is all about locating information relating to families and family connections, family researchers can be found clamoring for admittance at almost any archival institution.

Genealogical archives also differ from other public archives in the demographics of their patrons. Instead of attracting academic researchers, college students, or professional historians exclusively, genealogical collections draw researchers from a cross section of our varied, polyglot people, whose ethnic and cultural roots span the world. Although few of us can truly prove that European kings or African princes lurk in our family's past, we as Americans take an inordinate pride in the many just *plain* folks who populate our family trees, be they English convicts, French trappers, or Cherokee maidens. Researchers looking for these populist ancestors fit into no single ethnic, cultural profile, or age category. At any given time, archival search rooms and library stacks can be crowded with patrons with ages ranging from preteens to the elderly. Here the casually dressed tourist rubs shoulders with the business-suited professional. Generation X'ers work side by side with baby boomers and senior citizens. Unlike traditional academic researchers who may use a particular collection of primary source material once or twice during their professional careers, genealogical researchers, whose family history work is never done, often are daily visitors to the archives. In fact, many archival institutions call upon these kinds of patrons when seeking volunteers, fund-raisers, and goodwill ambassadors.

WHAT IS IT—GENEALOGY?

Genealogy, or family history (the terms are used interchangeably), is a popular American hobby that is slowly evolving into an auxiliary historical discipline. Its popularity has had an immense impact upon archives and libraries across the country. This is especially true for institutions that house large collections of biographical, religious, cultural, or ethnic material. A clear understanding of the basics of genealogical research coupled with some insight into the genealogical mindset or paradigm will benefit both the potential genealogist and the genealogical reference provider. Such an understanding is essential for the successful completing of a genealogical research project.

At its core, genealogy is an activity that seeks to locate, document, and preserve the story of one's ancestors; or in Alex Haley's immortal words, one's "roots." Genealogists search through collections of primary source materials seeking information on births, deaths, and marriages within their families with a view toward tracing direct descent from one generation to another. In the past, genealogists often ended their research after producing pedigree charts and family group sheets on their immediate family. However, within the past few years, as genealogical education has improved and genealogists have become more sophisticated in their approach to understanding historic sources, many family historians have expanded their interests into a number of allied fields. More than just a few now seek to understand the lives of their ancestors in the cultural and historical context of the period in which they lived. Searching for one's roots often serves as a springboard into an avid interest in military, religious, political, and cultural history.

More important than a textbook definition, is an understanding of the paradigm or the mindset of the genealogist. The "what makes the genealogists tick" definition. Interest in one's ancestors is at least as old as the Hebrew Bible and is a feature of many ancient and modern societies. During the Middle Ages, proving or disproving royal descent was one of the preoccupations of noble families of Europe. Americans, on the other hand, have historically been too busy taming the wilderness and establishing a new nation to devote much time to looking into the stories behind their own family's roots. However, this preoccupation with all things present changed about four decades ago as the result of a series of events that caught the public's attention and focused it upon the nation's past. One was the Civil War Centennial from 1961 to 1965, and the other was the American Revolution Bicentennial in 1976.

However, it was an airing of the dramatic story *Roots* that changed the face and character of American genealogy. Based upon the family history research of Alex Haley, *Roots* is the story of one family's journey from slavery to freedom. What had been a quirky hobby practiced by a few devotees suddenly mushroomed into a national mania that has since grown into a million-dollar industry, with its own publishing houses, jargon, literature, Internet Web sites, national conferences, and genealogical superstars.

None of these events by themselves can account for the fact that hunting for one's ancestors has become a national obsession in the United States. However, collectively, they convinced many people that their ancestors also had a lost story worth finding, recording, and preserving. For the first time, Americans from all lifestyles began to feel a vital connection with the events that shaped the story of the past. Curiosity about one's ancestors continues to lead researchers to libraries and archives throughout the country. It has spurred an unprecedented interest in the American Civil War. It has spawned a growing awareness of America's cultural and ethnic diversity and has given birth to the specialized subfields of African American and Native American research. Organizations based upon an ancestor's race, country of origin, religious affiliation, or prior military service attract thousands of members annually. It is often said to be the second most popular activity on the Internet.

However, there is more to America's new fascination with the past than just hunting for one's ancestors. It is a collective search for self-discovery, a quest for personal roots in a rootless society. It is a constant seeking for answers to the question, "Who am I and where did I come from?" For this reason, everyone in the United States is a prospective genealogist. It is this drive to establish a personal identity that creates for genealogists and family historians an intensity of interest and singleness of purpose that often perplexes archivists, librarians, record keepers, and county officials.

HOW DO I DO GENEALOGICAL RESEARCH?

Unfortunately, not all patrons who show up at genealogical archives are trained and experienced family historians. Many are researchers just beginning their journey in search of their roots. The following are a few basic rules of the road designed to help budding family historians prepare for the research experience.

Charts and Forms

Pedigree charts: The judicious use of pedigree charts and family-group sheets can aid both beginning researchers and the reference staff members they call upon for assistance. Most archives and libraries with genealogical patrons keep a supply of these forms on hand for patron use or for photocopying. Copies can also be downloaded from genealogical Web sites or printed from genealogical programs in commercial computers. Pedigree chart, fill-in-the-blank forms with origins in Medieval Europe, are simple devices that allow researchers to record information on each direct ancestor, generation by generation. They can be obtained in charts covering four, five, or more generations. Using known information, researchers begin their genealogy by recording data on themselves. They then work backward trying to record the birth, death, marriage, and so on, for as many generations as possible. Custom dictates that researchers record their paternal line at the top of the chart and their maternal line at the bottom. After completing this chart, the researcher can begin planning for the research needed to fill in the missing information.

Family-group sheets: A much more recent addition to the genealogical arsenal of charts and forms is the family-group sheet. This is a device used to collect expanded information on each couple recorded on the pedigree chart. When it was introduced into the field of family history after World War II, it brought about a revolution in research by encouraging genealogists to shift from collecting data on one individual ancestor at a time to collecting data on the ancestral family. Unlike pedigree charts that more or less have a standard form, family-group sheets come in a variety of configurations, sizes, and shapes. Researchers should shop around for a style that meets their particular research needs. Genealogical reference sections often have a variety of styles for patrons to copy. The most effective ones are those that provide space for recording the source or documentation of each piece of information recorded on the form. See William Dollarhide's *Genealogy Starter Kit* for several inexpensive forms.

The research log: One of the newer tools for the family history researcher is the research log. This is a simple form that allows the researcher to keep a running list of the records searched, the rolls of microfilm viewed, and the titles of publications scrutinized by day or by research trip. Keeping a good research log can be a lifesaver when trying to identify a photocopy that has no source information or when trying to decipher a strange notation on one's family-group sheet. It can also save research time by preventing duplication of research effort. There are several commercial versions of research logs available or researchers can make their own. Everton Publishers, Inc., at P.O. Box 368, Logan, Utah, 84323-0368, has a number of different styles of charts, group sheets, and research logs.

Computer genealogy programs: A number of genealogy programs are currently on the market. Researchers should compare several versions to see which meets their particular needs. The most expensive is not necessarily the best. Laptop computers loaded with a genealogical program are useful tools for research trips. However, not all archives permit their use. Older facilities may not have electrical outlets suitable for laptops. Getting them past security checks at airport and in public buildings may also be a problem. The careful researcher always has pencil and paper on hand as backup equipment.

"WHERE DO I BEGIN?"

The most frequently asked question by beginning genealogists is "Where do I begin?" Since successful genealogical research is based upon a systematic research plan, it is one of the most important questions. Unlike a typical historical research project, which is preoccupied with the past, genealogical research is all about connecting the present to the past and finding the *connections* between the researchers and their ancestors. Thus, the correct place to begin is with oneself, and the proper direction for research is *from* the present *to* the past. Avoid the mistake of trying to begin with some assumed ancestor in hopes of finding a link between the past and present. This approach typically leads to frustration, disappointment, and a search for a new hobby. A much more productive approach is to begin with oneself, one's parents, one's grandparents, and so on, and then work backward. The old genealogical adage is correct, "the successful road to the past begins in the present."

Lack of preparation is another mistake often made by beginning genealogists. It is the leading cause of researcher disappointment and burnout. Unfortunately, many would-be genealogists arrive at an archive without a clear idea of what they are seeking. According to the Arlington, Va.: National Genealogical Society's (2003) tips for beginners, http://www.ngs genealogy.org/edugetstart.htm "Getting Started...," "Personal knowledge can form the first limbs of your family tree." A search of family sources usually turns up family surnames, dates of births and deaths, and other information that provide additional clues to interfamily connections. Family Bible records, copies of birth, death, and marriage certificates may also be located. Do not overlook obituaries, wedding invitations, anniversary articles, and so on. Collections of photographs are also rich sources of genealogical information. This type of information can be used to begin the process of filling out pedigree charts and family-group sheets. As the charts take shape, questions will emerge that will help give direction to the overall research. According to the Maryland State Archives in "The First Steps to Take," http://www.mdarchives.state.md.us/msa/refserv/genealogy/html/genstart.html, researchers should "analyze exactly what objects need to be achieved" with their research. "What do I want to find out with this research?" is always an appropriate question to ask.

Networking with Family and Friends

Family members can also be a vital source of genealogical information. The National Genealogical Society suggests, "Contact family members" and "ask questions about their lives and those of other family members. Where did they live—what part of the country—what kind of dwelling? Did they move around while growing up? When were their relatives born; when did they die?" (National Genealogical Society Web site). Ask family members about photographs, old letters, and other memorabilia. Inquire if anyone else in the family has already conducted genealogical research. Write letters, make telephone calls, and use E-mails to ask questions about long lost family members. Genealogical Web sites on the Internet, though they should not be substituted for genuine genealogical research, often contain useful information for the beginner. Some popular Web sites are http://www.familysearch.org/, http://www.usgenweb.com/, and http://www.ancestry.com/. Some Web sites contain free information, while others require the user to register and pay a fee. Explore the free Web sites first.

Using Oral History

Some cultures have a rich heritage of passing along family history and family traditions through song, storytelling, and even dance. Such oral traditions can be a gold mine of genealogical data as they retell important positive events, such as marriages, births, emancipations, and so on, or significant negative events, such as crime, incest, murder, hard times, and so on. Regardless of the nature of such traditions, the family researcher can ill afford to ignore them. The researcher must use these oral histories as positive signposts to important milestones in the family history and avoid making moral judgements concerning an ancestor. Oral history is especially useful in researching members of cultures that often operated outside the traditional network of record keeping, such as those of African American and Native American cultures.

Collections of historical oral material often find their way into genealogical archives. Two excellent examples are the narrative biographies of ex-slaves housed at the Library of Congress, now published in *The American Slave: A Composite Autobiography* (Westport, Conn: Greenwood Publishing Company, 1972) series, and the reminiscent personal histories in the Indian Pioneer History Collection at the Oklahoma Historical Society. Information gleaned from oral history, as useful as it might be, should always be examined in the light of the historic record. Some family stories may prove to be more fancy than fact. Others may attribute actions of one ancestor to someone else entirely.

Read a Good Book

There is currently an excellent selection of books about all aspects of genealogical research on the market. They range from those designed for the beginning researcher to the works dealing with African American and Native American research. (See the bibliography at the end of this chapter for a selected list.) Instructional videos and audiotapes are also available. One can also access instruction on family history research over the Internet. Many local historical and genealogical societies and community colleges have periodic classes and workshops on the subject. The well-prepared researcher finds genealogy an absorbing and fulfilling hobby. Time invested in doing one's homework and learning the basics of research is time well spent.

RULES, REGULATIONS, AND PROCEDURES OF GENEALOGICAL ARCHIVES

Since most genealogists begin their research in local libraries, a first visit to an archival institution often results in cultural shock. Although both libraries and archives may have many collections of books and other publications, the two institutions can differ widely in their operating procedures. Archives, because they deal with irreplaceable historical material, are by nature more restrictive then some other institutions. The regulations may also differ from archive to archive. Genealogical patrons commonly complain about the restrictive nature of the policies in archives. This usually arises when the patron is not aware of the policies in advance. A very useful tactic on the part of genealogists is "always know before you go." Information on rules, regulations, and procedures can easily be obtained through a telephone call, a letter, or an E-mail to the institution at hand. A search on the Internet is also an excellent way to obtain copies of archival policies. New patrons should always read all information carefully and ask for any clarifications or exceptions in writing before they visit. Those who feel that archival restrictions are burdensome should pursue their research interest elsewhere.

Registration and Security

By the nature of their operations, archives are very security conscious. Now, due to the threat of international terrorism, security at all public facilities, including archives, has been heightened. Most archives require all potential patrons to show a current driver's license or a military identification, a valid passport, or other photo identification before they enter any research area. Patrons may also be required to complete a registration application, giving complete name, current address, and telephone number. In some institutions, patrons are required to wear a photo identification badge while in the facility. In many places, bags, purses, briefcases, boxes, packages, and so on, must be left in lockers outside of the research area or be subject to search upon leaving the facility. Firearms or weapons of any kind except those carried by law enforcement officers or military personnel on duty are usually not allowed. Most facilities do not allow pets of any kind in the archives.

Availability of Collections and Prior Approval

One major difference between archives and libraries is the availability of collections. In libraries research materials are usually available when the institution is open. Archives, on the other hand, often house manuscripts, publications, photographs, or even microfilm collections that may not be available without prior approval. While most traditional genealogical collections are usually unrestricted, use of other types of archival material may be much more limited. Besides prior approval, which may take the form of a letter of application stating the purpose of the patron's research or a letter of reference, some collections may require a signed release form from the original record holder. Patrons wishing to see a particular collection should inquire about its availability before finalizing their travel plans. Researchers may also encounter restrictions on photocopying original material, using computers, using tape recorders, using personal copiers and scanners, and so on, without prior permission. A simple telephone call, letter, or E-mail will save the potential patron countless hours of frustration and embarrassment.

Use of Material

Archival patrons are also often shocked to learn that they cannot bring items such as boxes, bags, suitcases, food, water bottles, hand-held scanners, laptops, and pets into research areas. Such items, except for pets, usually must be stored in lockers provided by the archives. Items taken into the research area are usually subject to search afterward. There may be additional restrictions on researchers wishing to use original manuscript materials. Patrons may be required to use pencils while taking notes. They may be required to ask for staff permission before making photocopies. In some instances, the researcher may be required to wear gloves while handling original materials. Such restrictions are designed to protect the archives' holdings and to prevent theft. Historians who are aware of archives' policies and procedures in advance will have far fewer surprises during their research than those who do not.

Hours of Operations

Unlike academic archives that often tailor their schedules to fit the school year, most archives with genealogical collections are usually open throughout the year. However, some may operate on a split schedule, being open on weekends but closed on Mondays or some other day during the week. Local historical societies and smaller archives may be open only one or two days per week. State, federal, and local holidays also affect archival operations. Public offices, including archives, are closed on Columbus Day in Alabama while those in Arkansas are open. It is a relatively simple matter for potential patrons to telephone beforehand or check with the appropriate archival Internet Web site for hours of operation and holiday schedules.

Orientation

Public research areas in genealogical archives are often divided into specialized work areas. There might be a section devoted to microfilm, an area for published material, another for manuscript items, and yet another for photocopying. Each area may have its own finding aids, collection catalogues, indexes, and even its own regulations. Other areas may be off limits to all but staff members and specially authorized patrons. It is always appropriate to ask a staff member or a volunteer for an orientation tour of public research areas, or at the very least, request a map that shows various research locations. It is also always appropriate to ask about the location of rest areas, drinking fountains, restrooms, and so on.

Special Needs Patrons

Research patrons with special needs should always contact the archive in advance of a visit. Most public facilities built within the past two decades are equipped to meet the reasonable needs of all users. However, many genealogical collections housed in older courthouses, on the upper floors of libraries, or in the basements of churches are not equipped to meet all special needs. Locating convenient handicap parking can also be a challenge, especially for older facilities that have no on-site parking. Patrons with special visual needs should inquire in advance about the availability of magnification lenses, enlargement equipment, and so on. Patrons in wheelchairs or on walkers should ask beforehand about available elevators, ramps, and handicap-accessible emergency exits.

Reference Requests

Many archives with genealogical collections employ staff members who can answer patron inquiries in person or by telephone, letter, or in some cases E-mail or fax. However, the responsibility for doing the research rests primarily with the patron. Archival staff members cannot do extensive research for patrons. In many cases, genealogical facilities can furnish out-of-town patrons with a list of professional researchers. Patrons who request information by telephone or mail are more likely to receive a positive answer if their request is in the form of a question. For example, a researcher asking for "all the information you have on the Baker Family" will usually receive a form letter referring the researcher to a professional researcher. However, a specific question such as "Do you have the Arkansas Confederate Pension records of Patrick Henry Baker of Pike County?" usually elicits a reply about the availability of such a record and the cost of receiving a photocopy. Patrons should also refrain from bombarding genealogical archives with lengthy letters containing numerous requests for information. The best inquiry is a short inquiry. Before

writing, keep in mind that not all records are published, abstracted, indexed, or are in a computer database. The answers to some genealogical questions may require years of devoted research.

Fees and Photocopies

Fees and the availability of photocopies vary from archive to archive. Some institutions have excellent photocopying equipment. Others have antiquated equipment or none available at all. Patrons should come equipped to copy material by hand if necessary. Some kinds of archival material may be copied while other kinds may not. In some institutions, staff members make all the photocopies; in others, patrons make their own. In some archives, patrons must bring their own change; others may have change machines. Some archives, especially those operated by private and religious organizations, may charge a daily or per-item use fee. Some may also charge a research fee for staff assistance. Other fees may cover parking or locker use. It is always convenient to inquire about archival fees in advance.

Copyright

Most historic material used for genealogical research is in the public domain. This includes records created by federal, state, county, and local governments at the public expense, which are not subject to the copyright laws. However, genealogical researchers should be aware of possible copyright restrictions if they plan to use private manuscript collections that contain twentieth- and twenty-first-century material. Usually copyright questions arise if patrons plan to publish sizable portions of a document or entire documents. Questions about copyright issues should be addressed to the archival staff in advance.

Behavior

An archive is not a place for casual chatter, family visits, or disruptive horseplay. It is an institution devoted to serious research. Noise from personal equipment should be kept to a minimum. Patrons with cellular telephones, laptops, tape recorders, or other electronic equipment should obtain permission in advance before using them in the archives. Research facilities are not usually equipped to meet the needs of patrons with babies or small children. Some archives only admit professional researchers to their search areas. Archival patrons should avoid loud and lengthy conversations with other researchers, family members, or reference personnel. Archive users should endeavor to keep a respectful demeanor toward staff members and cheerfully comply with their requests. Those who consistently violate posted rules and regulations may be asked to leave the archives. Patrons witnessing disruptive behavior should report it to a staff member at once.

BASIC GENEALOGICAL SOURCES

Archives in the United States are unusually rich in genealogical source material. Researchers who systematically search through the following six categories of historic records should find much of the information they need to conduct a successful and rewarding research. Potential archival patrons should inquire about the availability of these kinds of records before planning a research trip. A visit to the institution's Web site, a telephone call, or a letter asking for a description of genealogical holdings is always appropriate.

Vital Records

Vital records contain information about an individual's birth, death, marriage or divorce, and in some jurisdictions, adoption. They are usually created and maintained by an agency of local, county, or state government, such as a health department. Present-day researchers are often surprised to learn that preserving such records, now considered a necessity, was not often practiced in the past. While New Hampshire has some vital records that date back to 1640, Georgia did not begin keeping them until 1919. Vital records from the past are often more incomplete than their modern counterparts. Vital records relating to minority communities may be very incomplete or nonexistent.

Unlike many European counties, there is no central repository of vital records in the United States. Each state or locality has custody of its own records. Because of this, public access to such information varies from state to state. In some areas, records are open to all researchers. In others, their use is severely restricted or not permitted at all. In some cases, records must be more than 50 years old before they can be used for research. In some jurisdictions, duplicate copies of vital records are kept at the local or county level and may be used there. Copies of older records may also end up in archival collections. Thomas Jay Kemp's *International Vital Records Handbook* (Baltimore, Md.: Genealogical Publishing Company, many editions) is an extremely useful tool for locating vital

records of many Americans. Many state vital records bureaus also maintain Web sites. There are now several published statewide death indexes available for research. Death indexes tend to be much more accessible than birth records. Internet Web sites such as the USGenWeb Project (http://www.usgenweb.com) can yield additional information on state and local vital records.

Social Security and Railroad Retirement Records

Genealogical researchers looking for present-day vital records now have several additional resources available to them. These records are kept by the Social Security Administration and the Railroad Retirement Board. Within the past few years, the federal government has released certain information from the files of deceased social security beneficiaries. It includes the name, the date of death, the place of death, and the social security number of the deceased. These records are accessible at many genealogical archives through search databases or on the Internet. More detailed information, including full name, date and place of birth, names of parents, occupation, date and place of application, and so on, can be ordered from the Office of Central Records Operations in Baltimore, Maryland, 21201, by completing a form called "Social Security Number Record Third Party Request for Extract or Photocopy." This is an especially useful tool for locating family members that are currently missing. However, researchers should keep in mind that the social security system did not begin until 1936 and that not all Americans were required to participate in the system until the 1960s.

In the twentieth century, an additional government retirement system, the railroad retirement system, similar in many respects to social security, began operation for the benefit of retired railroad workers. Files for individual workers contain a gold mine of genealogical data. Contact the Railroad Retirement Board, 844 N. Rush St., Chicago, Illinois, 60611-2092, for more information.

U.S. Census Records 1790–1930

Population Schedules

Since the quality and quantity of vital records vary greatly from state to state, a much more consistent source for genealogical information within the United States is found in the records created by the decennial

U.S. Census Bureau. Individual and household information from these national enumerations, taken every 10 years since 1790, is currently available through 1930. These records form the most widely available source of historical data in the country. Microfilmed copies of the census records are a major part of the collections of most genealogical archives. Copies of some census records are also available on CDs and on the Internet. The census records that most genealogists use are *population schedules,* which list family information, such as names, ages, places of birth, as well as others. These population schedules are remarkably complete, except for those from 1890, which were mostly destroyed in a fire in 1921. They are arranged by territory or state, then by county, district, or parish. In many cases, they are further subdivided into minor civil divisions (MCD) called townships, districts, beats, or divisions. The publication of the first computer-generated indexes to these records, beginning about 1970, revolutionized genealogical research in the United States. In the 1990s additional census indexes began appearing on CDs and on the Internet. Currently there are census indexes available for most states from 1790 through 1870. However, the genealogical researcher should note that these indexes are often incomplete or distorted. Recently, several Web sites have started to offer digital copies and indexes of U.S. census records for a fee. One such site is http://www.ancestry.com/ (MyFamily.com, Inc.). Unfortunately, the quality of many of these digital copies leaves much to be desired.

Early population schedules, those from 1790 through 1840, usually only listed the name of the head of the house, the number of family members, age of persons, and the number of males, females, free persons of color, and slaves of the household. However, at the beginning of 1850, census records began listing more detailed information about each individual of each household. The list started to include the name, age, sex, race, and state or county of birth of each household member. In 1880, additional information was added detailing the state or county of birth of both parents. The 1900 schedules added information on the month and year of birth for each individual. Schedules from 1900 to 1930 also contain important information on immigration, marital status, home ownership, employment, and so on. Tax or voter registration records can often be substituted for missing or destroyed census. For more information, see William Dollarhide, *The Census Book* (Bountiful, Utah: Heritage Quest, 1999). A number of individual states, such as New York and Kansas, also conducted state censuses between the standard dates of the national census. For more information on state censuses, see Ann S. Lainhart, *State Census Records* (Baltimore, Md.: Genealogical Publishing Company, 1992).

Soundex Indexes

A series of Soundex indexes were added to the U.S. censuses during the 1930s that used a phonetic indexing system. These indexes cover most states and territories for censuses that were taken from the years 1880 through 1920. The 1930 Soundex index covers only some southern states. While these indexes are often incomplete, they are very useful for locating families whose whereabouts are unknown, especially those families with children. To use the Soundex indexing system, the family surname is coded into an alphanumeric number. For example, under this system, the surname Bowen and several similar family names become B500 and are listed under that code number. Consult Bradley W. Stuart, *The Soundex Daitch-Mokotoff Reference Guide* (Bountiful, Utah: Precision Indexing, 1994) for information on coding names.

Special Schedules

In 1850, a number of special census schedules were created along with the population schedule. Unfortunately, many special census schedules, except for those from 1850 through 1880, have not survived. These special schedules, available in many genealogical archives, are agriculture, or farm census, the slave schedules for southern states (1850 and 1860), the census of manufacturing, the mortality schedules, schedules entitled social statistics, among others. Of these, the two most important for genealogical research are the mortality schedules, a listing of persons who died the year the census was taken, and the agriculture census, an enumeration of farmers and farm operations. Check archival Web sites for information on these special census schedules.

Newspaper Files

U.S. newspapers date their beginnings back to 1690. Many genealogical archives possess excellent files of state, regional, and local newspapers, usually on microfilm. Searching these files most often produces obituaries, birth announcements, marriage notices, and other types of information rich in family connections. Additional clues to family affairs are often found in other sections of newspapers, such as legal notices, community news notes, and feature articles. The publication of abstracts and indexes to newspaper files has become common in recent years. Religious, professional, or fraternal publications should also be consulted. Internet sources often provide researchers with information on an institution's holdings of newspapers and similar publications.

County and Local Records

County and local records are other invaluable sources for genealogy and family history information. Records in this category usually include marriages, divorces, estate matters, deeds, tax records, court records, lawsuits, and so on. They can provide information useful in calculating the events of life such as death, marriage, and migration. They can also be used to show interfamily relationships. Most genealogical archives have collections of local county records available on microfilm or in hardcopy. Archives are usually more than willing to provide information on their holdings of county and local records to potential patrons. Similar information may also be available on the archives' Web sites.

Military Records

U.S. military service and pension records, which began during the colonial period, are yet another potential treasure trove of information for the family historian. While most genealogists are familiar with at least some of the records relating to service in the Revolutionary War or the Civil War, many do not realize that military service was much more common in the past than is often thought. Other U.S. wars include the Indian Wars, the Mexican War, the Spanish-American War, and a number of others during the twentieth century. Several different kinds of veterans' records were created during these conflicts. One was the military service record. It usually contains information about the veteran, but it rarely contains information on the veteran's family. However, it does contain information on the veteran's unit, company, battle service, military honors, and so on. The second potential record is a military pension or bounty land application. Throughout the history of the United States, veterans, and sometimes their widows, have received postmilitary service benefits. Some obtained grants for public lands while others received pension payments. These pension records, especially those dealing with widows' pensions, often contain information

of genealogical importance. Records relating to U.S. military service are usually available at the National Archives in Washington, D.C. Most archives with genealogical collections also have copies of service records relating to the men and women who lived in areas served by their institution. The Civil War confederate pension records are usually held in state archives in former confederate states. Local and state archives may also house information concerning veterans' organizations or inmates at local veterans' homes. Lists of obituaries, death notices, and location of burial for veterans are also commonly available. See James C. Neagles, *U.S. Military Records: A Guide to Federal and State Sources Colonial American to the Present* (Salt Lake City, Utah: Ancestry, 1994). The Internet is also a good source of information on military service information, unit histories, muster rolls, and so on, especially for the Civil War.

ADDITIONAL SOURCES

After searching through the basic types of records available for research, family historians may wish to look for additional information on family history in more nontraditional source materials. The following categories of such records are often available at the genealogical archives. Potential researchers should investigate guides, shelf lists, central card catalogues, finding aids, and possible Internet Web sites for possible holdings of this material. A telephone call, a letter, or an E-mail about the availability of certain kinds of records is always appropriate. Potential patrons should also keep in mind that some or all of these types of material may require advance permission to use or it may otherwise be restricted.

Local Business Records

Genealogical archives, especially local historical societies, often house records from local businesses in their collections. Genealogists will be particularly interested in those containing birth, death, burial, and relationship information. These include records of funeral homes, cemeteries, general stores, orphanages, insurance companies, railroad and transportation companies, and large area employers, among others.

Ethnic Records

Archival records that help establish race or ethnicity are as varied as the myriad of races and peoples who make up our nation. Among the traditional sources found in genealogical holdings for African Americans and Native Americans are the U.S. census slave schedules for 1850 and 1860 and the famous Dawes Rolls of the Five Civilized Tribes. Other U.S. census records, newspaper files, county and local public records, passenger lists, and religious records are all excellent sources for ethnic research. Most genealogical archives with large collections of race-specific records have special guides and handouts to assist their patrons in using them. Traditional archives that serve culturally diverse communities also maintain records of interest to the genealogists. A few examples are the large collections of records on European Jewry housed in Jewish archives in the New York City area and the Hispanic genealogical materials in the collections of the Family History Library of the Church of Jesus Christ of Latter-day Saints in Salt Lake City, Utah.

Fraternal Records

Many genealogical archives, especially local institutions, often house collections of fraternal organizations such as the Odd Fellows, the Masonic Lodge, the Grange, Knights of Pythias, and the Mosaic Templars of America, among others. Organizational minutes, histories, reports, newspaper files, and other types of records often provide age, residency, death information, and may also give clues to family relationships. See Alvin J. Schmidt, *Fraternal Organizations* (Westport, Conn.: Greenwood Press, 1980) for an exhaustive list of these organizations.

Migration/Immigration Records

Because the United States is a nation of immigrants, archives located in communities with large immigrant populations often house records relating to the culture, history, and genealogy of these groups. They may include port of entry records, immigration information, records of public and private immigration societies, materials relating to cultural and religious institutions, foreign-language newspapers, books, pamphlets, and other non-English publications, as well as manuscript collections, diaries, journals, and correspondences. Such archives may also have large collections of materials relating to the old country. Patrons may need a reading knowledge of a foreign language to access these records. Some types of records may also be restricted. Web sites operated by particular ethnic, religious, or cultural groups can supply additional information.

Photograph Files

Searching for photographs and similar visuals is an integral part of the genealogical research experience. A picture of an ancestor's house, a church the family attended, or the main street they strolled down, adds an entire new dimension to collecting dry family facts. Most archives with genealogical records also have collections of photographs. These collections can be arranged by name, location, or subject. Most archives have indexes, finding aids, or staff members to assist patrons with their use. Resourceful researchers may find copies of these indexes or guides, or even copies of the photographs themselves, on the Internet. Check with reference personnel for assistance in using this type of material.

Professional Records

Genealogical archives may also house collections of records relating to physicians, teachers, lawyers, judges, politicians, and other professionals. These collections can provide valuable clues to local community personalities and events. Physicians' records are particularly rich sources of vital record information. Teachers' records may contain the names and ages of students; records from lawyers' offices may contain information on estates, adoptions, divorces, real-estate transactions, and so on. Check through archival guides for this type of information; ask staff members for assistance.

Private Manuscript Collections

Genealogical archives may also hold collections of private manuscripts. Private manuscripts are collections of diaries, journals, letters, scrapbooks, legal documents, contracts, postcards, scrapbooks, tax receipts, clippings, and so on, produced by private citizens, families, businesses, or other nongovernmental entities in pursuit of their day-to-day activities. Although not usually created with a genealogist in mind, they can contain substantial family history information. Researchers lucky enough to find such a collection may find a collection of Civil War letters or the journals of a pioneer family crossing the Great Plains. Most private manuscript collections have guides or finding aids that will assist the genealogical researcher. See Library of Congress Catalogues, *National Union Catalogue of Manuscript Collections* [NUCMC] (Shoe String Press, Inc., Hamden, Conn.,—) and *Index to Personal Names in the Na-*

tional Union Catalog of Manuscript (NUCMC) Collections, 1959–1984, 2 vols. (Alexandria, Va.: Chadwyck-Healey, 1987).

Religious Records

Records relating to local churches and religious organizations, often found at genealogical archives, form one of the more useful categories of genealogical material. This can include parish registrars, church books, religious newspaper files, and congregational histories. It might also include records of church-owned cemeteries, religious schools, denominational publications, biographical sketches of local clergy, and even copies of their journals. Check with reference personnel about availability and restrictions before visiting the archives. Many larger U.S. religious denominations maintain their own archival agency. Most of the time, these institutions offer assistance to genealogical researchers. However, they may charge a fee for their services and some of their records may not be available for public use. Check denominational Web sites for additional information. Good examples of religious collections are the Quaker records at the Friends Historical Library, Swarthmore College, Swarthmore, Pennsylvania, and the church and organizational records housed at the Historical Foundation of the Presbyterian and Reformed Churches in Montreat, North Carolina. Different languages and strange social or religious customs may complicate the use of these records. Ask the reference staff for assistance.

School Records

Materials relating to schools and school-aged children often find their way into archives with genealogical collections. They may include information on private, religious, or industrial schools, as well as defunct colleges and universities, and may include records of individual schools or school classes, school-board minutes, records of defunct school districts, and school census records. Current records kept by active schools and school districts are not usually available for public use. Even those in archival custody may be restricted. Check with reference personnel for additional information.

Urban Sources

America's many large urban areas have always been a melting pot of race, language, culture, religion, and political outlook. Beginning in colonial times, they also served as ports of entry for countless immigrants whose wanderings eventually took them elsewhere. Fortunately, U.S. cities and urban areas are also rich in archives with religious, cultural, and ethnic genealogical collections. Larger city libraries, historical societies, and archival agencies house materials that will greatly assist the urban genealogical researcher. Larger cities themselves often create many of the same kinds of records that are usually associated with county governments. These may include marriages, divorces, adoptions, deeds, court cases, voter registration lists, naturalizations, maps, lists of city cemetery interments, and records relating to businesses and professions and may include birth and death records.

One of the most useful urban research tools is the city directory, which began in New York City in 1665. These publications can be found in most urban archives and libraries. Though often confused with telephone directories, they contain information on names, addresses, occupations, names of spouses, ownership of homes, and in some cases, race. City directories often also have crisscross reference sections that list similar information by street address or by telephone number. When used in conjunction with U.S. censuses, city directories make genealogical research in heavily populated urban areas easier then it would be otherwise. Foreign city directories and telephone books can also be found in some urban genealogical archives. Urban archives also usually house files of city newspapers and may have the morgues or clipping and photograph files of existing or defunct publications. They may also have files of Sanborn Fire Insurance or other maps showing business and residential locations. Many have extensive collections of biographical and historical material, as well as U.S. and local census records, immigration and migration records. See *City Directories of the United States 1860–1901: Guide to the Microfilm Collection* (Woodbridge, Conn.: Research Publications, 1983) and Estelle M. Guzik, ed., *Genealogical Resources in the New York Metropolitan Area* (New York: Jewish Genealogical Society, 1989).

The Internet, the World Wide Web, and the Computer

The virtual world of the computer and online genealogy is in the process of changing the face of American genealogy. These services are a gold mine of information for the armchair family historian. Researchers can use them to purchase a genealogical book or find a long lost ancestor. They often provide the genealogical researcher with instant information on an ancestor. They can also be used to locate local and county source materials or the hours of operation of state archival agencies. Most archival Web sites and some genealogical sites are free. Others are available only by subscription. Not all family history information, especially ones taken from other researcher's pedigree charts, is necessarily correct. The researcher should look critically at this information as well as information obtained from traditional genealogy publications, census records, or county histories. Check for information in Cyndi Howells, *Cyndi's List: A Comprehensive List of 70,000 Genealogy Sites on the Internet* (Baltimore, Md., Genealogical Publishing Company, 2001). However, remember that virtual research, no matter how useful and convenient, cannot take the place of an actual on-site research.

SELECTED BIBLIOGRAPHY

General Genealogical Works

Allen County Public Library, PERSI: Periodical Source Index. Fort Wayne, Ind.: Allen County Public Library Foundation, 1997. An index to published family history information found in local and regional genealogical periodicals. Also available on CD-ROM. The Allen County Public Library, Fort Wayne, Indiana, has also published a leaflet series entitled "Path Finder" designed for the beginning genealogist with titles such as "Sources for 20th Century Research," "Newspaper Research," etc. Contact the library for copies.

Everton, Walter M., et al. *The Handy Book for Genealogists: United States of America*. 10th edition. Draper, Utah: Everton Publishers, 2002. An extremely useful tool for anyone doing genealogical research, and especially helpful when using U.S. Census records.

Harris, Maurine, and Glen Harris. *Ancestry's Concise Genealogical Directory*. Salt Lake City, Utah: Ancestry Publishing, 1989. Useful work for definitions of obsolete, unused, and forgotten family history terms.

Herbert, Miranda C., and Barbara McNeil. *Biography and Genealogy Master Index*. 2nd edition. Detroit, Mich.: Gale Research Co., 1980. Index to many published biographical dictionaries.

Kaminkow, Marion J. *Genealogies in the Library of Congress: A Bibliography*. 5 vols. Baltimore, Md.: Genealogical Publishing Company, 2001. A very useful source for locating published family histories.

National Society of the Daughters of the American Revolution. *[DAR] Library Catalogue Family Histories and Genealogies,* and *State and Local Histories and Records,* 4 vols. (National Society of Daughters of the American Revolution, Washington, D.C., 1983–1986). Works that should be used in connection with the Library of Congress lists of genealogies.

Schreiner-Yantis, Nettie, compiler. *Genealogical and Local History Books in Print*. 4th edition. Springfield, Va.: N. Schreiner-Yantis, 1985. Another source of published genealogical data. Updated frequently. Features book, microfilm, and microfiche.

Szucs, Loretto Dennis, and Sandra Hargreaves Luebking, eds. *The Source: A Guidebook of American Genealogy*. Rev. ed. Salt Lake City, Utah: Ancestry Publishing, 1997. Long a mainstay for genealogical source information, this revised edition is a masterpiece.

Guides and Directories

Bowker, R. R. *American Library Directory: A Classified List of Libraries in the United States and Canada, with Personnel and Statistical Data*. 55th edition. New York: R. R. Bowker, 2002/2003. Although primarily a directory of libraries, it also contains a significant amount of information on local, regional, and state archival facilities. Researchers can use it to ascertain the extent of genealogical holdings of many local institutions.

Cerny, Johni, and Wendy Elliott. *The Library: A Guide to the LDS Family History Library*. Salt Lake City, Utah: Ancestry Publishing, 1988. A comprehensive look at records found in the world's largest genealogical collection at the LDS Family History Library, Salt Lake City, Utah.

Darnay, Brigette T., ed. *Directory of Special Libraries and Information Centers*. 26th edition. Detroit, Mich.: Research Co., 2001. Institutions are listed by name.

Dollarhide, William, and Ronald A. Bremer. *America's Best Genealogical Resource Centers*. Bountiful, Utah: Heritage Quest, 1998. Useful for planning a research trip.

Filby, P. William. *Directory of American Libraries and Genealogical and Local History Collections*. Wilmington, Del.: Scholarly Resources, 1988. Now a little dated but still a useful tool for locating genealogical collections.

Grundset, Eric G., and Steven B. Rhodes. *American Genealogical Research at the DAR, Washington, D.C.* Washington, D.C.: National Society, Daughters of the American Revolution, 1997. A discussion of one of Washington, D.C.'s often overlooked major genealogical collections.

Library of Congress Catalogues. *Index to Personal Names in the National Union Catalog of Manuscript [NUCMC] Collections, 1959–1984*. 2 vols. Alexandria, Va.: Chadwyck-Healey, 1987. NUCMC is a good place to begin looking for manuscript collections that contain family history information. However, keep in mind that it does not contain a complete listing of such records in the United States.

———. *National Union Catalogue of Manuscript Collections*. Ann Arbor, Mich.: J. W. Edwards, 1962–1993. See above.

National Archives and Records Service. *Guide to Genealogical Research in the National Archives.* Washington, D.C.: National Archives and Records Service, 1982. An excellent introduction to family history research using sources from the National Archives in Washington, D.C.

Neagles, James C. *The Library of Congress: A Guide to Genealogical and Historical Research.* Salt Lake City, Utah: Ancestry Publishing, 1990. A must-have guide for genealogical researchers visiting this institution.

Schaefer, Christina Kassabain. *The Center: A Guide to Genealogical Research in the National Capital Area.* Baltimore, Md.: Genealogical Publishing Company, 1996. A short but excellent guide to genealogical sources in and around Washington, D.C.

Szucs, Loretto Dennis, and Sandra Hargreaves Luebking, eds. *The Archives: A Guide to the National Archives Field Branches.* Salt Lake City, Utah: Ancestry Publishing, 1988. A very good introduction to sources available at National Archives branches across the country.

How-to Books

Dollarhide, William. *Genealogy Starter Kit.* 2nd ed. Baltimore, Md.: Genealogical Publishing Company, 1994. A brief introduction with sample charts.

Greenwood, Val D. *The Researcher's Guide to American Genealogy.* Baltimore, Md.: Genealogical Publishing Company, 1973. An excellent manual for the genealogical researcher.

Rose, Christine, and Kay Germain Ingalls. *The Complete Idiot's Guide to Genealogy.* New York: Alpha Books, 1997. Its title says it all. A must-have book for the beginning family historian.

Schaefer, Christina Kassabain. *The Hidden Half of the Family: A Sourcebook for Women's Genealogy.* Baltimore, Md.: Genealogical Publishing Company, 1999. Contains a state-by-state directory of sources for women's history and genealogy.

Stevenson, Noel C. *Genealogical Evidence: A Guide to the Standard of Proof Relating to Pedigrees, Ancestry, Heirship and Family History.* Rev. ed. Laguna Hills, Calif.: Aegean Park Press, 1989. Written by a lawyer who is also a genealogist.

Vital Records

Cerny, Johni, and Wendy Elliott, eds. *The Library: A Guide to the LDS Family History Library; Church of Jesus Christ of Latter-Day Saints Family History Library.* Salt Lake City, Utah: Ancestry, 1988, chapters 4–13.

Greenwood, Val D. *The Researcher's Guide to American Genealogy.* 2nd edition. Baltimore, Md.: Genealogical Publishing Company, 1990, chapter 10.

Kemp, Thomas Jay. *International Vital Records Handbook.* Baltimore, Md.: Genealogical Publishing Company,

2000. An important guide to vital records in the United States and other countries.

Rose, Christine, and Kay Germain Ingalls. *The Complete Idiot's Guide to Genealogy.* New York: Alpha Books, 1997, chapter 8.

Szucs, Loretto Dennis, and Sandra Hargreaves Luebking, eds. *The Source: A Guidebook of American Genealogy.* Rev. ed. Salt Lake City, Utah: Ancestry, 1997, chapter 3 and appendix F.

Census Records

The Church of Jesus Christ of Latter-Day Saints. *Familysearch 1880 United States Census and National Index.* Salt Lake City, Utah: Intellectual Reserve, 2001. A searchable CD database of abstractions made by LDS Church members from the 1880 U.S. Census.

Dollarhide, William. *The Census Book: A Genealogist's Guide to Federal Census Facts, Schedules and Indexes.* Bountiful, Utah: Heritage Quest, 1999. An especially useful guide for anyone using U.S. Census records.

Everton, George B. *The Handybook for Genealogists: United States of America.* 10th edition. Draper, Utah: Everton Publishers, 2002.

Greenwood, Val D. *The Researcher's Guide to American Genealogy.* 2nd edition. Baltimore, Md.: Genealogical Publishing Company, 1990, chapters 11 and 12.

Lainhart, Ann S. *State Census Records.* Baltimore, Md.: Genealogical Publishing Company, 1992. A very useful source for locating nonfederal census records.

Rose, Christine, and Kay Germain Ingalls. *The Complete Idiot's Guide to Genealogy.* New York: Alpha Books, 1997, chapters 9 and 10.

Szucs, Loretto Dennis and Sandra Hargreaves Luebking, eds. *The Source: A Guidebook of American Genealogy.* Rev. ed. Salt Lake City, Utah: Ancestry, 1997, chapter 5.

Thorndale, William, and William Dollarhide. *Map Guide to the U.S. Federal Census, 1790–1920.* Baltimore, Md.: Genealogical Publishing Company, 1987. A must-have source of using census records.

County/Local Records

Bently, Elizabeth Perry. *County Courthouse Book.* 2nd ed. Baltimore, Md.: Genealogical Publishing Company, 1995. A useful tool for planning a genealogical road trip.

Cerny, Johni, and Wendy Elliott, eds. *The Library: A Guide to the LDS Family History Library; Church of Jesus Christ of Latter-Day Saints Family History Library.* Salt Lake City, Utah: Ancestry, 1988, chapters 4–13.

Greenwood, Val D. *The Researcher's Guide to American Genealogy.* 2nd edition. Baltimore, Md.: Genealogical Publishing Company, 1990, chapters 13–19.

Hone, E. Wade. *Land and Property Research in the United States.* Salt Lake City, Utah: Ancestry, 1997. Excellent guide to using deed and property records in genealogical research.

Rose, Christine, and Kay Germain Ingalls. *The Complete Idiot's Guide to Genealogy.* New York: Alpha Books, 1997, chapter 13.

Szucs, Loretto Dennis and Sandra Hargreaves Luebking, eds. *The Source: A Guidebook of American Genealogy.* Rev. ed. Salt Lake City, Utah: Ancestry, 1997, chapters 6–8.

Newspaper Files

Greenwood, Val D. *The Researcher's Guide to American Genealogy.* 2nd edition. Baltimore, Md.: Genealogical Publishing Company, 1990, chapter 9.

Henritze, Barbara K. *Bibliographic Checklist of African American Newspapers.* Baltimore, Md.: Genealogical Publishing Company, 1995. A state-by-state listing of African American newspapers.

Library of Congress. *Library of Congress Catalogs Newspapers in Microform United States, 1948–1983.* 2 vols. Washington, D.C.: Library of Congress, 1984. A dated but still valuable listing of microfilmed American newspaper files.

Rose, Christine, and Kay Germain Ingalls. *The Complete Idiot's Guide to Genealogy.* New York: Alpha Books, 1997, chapter 15.

Sumner, Jeff, ed. *Gale Directory of Publications and Broadcast Media (Formerly Ayers Directory of Publications).* 135th edition. Detroit, Mich: Gale Group, 2001. Standard reference for American newspapers.

Szucs, Loretto Dennis and Sandra Hargreaves Luebking, eds. *The Source: A Guidebook of American Genealogy.* Rev. ed. Salt Lake City, Utah: Ancestry, 1997, chapter 12.

Military Records

Brown, Brian A. *In the Footsteps of the Blue and Gray: A Civil War Research Handbook.* Shawnee Mission, Kans.: Two Trails Genealogy Shop, 1996. An excellent how-to book for the Civil War genealogical researcher.

Greenwood, Val D. *The Researcher's Guide to American Genealogy.* 2nd edition. Baltimore, Md.: Genealogical Publishing Company, 1990, chapters 22–23.

Hewett, Janet B. *The Roster of Confederate Soldiers, 1861–1865.* Wilmington, N.C.: Broadfoot Publishing Company, 1995–96. Basic source for Confederate military service records.

———. *The Roster of Union Soldiers, 1861–1865.* Wilmington, N.C.: Broadfoot Publishing Company, 1997–2000. Basic source for Union military service records.

———. "United States Colored Troops." In *The Roster of Union Soldiers, 1861–1865.* Wilmington, N.C.: Broadfoot Publishing Company, 1997. Basic source for Union military service records.

National Archives and Records Service. *Guide to Genealogical Research in the National Archives.* Washington, D.C.: National Archives and Records Service, 1982, chapters 4–9.

National Archives Trust Fund Board, National Archives and Service Administration. *Military Service Records: A Selected Catalogue of National Archives Microfilm Publications.* Washington, D.C.: National Archives Trust Fund Board, 1985. An exhaustive listing of microfilmed records relating to American military activity, especially during the Civil War.

Neagles, James C. *U.S. Military Records: A Guide to Federal and State Sources Colonial American to the Present.* Salt Lake City, Utah: Ancestry, 1994. Contains a useful listing of state resources.

Rose, Christine, and Kay Germain Ingalls. *The Complete Idiot's Guide to Genealogy.* New York: Alpha Books, 1997, chapter 16.

Szucs, Loretto Dennis and Sandra Hargreaves Luebking, eds. *The Source: A Guidebook of American Genealogy.* Rev. ed. Salt Lake City, Utah: Ancestry, 1997, chapter 9.

Migration and Immigration

Angus Baxter, *In Search of Your European Roots: A Complete Guide to Tracing Your Ancestors in Every Country in Europe.* 3rd edition. Baltimore, Md.: Genealogical Publishing Company, 2001. Standard how-to book on European research.

———. *In Search of Your British and Irish Roots: A Complete Guide to Tracing Your English, Welsh, Scottish, and Irish Ancestors.* 4th edition. Baltimore, Md.: Genealogical Publishing Company, 1999. Standard how-to book on European research.

———. *In Search of Your Canadian Roots.* Baltimore, Md.: Genealogical Publishing Company, 2000. Standard how-to book on Canadian research.

Cerny, Johni, and Wendy Elliott, eds. *The Library: A Guide to the LDS Family History Library; Church of Jesus Christ of Latter-Day Saints Family History Library.* Salt Lake City, Utah: Ancestry, 1988, chapters 14–27.

Dollarhide, William. *Map Guide to American Migration Routes.* Bountiful, Utah: AGLL, Heritage Quest, 1997. Especially useful for migration routes east of the Mississippi.

Filby, P. William, and Mary K. Meyer. *Passenger and Immigration Lists Index.* Detroit, Mich.: Gale Group, 2000. A basic source for immigrants to the United States.

Greenwood, Val D. *The Researcher's Guide to American Genealogy.* 2nd edition. Baltimore, Md.: Genealogical Publishing Company, 1990, chapter 21.

Herber, Mark D. *Ancestral Trails. The Complete Guide to British Genealogy and Family History.* Baltimore, Md.: Genealogical Publishing Company, 2000. An excellent new guide to research in the British Isles.

National Archives and Records Service. *Guide to Genealogical Research in the National Archives.* Washington, D.C.: National Archives and Records Service, 1982, chapters 2–3.

Newman, John J. *American Naturalization Records, 1790–1990.* Baltimore, Md.: Genealogical Publishing Company, 1998. An update of a standard work.

Szucs, Loretto Dennis and Sandra Hargreaves Luebking, eds. *The Source: A Guidebook of American Genealogy.* Rev. ed. Salt Lake City, Utah: Ancestry, 1997, chapter 13.

Urban Genealogy

City Directories of the United States, 1860–1901: Guide to the Microfilm Collection. Woodbridge, Conn.: Research Publications, 1984.

Guzik, Estelle M., ed. *Genealogical Resources in the New York Metropolitan Area.* New York: Jewish Genealogical Society, 1989.

Szucs, Loretto Dennis and Sandra Hargreaves Luebking, eds. *The Source: A Guidebook of American Genealogy.* Rev. ed. Salt Lake City, Utah: Ancestry, 1997, chapter 19.

Ethnic Genealogy

Burroughs, Tony. *Black Roots: A Beginners Guide to Tracing the African American Family Tree.* New York: Fireside Book/Simon & Schuster, 2001. An excellent new book on the African American genealogical experience.

Byers, Paula K., ed. *African American Genealogical Sourcebook.* New York: Gale Group, 1995. This guide offers the beginning researcher basic information on ethnic genealogy.

———. *Asian American Genealogical Sourcebook.* New York: Gale Group, 1995. This guide offers the beginning researcher basic information on ethnic genealogy.

———. *Hispanic American Genealogical Sourcebook.* New York: Gale Group, 1995. This guide offers the beginning researcher basic information on ethnic genealogy.

———. *Native American Genealogical Sourcebook.* New York: Gale Group, 1995. This guide offers the beginning researcher basic information on ethnic genealogy.

Mooney, Thomas G. *Exploring Your Cherokee Ancestry: A Basic Genealogical Research Guide.* Tahlequah, Okla.: Cherokee National Historical Society, 1987. An excellent case study on American Indian genealogical research.

National Archives and Records Service. *Guide to Genealogical Research in the National Archives.* Washington, D.C.: National Archives and Records Service, 1982, chapters 11 and 12.

National Archives Trust Fund Board. *American Indians: A Selected Catalog of National Archives Microfilm Publications.* Washington, D.C.: National Archives Trust Fund Board, 1984. An excellent guide to ethnic material available on microfilm from the National Archives.

———. *Black Studies: A Selected Catalog of National Archives Microfilm Publications.* Washington, D.C.: National Archives Trust Fund Board, 1984. An excellent guide to ethnic material available on microfilm from the National Archives.

Smith, Jessie Carney, ed. *Ethnic Genealogy.* Westport, Conn.: Greenwood Press, 1983. A very scholarly treatment of the subject.

Szucs, Loretto Dennis and Sandra Hargreaves Luebking, eds. *The Source: A Guidebook of American Genealogy.* Rev. ed. Salt Lake City, Utah: Ancestry, 1997, chapters 14–17.

Computer Genealogy

Arends, Martha. *Genealogy Software Guide.* Baltimore, Md.: Genealogical Publishing Company, 1998. A useful tool for the computer genealogist.

Howells, Cyndi. *Cyndi's List: A Comprehensive List of 70,000 Genealogy Sites on the Internet.* Baltimore, Md.: Genealogical Publishing Company, 2001. A guide to finding genealogy and family history information on the World Wide Web.

Selected Publishers of Genealogical Material

Ancestry.com
P.O. Box 990
Orem, UT 84095
800-262-3787
http://www.ancestry.com/

Broadfoot Publishing Company
1907 Buena Vista Cir.
Wilmington, NC 28411
800-537-5243
http://broadfoot.wilmington.net/

Chadwyck-Healey Inc.
1101 King St.
Alexandria, VA 22314
http://www.chadwyck.com/

CIS UPA Lexis-Nexis Universe UPA
Congressional Information Service, Inc.
(Formerly UMI)
4520 East-West Highway
Bethesda, MD 20814-3389
800-638-8380
http://www.lexisnexis.com/academic/research_resources/terrorism/default.htm

Clearfield Company
200 East Eager St.

Baltimore, MD 21202
http://www.genealogical.com/

Everton Publishers, Inc.
P.O. Box 368
Logan, UT 84323-0368
800-443-6325
http://www.everton.com/

Family and Church History Department
LDS Church
50 East North Temple St.
Salt Lake City, UT 84150-3400
http://www.familysearch.org/

Frontier Press
P.O. Box 126
Cooperstown, NY 13326
800-772-7559
http://www.frontierpress.com/frontier.cgi/

Gale Group
P.O. Box 9187
Farmington Hills, MI 48333-9187
http://www.gale.com/

Genealogical Publishing Company
1001 N. Calvert St.
Baltimore, MD 21202
800-296-6687
http://www.genealogical.com/

Heritage Books, Inc.
1540 Pointer Ridge Place
Bowie, MD 2071
800-276-1760
http://www.heritagebooks.com/

Heritage Quest
P.O. Box 540670
North Salt Lake City, UT 84054-0670
800-760-2455
http://www.heritagequest.com/

Higginson Book Company
148 Washington St.
Salem, MA 01970
http://www.higginsonbooks.com/

Morningside Book Store
P.O. Box 1087
Dayton, OH 45401
http://www.morningsidebooks.com/

National Historical Publishing Company
P.O. Box 539
Waynesboro, TN 38485

New England Historical Genealogical Society
101 Newbury St.
Boston, MA 02116-3007
888-286-3447
http://www.newenglandancestors.org/

Scholarly Resources Inc.
104 Greenhill Ave.
Wilmington, DE 19805-1897
http://www.scholarly.com/

Southern Historical Press
P.O. Box 1267
Greenville, SC 29602-1267

Tuttle Antiquarian Books Inc.
28 S. Main St.
Rutland, VT 05701
http://www.tuttlebooks.com/

CHAPTER 3
Science Archives

Elisabeth Buehlman

INTRODUCTION

In 1912, just before World War I, Frenchman George Sarton emigrated to the United States and founded a review entitled *ISIS: revue consacrée à l'histoire et à l'organisation des sciences.* After the war Sarton tried to develop his new discipline at the Carnegie Institution of Washington. But it was only during the 1930s that a new discipline appeared at Harvard University—a doctorate in the history of science. Even though science and technology are as old as humankind, the study of their evolution dates to the beginning of the social history movement in the twentieth century. In earlier times, histories were often written by non-historians. In the case of science, they were retired scientists and researchers who were proud of their work and wanted to share their knowledge of the evolution of the discipline or to explain the origins and consequences of advances in science and technology. Just after the Second World War in France, Frédéric Joliot-Curie published in collaboration with other colleagues the whole history of their research concerning nuclear energy and its military use. Historians gradually became interested in the history of science and technology because of its impact on the other domains of history and the general trend toward seeing the world in scientific terms.

For writing history, arguments should be based on facts and tangible proofs, implying the use of primary sources. The French say "dépouiller des archives," meaning "to denude or skin." In other words, the themes that reflect the evolution of a subject are extracted from the sources. It was expressly because of their utility that scientific archives services were created in institutions.

The development of scientific archives was caused by three main things. First, institutions, deliberately or in connection with their retired or famous staff, wanted to enhance their patrimony and appear prestigious. The opportunity to advance such an agenda can be an anniversary or the celebration of the institution's staff. For example, the European Organization for Nuclear Research (CERN) established its archives services when a history study group was created in order to publish CERN's history on its 40th anniversary.

Secondly, institutions must keep track of documents for legal reasons. Many professional archivists take the opportunity to develop a complete archives service, which preserves traces of all activities of the institution.

The third cause is relatively new and comes from cognitive science and its application in corporate environments: knowledge management. The idea that past history can be reused in the future to increase the efficiency and professionalism of an institution requires that the institution reference a past that is stored in the archives.

Due to the plethora of motivations for the establishment of archival services, historians should keep in mind that they will have to deal with various types of archives governed by differing national rules, especially if services are not geared to the public. That is why, before listing all the fruitful places to find primary sources related to a subject, the relation of historians of science and technology to their archival material must be studied in depth. What should the historian take into account before going through primary sources? Which are the likely possibilities for finding out the location of primary sources relevant to the subject? Historians who know where to go and are aware of the various situations they could encounter will be far more efficient at finding needed documents in the jungle of information available. They will also be able to extract greater value from the accessed documents.

HISTORIANS OF SCIENCE AND THEIR SOURCES

Preparing a research report through the study of archival material is generally a time-consuming process, as primary sources are rougher than published material, in which information is processed and arranged. One of the first issues that will impact research is whether the scholar is dealing with a person or a process.

Studying a famous character in science implies reconstructing the entire contacts network of the person studied. For scientists, however, the network is commonly wide, so scholars have to navigate between many sources. Thus researching a person will require mobility. It is also very rare for a scientist to remain in the same place for an entire career because of both professional and political issues. This is typical for contemporary European scientists who migrated to the United States before and during World War II. The Albert Einstein Archives at http://www.albert-einstein.org/archives2.html are a good example of all the possible moves of archives between several continents. Both Einstein himself and the archives documenting his life traveled around. Scholars who are focusing on medieval and modern history of science face the same problem, because most of the sources are near the locations where they were created.

If a process or an experiment is to be studied, then archival material is more likely to be located in one or two places, because experiments commonly take place at one or two focal points. Added to this concentration, an important part of the research is likely to be widely published in the scientific literature. Additional material may be available as circulated manuscripts with attached comments from peers. The scientific habit of sharing knowledge allows duplication and dissemination of information that may render archive material more accessible. However, locating the sources is not enough. The scholars must also be able to understand them.

CRITICAL AND ASSESSMENT OF PRIMARY SOURCES

Before diving into the sea of information contained in primary sources, scholars should assess the quality of archives and their potential interest and relevance for the research. Like other modern historians, historians of science must be able to decipher what is in the sources. There may be a paleography issue, as scientists are famous for their unreadable handwriting. There could be a knowledge issue, which hinders the researcher in his or her quest. In scientific archives, various types of documents can be found and used in different ways. The famous laboratory notebook, which contains information in serial form, can be processed with methods and tools used to make a quantitative history. Working papers and linked bibliographic documentation can be useful for the comprehension of the process, which is suggested by the notebooks. Letters, articles, books, lectures, and documents written to be published, whether widely or not, can either act as a good synthetic communication of the ideas of scientists or an explanation of a specific point. But their contents are not always easily usable and interesting. Instruments, experiments, and samples in applied sciences and technology have value for illustrating research, as they can be a tangible way to understand a theoretical explanation or description that might otherwise remain abstract by reading only results.

A history of science that is developed using scientific archives is an extensive work requiring a clearly defined scope of study. Scholars should be aware that going through primary sources can be very time-consuming and they should adopt a strategy for accessing sources without neglecting articles and correspondence, which are often a way for scientists to share information, progress in experiments, and theory. The following table presents the various types of sources and their potential uses.

PRELIMINARY QUESTIONS REGARDING THE SOURCES

Scattered or Concentrated Primary Sources?

Based on the scope of the research and the defined accurate sources on which to base the study, scholars must find the location of sources. As explained earlier in this chapter, sources are often scattered in distant places. Scholars should therefore think about the central location of their research and the opportunity to consult sources located elsewhere. If it is necessary to consult remote sources, scholars must consider the relevant expenses in terms of both time and money. Scholars have two choices in reviewing remote original sources. One is to visit the materials. The other is to seek reproduction of the documents by the institu-

TABLE 3.1 TYPOLOGY OF SCIENTIFIC ARCHIVES

Type of document - name	Type of contents	Contents	Comments and observation
Laboratory notebook and assimilated	Formal	Very technical data. Observations on the spot.	Require understanding of experimental process. Can be difficult to read and in bad condition.
Working files	Half-formal	Research and working notes. Bibliography and literature.	Chronological or thematic filing. Illustrate intellectual progress. Can contain administrative papers. Can be very time-consuming to go through.
Articles and books	Formal	Synthetic documents.	Reveal publication rhythm of the scientist. Can help to understand raw material: valuable for working backward through the scientist's career: i.e., start from his or her publications and work back to unpublished material.
Lectures and courses, teaching material	Formal	Pedagogical documents.	Same use as published material. Can have less value if only for general public.
Correspondence	Half-formal	Hypothesis and conclusions. Trivial subjects.	Mix of trivial and scientific subjects can make study of the sources very time-consuming. Can be very valuable if scientist often uses this method to communicate and share information.
Instruments, samples of experiments	Formal or informal	Instruments used for experiments. Samples, results of experiments.	If kept but not cataloged source may be unusable. Illustration role. Explanation role.
Administrative files	Formal	Budget, accounting, human resources, orders.	Either chronological or subject filing. Can help to understand research rhythm (budget aspects). Give essentially contextual elements.
General archives of experiments and institutions	Formal	Administrative, scientific, and technical documents.	Give essentially contextual elements. Position and role of experiment/ scientist in the institution (integration or not, etc.).
Oral history, interviews	Half-formal	Either vulgarization or very technical.	Reminder of chronology of facts. Can be very subjective, but gives potential new views on the subject.
Knowledge management interviews	Half-formal	Technical and scientific documents.	Focused on explanation of phenomenon. Very technical, as target is successor in the position.

AS THE SOURCES ARE VERY DIVERSE, SCHOLARS MUST SELECT AMONG THE ABUNDANT RESOURCES BY FOCUSING ON ARCHIVES THAT ADD VALUE TO THEIR RESEARCH. PROPORTIONS OF EACH TYPE OF SOURCE DEPEND ON THE BEHAVIOR OF THE SCIENTIST OR THE EXPERIMENT TEAM AS WELL AS THEIR PRESERVATION OVER TIME. LABORATORY NOTEBOOKS, INSTRUMENTS, AND SAMPLES OF EXPERIMENTS ARE THE ONLY ROUGH DATA. THE REST OF THE ARCHIVES, CONSCIOUSLY OR NOT, CONTAIN INTERPRETED INFORMATION. THE LAST FOUR TYPES OF DOCUMENTS GIVE MORE CONTEXTUAL ELEMENTS TO THE RESEARCH, BUT THEY SHOULD NOT NECESSARILY BE NEGLECTED BECAUSE THEY CAN ANSWER QUESTIONS REVEALED IN THE STUDY.

tion housing them. If they wish to consult the documents themselves, they should consider the following issues:

- When is it most appropriate to go through these sources?
- Should the scholar return to the sources several times during different stages of the research?
- What alternative possibilities provide the same outcome? If archives are abroad, is there a possibility to copy documents or to have contacts there to help? If the remote sources are of great interest, the scholar may have the opportunity to ask other researchers or archivists in the institution or freelance historians to do the research. In any case, scholars must consider the option of requesting assistance before choosing any solution.

Public Domain Collections or Not?

Other difficulties for the historian of science are communication and copyright issues, which could interfere with the advancement of his or her research. For institutional, national, and assimilated archives services, the 30-year limitation on public disclosure applies. However, private and corporate archives services are not always obliged to follow national rules, and obtaining access to files in those locations can be tricky. For scientific questions linked to military applications, confidentiality (national security) is also a roadblock to accessing the documents. If the family or the firm intends to publish the sources on their own, then use of material may be restricted even if it is made available for consultation. Those issues should be dealt with at the very beginning of the research, because they can radically interfere with the project.

Accessible Collections or Not?

After having resolved the issues of confidentiality and copyright, scholars may come up against another problem, that of physical access to the sources. Access has both physical and intellectual implications. Physically, the sources may be very fragile due to aging and climate effects or insect damage, and the archivist can block access to documents that may disintegrate with inexperienced handling. Conversely, sometimes the archival material can be harmful to the researcher. For example, documents held by nuclear physicists in the beginning of the twentieth century are frequently hyper-radioactive. All the instruments and notebooks of Pierre and Marie Curie are kept under leaden glass

to protect users from radiation. Sometimes archives are not yet sorted, and archivists may deny access to them until they are processed. The historian may be able to negotiate access by offering to organize the material or to at least create a basic finding aid in collaboration with the archivist.

The status of archives suggests the type of work and the time scholars will spend on them. As finding aids are theoretically based on the original filing pattern, the structure of the document itself can suggest the general state of mind of the scientist or the experimental team. This structure also reveals the type of documents scholars will find in the collection and the type of work needed to extract value from the archive material.

Conclusions to Parts Dedicated to Sources

It is crucial to keep in mind every aspect mentioned in the last two sections before starting research because they are mandatory conditions of a successful research project. If the documents are difficult to access, scholars must ask whether there are accessible duplicates elsewhere. If there are not, scholars should discuss with colleagues whether the research has enough interest to justify the predicted difficulties of dealing with sources. History of science is large enough to allow a withdrawal strategy even if there is associated disappointment. There is no value in continuing if difficulties already exist at the access level of primary sources.

MASS WEB SEARCH FOR PRIMARY SOURCES IN HISTORY OF SCIENCE

Note: unless otherwise stated, all Web pages described in this subchapter are free of charge.

General Research

Having chosen a subject, most scholars already know the location of the main corpus of relevant sources. If they do not, they can still proceed by successive refinements using all available tools. The exponential increase of Web pages since the middle of the nineties means that the Internet is a good place to start for general searching. It is probably more productive than searching a basic university library catalog. But success remains uncertain even if the main corpus of sources appears in the top results. At least one can assess the general interest in a subject by analyzing the answers rate and type of results received. Because of its method of listing and ranking the results, Google http://www.google.com/ is probably the most valuable product for getting results that can be browsed in depth in the continuation of the research. Google also offers the possibility of browsing an open directory by naming the category where the engine has found the most accurate results (for comments on open directory, see Browsing the Web). In order to ensure relevant results, the word "archives" should be ignored, as it generates much noise in the results (mailing list archives, Web page archives, etc.). The term "manuscripts" is far more effective. This applies to all search engines and other similar Web resources.

Focused General Research

In researching scientific archives, scholars should know that they may use specific scientific search engines, which may have some advantages.

Scirus
http://www.scirus.com/

The well-known and respected Scirus, produced by Elsevier Science, is a search engine containing approximately 69 million institutional, educational, and private Web pages with scientific content as of Spring 2002. It is free to submit a page, though Elsevier retains the right to reject submissions. This allows a large panel of potential sites and ensures that only scientific sites are listed in the database. The results ranking is the same as for Google, as it analyses the frequency of hits of the keywords searched and the number of Web pages referring to that page.

Search4Science
http://www.search4science.as/

Search4Science is a Norwegian product under development that intends to offer access to the most accurate information on science. A feature called "dynamic search" allows a search using specific scientific and technical terms or concepts. The site is currently down because the development team is seeking financing. It is uncertain whether they will complete the site.

Browsing the Web

One issue that has divided Internet researchers for a long time is whether it is better to browse or search the Web. For scientific searches, general directories have the same accuracy as search tools. As usual, the re-

searcher must use the right one to achieve good results. Directories have the advantage of allowing extremely fast refinement of the research by only crawling through categories. But categories may have the disadvantage of being arbitrarily defined by people inexperienced in the subject area. This is especially true for history of science, as the scholar must choose among science, history, and references categories. In fact, one has to browse all three categories to assess their potential interest. But directories always give the possibility of searching the directory instead of browsing it. Google offers resolution by compiling searching and browsing features. Among the directories, the most valuable for scientific archives are those produced by dmoz and Yahoo!

Open Directory Project
http://dmoz.org/

Begun in 1998, Open Directory Project is a general catalog for the Web, maintained by groups of editors focused on more than 400,000 categories and subcategories. Many search engines are based on this directory, which contains more than 3.8 million sites. The dmoz catalog also can be immediately refined by geographical area.

Yahoo!®
http://www.yahoo.com/

"Yahoo" is the acronym for Yet Another Hierarchical Officious Oracle. Started in 1994, it is the oldest directory on the Web. The firm changed the algorithm of research in October 2001, and the tool has increased its capacity by integrating Google technology and analysis of keywords in title and URL metadata and also by more general reworking of the directory. The number of sites listed is not directly available, but it is probably around 2.5 million. The search is powered by Google and lists the related category in the Yahoo directory if there is one. The general structure of the directory is the same as dmoz.

Sciseek
http://www.sciseek.com/

Created in 1998 by Magnolia Scientific Services, Sciseek is a directory using Hyperseek as a search engine. The scope has scientific information online and the directory is divided by the main subjects of science. Regarding archives and other sources, it allows narrow searches.

New Generation of Search Engines

With the exponential increase of Web pages, computer engineers have tried to develop intelligent search engines, the so-called Web meta-search engines, compiling various approaches of searching and displaying results. Although the researcher, using basic search engines, analyses the various results he or she gets, meta-search engines may provide a new approach to the list of hits. On the other hand, if the subject is unknown, the Web meta-search engine compiles results of other independent search engines and thus widens the panel of indexed Web pages searched.

Kartoo
http://www.kartoo.com/

Kartoo, developed by a French firm, is a product based on a cognitive approach. As opposed to Google, which offers the one step search with the "I'm feeling lucky" button that directly routes the Internet searcher to the most accurate URL hit found, Kartoo displays a series of results schemes linked by keywords and customizes in various ways new keywords in the search sentence or increases the importance of certain keywords found in the hit set. With such engines the results are already analyzed and integrated in a context. This is a typical systemic approach. This product is very useful to trace a route of archives or see where the main nodes of a subject are located. A small description of each site appears when an URL in the scheme is highlighted.

Ixquick
http://ixquick.com/

Ixquick, developed by a Dutch firm, is a one-step meta-search engine searching ten of the biggest world search engines. The results are listed like any other search engine, but it also lists the search engine where the result was found and gives an accuracy rate with stars. The search cannot be refined. However, for a very precise search this tool is the most appropriate.

SOURCES FOR GENERAL HISTORY OF SCIENCE (MACRO-LEVEL)

Thematic Sites: Guide of Primary Sources, Guide for Historians of Science

Historians since Herodotus have experienced the difficulty of obtaining and studying valuable primary sources. Scholars have developed tools to help them locate these materials, and historians of science can also benefit from such tools. At the macro-level, international professional associations of archivists and preservation specialists and groups of people who specialize in compiling information about science and history of science create these tools.

Echo
http://echo.gmu.edu/

Echo, which stands for Exploring and Collecting History Online, is an initiative funded by the Alfred P. Sloan Foundation. The aim is to ensure the preservation of contemporary history. Among other resources for historians of science, they have developed a virtual center that contains links to digitalized archives in technology and applied science. A search engine ensures easy access to the directory and the results are displayed in a list with the following pieces of information: the URL, the name of the person or organization that created the page, and a qualitative description of the context, contents, and organization.

HSSOnline
http://www.hssonline.org/teach_res/resources/archives.html

The History of Science Society, founded in 1924 by George Sarton, is probably the largest association of the history of science. They have a database accessible to society members that includes all bibliographic and information resources on the history of science. The resources pages list archives and famous collections under the following categories: archives and collections, organizations and societies, and papers and manuscripts of noted scientists.

Uidaho
http://www.uidaho.edu/special-collections/iil.htm

This is a main reference for lists of primary sources. Created in 1995, it contains at present 4,500 links to archival repositories and lists of archives. URLs are classified by geographical area and country, but there are also additional lists by institution type. One is specifically dedicated to the history of science, but the URLs are listed by location without distinction by state. The URLs are rarely described. The Web site is constantly updated and allows access to more specific directories, such as physics or astronomy.

Professional Sites

At the macro-level, the international cooperation of historians, archivists, and preservation specialists has led to the creation of directories that detail the network and act as a list of contacts. These directories may be very useful to the historian of science to the extent that scientific archival repositories are not as visible as national archives.

UNESCO Archives portal
http://www.unesco.org/webworld/portal_archives/

At the end of the 1990s, UNESCO (United Nations Educational, Scientific and Cultural Organization) created a directory listing archival services by types of institution. The directory allows basic searching and gives results with a description of the repository and its position in the UNESCO Archives directory. The newly created category "archives of Museums" has 161 links sorted by geographic area and country. This may be useful for historians of technology and of natural sciences. A new section titled "primary sources online" lists 326 links of online finding aids and exhibits. They are classified by geographical region and each category primarily contains links to national archives. There is a specific section for international organizations.

Library of Congress, portals to the world
http://www.loc.gov/rr/international/portals.html

The largest library in the world has also created a gateway to Internet resources. Each country listed contains a section titled "libraries and archives" which lists and briefly describes main links in the country. A map with the listed locations allows users to see locations of repositories. If there are online searchable databases for primary sources in the country, they are linked in the description. This is not a specific tool for finding scientific primary sources but can be very useful in finding associations that are dedicated to history of science at the country level.

CASE
http://www.bath.ac.uk/Centres/NCUACS/esearch.htm

In 1998, on behalf of the International Council of Archives (ICA-CIA), a working group known as CASE (Cooperation on Archives of Science in Europe) was created to develop and promote interest in scientific archives in Europe. The final aim is to offer a gateway on this subject. For the time being, they have put online a list of scientific archives sorted by country. For each site there is a short description of the general collections of the repository and the contents of the Web site. In 1996, a more generic group for scientific archives had been created with the same goal, but it has not yet produced any sustainable document

for historians of science (see STAMA, Science, Technology and Medicine Archives working group http://www.asap.unimelb.edu.au/asa/stama/stama_int/intstama.htm). Note also that the CASE directory is hosted by NCUACS, a reference for history of science in the United Kingdom (see below under Resources by Country, United Kingdom).

Resources by Country

At the country level, there are various avenues to finding primary sources. First, there are institutional archives. National or state archives often keep scientific archives. Material for the history of science can also be found in the institutions such as academies of science, engineering schools, universities and research institutes, laboratories, and museums. In some countries, scientific archivists and librarians have created groups and directories of resources for history of science. But professional sites are not the only route to access resources. Amateur historians and retired scientists and engineers may create societies and associations to collect, preserve, and promote sources for the history of science. It is a huge task to list all the potential locations of material for history of science everywhere in the world. However, each historian of science should keep in mind the variety of places where sources for his or her work may be found. The following list presents links and references to find accurate primary sources and gives examples of potential resources that can be found on the Web.

Australia

Australia is a typical location of projects initiated by academics suffering from lack of physical access to sources.

Bright Sparcs
http://www.asap.unimelb.edu.au/bsparcs/bsparcshome.htm

In 1985, the Department of Philosophy and History of Science at the University of Melbourne founded the so-called ASAP, or Australian Science Archives Project, in order to identify scientific archives in Australia and to ensure their preservation and promotion. In 1999 the ASAP created the Australian Science and Technology Heritage Centre and developed a searchable and browsable resource for historians of science called Bright Sparcs. This resource contains more than 4,000 entries on major figures in Australian science since the eighteenth century. For each person, the list of archives locations is linked with a complete description: place, range date, description of contents, size of collections, and place and name of repository. The search can be simple, with the name only, but the directory can also be browsed by functions (such as "agricultural engineer") and genre with sort options. For finding aids that could not appear on Bright Sparcs, ASAP also published guides to primary sources (see http://www.asap.unimelb.edu.au/pubs/asap_pub.htm). A mailing list is available to contact members of ASAP if needed.

Germany

Kalliope, Verbundinformationssystem Nachlässe und Autographen
http://kalliope.staatsbibliothek-berlin.de/

Kalliope is the German part of the integrated European network project on autographs and manuscripts collections (Malvine). It compiles collections kept by 150 institutions in Germany. The search tool is available in German only but allows a large panel of searches by name, dates, function, and location. A search tool specific to correspondence between people and institutions can be very useful for detailed searches.

Russia

The Russian State Archive of Scientific and Technical Documentation (RGANTD)
http://www.russianarchives.com/rao/archives/rgantd/coll.html

Issued from a U.S.-Russian project of digital archives, Russian Archives Online started in 1997 with the aim of allowing worldwide access to representative cultural elements of Russia. RGANTD is one of the catalogs available in this gateway. For the time being, only samples are available in English; the rest of the collection is described in Russian only. The archive has collected historical documents concerning energy and space program development in Russia from entities such as the famous laboratory Baikonour Space and Launch Complex.

United Kingdom

The following works and links show how national archives can develop tools to ensure access to sources. If scholars do not find at the country level an organization dedicated to sources in history of sciences, they should check the state holdings for possible links to specific scientific archives.

Summers, Anne. *How to Find Source Materials: British Library Collections on the History and Culture of Science, Technology and Medicine.* London: The British Library, Science Reference and Information Service, 1996.

As the title clearly states, this book presents each department's scientific collections in the second largest library in the world. It also lists finding aids and other useful reference tools.

The Royal Commission on Historical Manuscripts. *The manuscript papers of British scientists, 1600–1940, Guides to sources for British history, 2.* London: Her Majesty's Stationary Office, 1982.

In the digital age, inventories and printed guides are losing ground to online finding aids. This catalog has been replaced by the NCUACS, available online and presented below.

NCUACS
http://www.bath.ac.uk/Centres/NCUACS/lists.htm

The National Cataloguing Unit of Archives of Contemporary Scientists was begun in 1987, succeeding the Contemporary Scientific Archives Centre in Oxford in its mission of identifying, collecting, preserving, and promoting the history of British science. NCUACS, which at first published a catalog in hardcopy only, now offers a detailed browsable online catalog listing in alphabetic order scientists and their archival collections. The catalog can be accessed by name, discipline, repository, and date of compilation. A complete description for each scientist includes name; dates; function; archival description (reference codes, repository, title of collection, date of material, level of description, and extent); context information, such as biography; custodial history; content information, such as scope, arrangement, conditions of access and use; access; language; finding aids; and allied material. This is the ultimate source for accessing material on contemporary British scientists.

Archives Hub
http://www.archiveshub.ac.uk/

The Archives Hub, as part of the United Kingdom's national archives network, offers access to descriptions of collections held by institutions of higher education in the United Kingdom. The catalog of collections is searchable and browsable in the same way as NCUACS. This can be useful for finding personal papers of professors, whose collections are not mentioned in NCUACS list.

Access to Archives (A2A)
http://www.a2a.pro.gov.uk/

A2A is part of the United Kingdom's national archives network. The searchable database contains more than 20,000 collections from 251 records centers, including scientific societies like the London Geological Society. The search, which can be simple or advanced, is done at the file level. When accessing a hit, it is possible to go to the collection level and access the table of contents.

United States

Rider, Robin E., and Henry E. Lowood, eds. *Guide to the Sources in Northern California for the History of Science and Technology.* Berkeley: Office for the History of Science and Technology, University of California, 1985.

This book lists and describes over 1,000 collections of manuscripts in northern California.

Society of American Archivists (SAA)
http://www.hunterinformation.com/corporat.htm

After having searched the Library of Congress catalog and the National Archive and Records Administration collections, scholars can turn to professional listings such as this one, which is constantly updated by the Society of American Archivists. The directory is accessible by geographical area, name of the archivist, and corporate name. It applies to corporate archives in the United States and Canada. Each entry contains the address, names of contacts, and hours of service. A short description lists the type of holdings, their extent, and any conditions of access.

American Association for Advancement of Science (AAAS)
http://archives.aaas.org/resources/

The AAAS can be valuable when searching for information on history of science. Their list of links is quite short but has the advantage of routing the searcher to the most common known repositories of scientific archives in the United States.

Locations of Sources within a Country

Be aware that searching these sites generally requires knowledge of the native language where the finding aids were developed.

Digital Archives Projects

British Columbia
http://bcdlib.tc.ca/links-subjects-science_tech.html

The British Columbia digital library is compiling links to online collections of primary sources. In the science and technology area, links are mixed and Linné correspondence is listed at the same level of high-energy physics conferences proceedings. Scholars should know that more and more collections of common interest will be published over the Internet and they should not be surprised to find material in such digital libraries.

National Archives and Similar Institutions

Germany
http://www.bundesarchiv.de/bestaende_search.php/

When searching for private collections, keep in mind that state archives may have collected archives of both scientists and scientific associations or state offices. The German State Archives allows online searching in their holdings, which are kept in various locations in Germany. Collections are described according to archival standard with reference code, dates, extent, location, history and contents of the collection, finding aids available, and allied sources.

Italy, Tuscany region
http://www.cultura.toscana.it/bibl/cataloghi/cafos/cafos1.html

In this case we see a regional initiative to list all scientific collections available in Tuscany in every possible type of institution. The catalog is an OPAC (Online Public Access Catalog) and allows standard searches by name, subject, title, and dates.

Science Academies

Many countries have their own science academies, which are divided into various disciplines. As academies often receive private papers of famous scientists and rare manuscripts in the history of national science, they house interesting collections for the historian of science and should not be forgotten during a search for primary sources. Not all have an online catalog, but most of them describe their collections and give links to their allied offices (see U.S. example).

Royal Society of London. *Catalog of Scientific Papers, 1800–1900.* Metuchen: Scarecrow Reprint Corp., 1968.

An accompanying subject index published by the same author and editor is also available to help scholars searching the holdings of the Royal Society.

Academy of Sciences of the Czech Republic
http://www.cas.cz/

The Czech Academy of Sciences in Prague holds large collections of both institutional and personal papers in mathematics, physics and astronomy, astrophysics, and biology. The collections are listed in a directory. A brief description is given for each collection, including bibliographical note, collection extent, dates, and type of finding aid.

Australian Academy of Science—Basser Library
http://www.science.org.au/academy/basser/bass_lis.htm

The Basser library, located in Canberra, lists all collections by reference number. For each reference number, the creator (people or institution), dates, and extent are given. Clicking the reference number link accesses a brief history of the collection and items included. For items with a generic title, a comment on the contents is added.

United States National Academies Archives collections
http://www7.nationalacademies.org/archives/collections.html

This site allows access to the holdings either by using a simple search engine or by browsing the directory. The directory is sorted by functions: council, projects, and small collections. Each collection has a short historical introduction and a listing of files described by a title and a date.

Higher Education, Research Institutes, and Laboratories

As previously mentioned, sources are generally located where they have been produced. Universities or institutions with a long history or famous research institutes often pay attention to their patrimony and preserve archives that document their history. Depending on the structure of higher education in the particular country and the particular institution's private or public status and celebrity, archives may be kept in the institution itself or in national archives. In the United States especially, well-known colleges and universities centralize their historical collections in their libraries, which act as a manuscripts repository. As these primary sources are kept by information managers they are often well described and can be found under the section called "rare and manuscript collections" or "special collections."

California Institute of Technology (CALTECH)
http://archives.caltech.edu/collections.html

CALTECH holds multimedia collections about its members and projects. Most of the material is described in a searchable online catalog and a directory list of collections. A basic search returns descriptions that contain in their detailed views the following pieces of information: title, date, bibliographical note, extent, short description of type and subject of archives, and finding aid availability. At that point the researcher can automatically narrow his or her search to the pictures database or get a list of material related to the described item.

Cornell University
http://rmc.library.cornell.edu/

Cornell University in New York has a "rare and manuscripts collections" division which also hosts the University Archives. The section dedicated to history of science holds a fine collection of books and scientific papers related to chemistry, physics, medicine, ornithology, and botany since the sixteenth century. A small but fine collection of material on civil engineering is also preserved by the university library. A searchable online catalog groups most of the collections, except for a few descriptions that are only accessible on a subject card catalog in the library. The library offers an inquiry service that will answer remote questions on holdings. Finding aids have not been digitalized yet, but the online catalog gives a good overview of each collection. The online description contains the following information on the collection: title (producer name), dates, extent, and typology and subject.

Harvard University
http://oasis.harvard.edu/

Harvard University created OASIS, the Online Archival Search Information System, to allow remote research on sources belonging to archives and repositories at Harvard. The search can be focused on individual repositories or broadened to include contents of all finding aids using various indexes to narrow the search (date, name, keyword, subject, genre, etc.). The finding aids are put online in a very complete form using Encoded Archival Description (EAD). This allows an excellent preparation of sources to be read before going through the primary material itself. However, scholars must keep in mind that not all repositories are participating in the EAD project and should not consider the results of their search as being complete for all material at Harvard.

Massachusetts Institute of Technology (MIT)
http://libraries.mit.edu/archives/research/manuscripts-list-a-f.html

MIT holds institute archives with official records, professional and personal papers from staff and students in MIT, and external collections related to the history of science. Three online catalogs allow access to the collections:

- The RLIN-NUCMUC catalog
- The AIP catalog for collections related to physics (see below in sources for physics)
- Alphabetical list of collections with bibliographical note, extent, and scope and content note (type and subject of archive material)

Complete finding aids, with the exception of the one related to physics, are for sale or made available in the archives reading room.

Polytechnic Schools

In countries such as Switzerland and France, there are prestigious technical high schools that contain their own archives, institutional archives, collections of gifts to the state, and papers of members of the institution. Unless they have a strong public outreach, remote and even direct access are not easy and require specific recommendations. But as these schools are an inevitable gateway to their disciplines, scholars should not hesitate to inquire in this area.

French Polytechnic School
http://www.patrimoine.polytechnique.fr/historique
collections/historique.html

"L'école polytechnique," located in Palaiseau near Paris, compiles in its library over 200 years of museo-logic material and notebooks inherited from the French Academy of Science and State Treasure.

Swiss Polytechnic School—Zurich (Switzerland)
http://www.ethbib.ethz.ch/eth-archiv/nachlaesseb_e.html

The famous "Polytechnikum" where Einstein and Jung taught holds in its library large collections of papers of scientists, professors, and visitors to the school. A list of collections of personal papers is available online with name, dates, function, and reference code. The reference code is a hyperlink to the NEBIS catalog (German or French only), which briefly describes the collection by its type, extent, and availability.

Museums

In addition to academic institutions, scholars who are researching the history of science should not forget museums. Technical museums, museums of natural history, and museums of natural sciences are often repositories of major archival collections.

Deutsches Museum Archives
http://www.deutsches-museum.de/bib/archiv/e_archiv.htm

The Deutsches Museum holds the largest collections in the history of science and technology in Europe. Located on an island over the Isar in Munich, the museum preserves museological and archival material related to physics, chemistry, and technology. No online catalog is available. For each type of collections a list of available finding aids is given. For some of the collections (private papers, etc.), an alphabetical directory has been put online. It contains a short description with name, dates, short bibliographical note, short description of type of archives, and sometimes a mention of allied archives. However, the archives service welcomes external requests on holdings and copies of material.

Technisches Museum Wien—Library and Archives
http://www.technischesmuseum.at/

The Technisches Museum in Vienna, Austria, holds a large collection of archives related to the history of science and technology. Its strength is in technical and engineering collections as well as in natural history archival material produced by its members or obtained by donation. There is no online catalog, but requests on holdings can be sent to the institution.

National Air and Space Museum—Smithsonian Institution
http://www.nasm.si.edu/nasm/arch/archdiv.htm

As its title suggests, the National Air and Space Museum Archives in Washington, D.C., seeks to preserve archival material in air and space flight. Its strength is in photographs, motion picture film, and technical drawings. A few finding aids and graphic archives can be accessed online. The finding aids are professionally structured, listing origin, scope and content note, extent, dates, bibliography, and related collections. For some of them, other appendices are added, such as listing of officers.

Conclusions on Locations of Sources at the Macro-Level

The search for sources in history of science can be broken down in various ways, from wide sweeping research to timely geographical research. Archivists and records managers have created groups specializing in scientific archives or corporate archives. Such groups often publish an international or national contact list, which may be very useful for scholars in locating sources. Even if contemporary science is largely developed by the private sector, scholars should not omit consulting national archives catalogs, as they may have major collections from national institutes or laboratories, scientific academies, and private gifts from great scientists' families. The difficulty with university libraries, private research institutes, laboratories, and corporations is the lack of organization and publication of their collections. Scholars should not forget museums and other exhibitions if they want to illustrate their work or make it more lively.

SOURCES BY DOMAIN OF SCIENCE AND TECHNOLOGY (MICRO-LEVEL)

In this section, examples of reference tools are listed in alphabetical order by subject area and institution name. As in the former section of this chapter, printed reference publications appear before Web links. This list is based on commonly accepted distinctions of scientific disciplines.

Astronomy

Astronomical Institute of Bonn University (Germany)
http://www.astro.uni-bonn.de/~pbrosche/hist_astr/ha_arch.html

A different update of this page is also available at the University of Idaho, in the History of Astronomy subsection under the Additional Lists section http://www.uidaho.edu/special-collections/ill.htm. The list enumerates most individual archives and libraries on astronomy located in the world. For some links, a short note describes the type of collections held. As the list is alphabetical, it is difficult to see the volume of archives owned at a country level.

Lowell Observatory Archives
http://www.lowell.edu/Research/library/paper/archive_home.html

This observatory was founded in 1894 and is located in Flagstaff, Arizona. The Archives hold complete collections of Lowell Observatory members.

Scholars can access short descriptions of the collections by name of scientist. A search in the correspondence archives by subject or content keywords and name is also available.

Royal Greenwich Observatory
http://www.lib.cam.ac.uk/Handbook/D12.html

The Cambridge University Library preserves the Royal Observatory Archives. The collections contain personal papers and a few institutional records. The Web page presents the collections and lists all potential restrictions to access, such as no finding aid available, restricted access due to legal provisions, and so on.

Biology

Florida Museum of Natural History
http://www.flmnh.ufl.edu/research_collections.htm

The Florida Museum, located in the University of Florida campus in Gainesville, holds large collections on zoology: birds, butterflies and moths, fishes, mammals, mollusks, reptiles, and amphibians. For each type of collection, there is a description online. Examination of specimens is by request even if virtual exhibitions have been designed for some themes (birds, butterflies, etc.). The Florida Museum also preserves collections on anthropology and paleontology that may be of interest for scholars researching evolution.

Institut Pasteur
http://www.pasteur.fr/infosci/archives/

The French Pasteur Institute, located in Paris, keeps in its holdings all the scientific collections of the Pasteur laboratory and satellite or linked institutions and personal papers relating to Louis Pasteur and Théodore Monod. On the Web site scholars can search by subject or name or can access the detailed inventory of the collection (professional archivist standard ISAD-G).

National Wildlife Research Center (NWRC)
http://www.aphis.usda.gov/ws/nwrc/is/archives.html

The NWRC, located in Fort Collins, Colorado, is a research and information center within the U.S. Department of Agriculture's (USDA) Animal and Plant Health Inspection Service's (APHIS) Wildlife Services (WS) program. The archives of NWRC preserve all records of the research center's activities, as well as archival materials related to studies conducted by the Federal Insecticide, Fungicide, and Rodenticide Act (FIFRA) Good Laboratory Practice Standards and pesticide registration files. There is an online searchable database of all NWRC's published and unpublished reports.

Chemistry

Tselos, George D., and Colleen Wickley. *A Guide to Archives and Manuscript Collections in the History of Chemistry and Chemical Technology.* Philadelphia: Center for History of Chemistry, 1987.

Focused on American collections, this book compiles all types of sources, from personal papers to institutional records on history of chemistry.

Classic Papers in Chemistry
http://webserver.lemoyne.edu/faculty/giunta/
http://dbhs.wvusd.k12.ca.us/Chem-History/Classic-Papers-Menu.html

These two sites consist of a virtual library of major texts in the history of chemistry since the sixteenth century. Documents can be browsed by author's name or subject.

Royal Society of Chemistry Library
http://www.rsc.org/lic/histuk.htm

This page lists institutions in the United Kingdom where archival collections on chemistry are located. Each entry is described with name, URL, contact references, type of collections held, and access rules.

Computing

Cortada, James W., ed. *Archives of Data-Processing History: A Guide to Major U.S. Collections.* New York: Greenwood Press, 1990.

This book provides a short description of major archival collections housed in the United States. Scholars can also find practical information on accessing these collections. The book is arranged by area of interest (hardware, software, information processing industry, etc.), but it can also be accessed by author and subject.

Charles Babbage Institute (CBI)—Center for the History of Information Technology
http://www.cbi.umn.edu/collections/archmss.html

This archive and research center of the University of Minnesota was founded in 1978 to promote the study of history of information technology and information processing. With a strong policy of collecting archival material, the CBI keeps in its holdings an ever-increasing number of collections from various sources: institutional, academic, personal papers, and so on. Finding aids for each collection are available online in alphabetical format. A simple subject search is also available. Each collection is precisely described according to the following criteria: archives format, creator, processor, acquisition, access rules and copyright, historical note, scope and content of collection, arrangement of the collection, and related collections in the CBI. The CBI has also published sourcebooks for collections related to history of computing (see Bruce Bruemmer, *Resources for the History of Computing: A Guide to U.S. and Canadian Records,* 1987). Finally, the CBI Web site contains a directory of links to other relevant institutions and resources.

Computer History Museum
http://www.computerhistory.org/

This Museum is still developing its Web site, though it has been around since the late seventies. Scholars are able to look through the artifacts collection online database using a simple search form. The museum also offers remote searches in the other catalogs for media, documentation, and archives that are not available online via an e-mail address. The museum itself is located in the heart of Silicon Valley, in Mountain View, California.

National Archive for the History of Computing
http://www.chstm.man.ac.uk/nahc/catalog.htm

The University of Manchester in the United Kingdom hosts the national archive for the history of computing. The collections consist of public, academic, and private archives. A catalog of manuscripts is available online. It contains a detailed description of each collection that includes summary, provenance, items descriptions, and bibliographic references.

Engineering

Academy François Bourdon
http://www.afbourdon.com/frame_consultfonds.htm

This French society is collecting papers from companies located in the major industrial area of Le Creusot, France. The main collection is the fonds of Schneider Electric S.A., a firm that existed from 1836 to 1967. Historical notes are presented for each collection, and each finding aid is available online in PDF format.

Bedi, J.E., R.R. Kline, and C. Semsel. *Sources in Electrical History: Archives and Manuscript Collections in U.S. Repositories.* New York: Center for the History of Electrical Engineering, 1989.

This book, issued by the IEEE, describes more than 1,000 archival repositories that hold primary sources in electrical history. Three indices by name, subject, and geographic location allow access to this catalog, which has been made available online at http://www.ieee.org/organizations/history_center/research_guides/sources1/sources1_menu.html.

Institute of Electrical and Electronics Engineers, Inc. History Center
http://www.ieee.org/organizations/history_center/

The History Center of the IEEE, located in New Brunswick, New Jersey, has created a virtual library and a clearinghouse of information, both online and printed, for researchers in electronic engineering.

The Science Museum
http://www.sciencemuseum.org.uk/library/archive.asp/

The British Science Museum, located in London, keeps in its repository large collections relating to famous engineers and scientists, as well as industrial and company records. Collections can be searched by item in the Web catalog at http://www.lib.ic.ac.uk/catalog/cataccess.htm by using the complex search function and selecting archives as the format.

Geology

American Heritage Center—University of Wyoming
http://uwadmnweb.uwyo.edu/AHC/depts/reference/anaconda.htm

The Anaconda Copper Mining Company donated its entire collection of geological archives to the University of Wyoming in 1987. This collection contains more than 1.8 million documents on prospecting and analysis, studies, and reports on American and worldwide locations. Scholars may search the collection online at no cost by completing a request form, but there is a charge for physical access. Students and academic researchers are charged a preferential rate of $15 per annum.

Bundesanstalt für Geowissenschaften und Rohstoffe
http://www.bgr.de/z7/homepage.htm

The German Federal Office for Geology, located in Hannover, holds a major collection of reports and maps on German geology. Some thematic catalogs (themes, subjects) are available online, but the catalog ORBIT that allows searches in all manuscript collections is internal only.

Mathematics

Albree, Joe, et al., eds. *A Station Favorable to the Pursuits of Science: Primary Material in the History of Mathematics at the United States Military Academy.* Providence: American Mathematical Society, 2000.

This book is dedicated to mathematical archival material in the West Point collection. After a chapter introducing the collection and giving historical background information, the catalog lists all available collections in chronological order. As there is no index, scholars may have difficulty retrieving information related to their subjects.

AMS-MAA Joint Archives Committee
http://www.ams.org/mathweb/History/collections.html

The Web site of the American Mathematics Society contains an alphabetical list of archival collections of mathematicians in Northern America. Each entry gives the name and dates of the mathematician, the location of the collection, and reference to related collections. The list is not cross-referenced.

Medicine

Tunis, Elizabeth. *A Directory of History of Medicine Collections.* Bethesda: U.S. Department of Health and Human Services, 1997.

This directory, which lists archival repositories by geographical locations, has been made available online at http://www.nlm.nih.gov/hmd/directory/directoryhome.html. Each institution is briefly described with a historical note, a contact address, and the contents and extent of its holdings. If the institution has a Web site, the directory has a link to it.

There are associations and societies that are dedicated to general history of health sciences or to a specific domain. They may be a contact resource when searching for primary sources.

American Association for the History of Medicine
http://www.histmed.org/

History of Dermatology Society
http://www.dermato.med.br/hds/

History of Anesthesia Society
http://www.histansoc.org.uk/

Archivists and Librarians in the History of the Health Sciences (ALHHS)
http://www.library.ucla.edu/libraries/biomed/alhhs/iresources.htm

This is a general list of online resources related to the history of medicine. This can be a starting point for scholars looking for archives on the subject.

Dittrick Medical History Center
http://www.cwru.edu/artsci/dittrick/archives.htm

Based on material collected by the Cleveland Medical Library Association, Dittrick Medical History Center tries to centralize and preserve the medical heritage of Northern Ohio. Each collection is listed by type and subject and is shortly described with a note about its origin, extent, and dates.

Dundee University Archives
http://www.dundee.ac.uk/archives/a-thb.htm

In the United Kingdom, the University of Dundee keeps collections of the Tayside Health Board dating to the middle of the nineteenth century. Each institutional collection is composed of administrative material (minutes, reports, and registers), manuscripts, project papers, and statistics. A simple search allows online access to short descriptions of collections including types of documents and dates. The archives service also welcomes online inquiries. This collection includes an exhaustive set of document types that scholars can retrieve in medical institutions.

French National Academy of Medicine
http://www.academie-medecine.fr/bibliotheque/bibliotheque3.asp/

The French National Academy of Medicine, located in Paris, preserves in its holdings archival material dating from the eighteenth century. Collections come from French academies and societies, academicians' personal papers, and donations. Each collection is shortly described with a note on its origin, general structure, and dates. A small online database, HISTMED, allows a simple name search. The results given correspond to the type of holdings (papers, graphics, sculptures, etc.) kept by the Academy http://www.academie-medecine.fr/base.htm.

International Network for History of Occupational and Environmental Prevention (INHOEP)
http://users.unimi.it/~netprev/sugl/sugl.htm

This Milanese Web page is divided into three parts: generic links, health sciences museums, and historical archives. It gives major resources for each theme and is geared toward Italian institutions.

Medical Library Association—History of the Health Sciences section
http://www.mla-hhss.org/histloca.htm

This directory lists by state and country or by institutional name large collections on history of health sciences. Many links for the United States are to academic collections. There is no description of collections given, but the name of the repository is provided.

National Library of Medicine (NLM)
http://www.nlm.nih.gov/hmd/manuscripts/asaio/index.html

In collaboration with the Smithsonian Institution and the American Society for Artificial Internal Organs, the United States Library of Medicine in Bethesda, Maryland, has developed "a guide to collections relating to the history of artificial organs." In alphabetical order, this guide lists worldwide repositories of archives, literature, and specimens. The Web page allows direct access to major collections. At an upper level in the library and archives section of the Web site, the NLM provides a descriptive list of large resources in the history of medicine.

Natural Science

British Museum Library. *Catalog of the Books, Manuscripts, Maps and Drawings in the British Museum (Natural History).* London, 1992.

This catalog describes personal papers and collections held by the Museum of Natural History. It is available online at http://www.nhm.ac.uk/library/index.html (select Catalog). The catalog is a search tool that allows access to comprehensive descriptions of collections.

Linnean Society of London Library. *Catalog of the Manuscripts in the Library of the Linnean Society.* London: Linnean Society, 1934–48.

This catalog lists the Smith and Ellis papers and part of the Linné papers retained by the society.

Phillips, Venia T., and Maurice E. Phillips. *Guide to the Manuscript Collections in the Academy of Natural Sciences of Philadelphia.* Philadelphia: Academy of Natural Science, 1963.

This book lists alphabetically collections kept by the academy. There are indexes by subject and authors (originator or recipient of documents).

Physics

Curie Museum
http://musee.curie.fr/presentation/archives.html

The Curie Museum in Paris contains the archives of the Curie Laboratory dating from its creation in 1914. It contains part of the Pierre and Marie Curie collection, Frédéric and Irène Joliot-Curie collections, archives from their collaborators, and the library of the laboratory. The finding aid is available only in hardcopy, and access to the archives is by appointment.

ICOS Database
http://libserv.aip.org/webpac-bin/wgbroker?new+-access+top.icos/

ICOS, the International Catalog of Sources for History of Physics and Allied Sciences, maintained by the American Institute of Physics (AIP), is the reference resource for locating primary sources in physics and related disciplines since 1890. A basic search gives access to a complete description of the collection, including title, repository name and location, archival organization, item size, content summary, notes, and access rules. A subject field with related names allows a direct search to names throughout the catalog.

Max Planck Society
http://www.mpg.de/deutsch/general/archiv.html

The archives for history of the Max Planck Society, located in Munich, Germany, preserve all collections related to the history of the institution and papers of its members. The society holds collections of famous physicians and Nobel Prize winners such as Otto Hahn, Max von Laue, and Werner Heisenberg. There is no catalog online, but requests on holdings may be sent to the archives services.

Niels Bohr Archive
http://www.nbi.dk/NBA/webpage.html

This archive holds all surviving material from Niels Bohr: his correspondence and manuscripts and external resources such as newspaper clippings, interviews, and so on. The archive also preserves collections created by other physicists. All collections may be searched in ICOS or browsed directly from the Niels Bohr Archive Web site.

PSI Gate: Physical Sciences Information Gateway
http://www.psigate.ac.uk/homenew.htm

This gateway to science information was launched in September 2001. It is a basic search engine for the physical sciences: physics, astronomy, chemistry, and earth sciences. It has the advantage of focusing on physical sciences and gives detailed descriptions of Web sites included in the catalog.

Wheaton, Bruce R. *Inventory of Sources for History of Twentieth-Century Physics: Report and Microfiche Index to 700,000 Letters.* Stuttgart: Verlag für Geschichte des Naturwissenschaften und der Technik, 1993.

This microfiche index is arranged by name, and its guide contains citations of correspondence and holding information for approximately 6,000 physicists' papers worldwide. It has also been published as a CD-ROM with an additional index by collections.

Telecommunications

Bracken, J. K., and C. H. Sterling. *Telecommunications Research Resources: An Annotated Guide.* Mahwah, N.J.: Lawrence Erlbaum Associates, 1995.

This is a comprehensive book listing and describing sources available in the United States for scholars studying telecommunications. With several indices, this handbook compiles background information on the history of telecommunications and provides a bibliography and list of primary and secondary sources on the subject.

International Telecommunication Union (ITU)
http://www.itu.int/

The oldest international organization, founded in 1865, keeps in its holdings historic material and a large collection of worldwide maps of telecommunication networks up to the development of satellite networks (1960). There is no open access finding aid, but the archives, located in Geneva, Switzerland, can be contacted in preparation for research.

Telecommunications History Group
http://www.telcomhistory.org/

The Telecommunications History Group in Denver, Colorado, has compiled a list of telecommunications archives and resources. For each institution, address, contacts, structure of collections, access rules, and hyperlinks are provided. The list is available upon request at the group's Web site. This group should not be confused with the British Telecommunications Heritage Group, which provides in its Web site a directory of links on the history of telecommunications: http://www.thg.org.uk/.

CONCLUSION

In contrast to some other history disciplines, the history of science requires broadminded scholars to access sources that consist of extremely varied types and origins. Archival material is often scattered because of the professional mobility of scientists and their tradition of sharing information with colleagues. These sources need specific treatment, and scholars should be able to limit their focus to relevant items and to read and understand the sources. The study of technical data in notebooks and an analysis of scientists' correspondence can be very beneficial but are also very time-consuming. Scholars must be aware of that before diving into the vast sea of resources. Scholars can also easily encounter other problems, such as access and copyright restrictions. Most of the time the 30-year rule is applied even in the private sector. If access is limited because the collection has not been processed, scholars can negotiate access on the condition that they help to create a finding aid or index. As in any other discipline, the success of historical research is based on the responsibility and awareness of the researcher with regard to issues underlying the process of study and use of background materials. An understanding of the issues will help the scholar in negotiating access or publication rights for archival material.

There are some specific search engines and directories on the Internet specializing in scientific information. Scholars can use such tools to limit their search and access references that may be invisible using common search engines. As researchers become increasingly interested in science, thematic guides on science and history of science are multiplying. However, one should take into account that some guides are pay-per-view directories. Museums that develop virtual exhibitions are also a valuable source of information. With the exception of physics and allied sciences and health sciences, there are few guides on primary sources for particular scientific disciplines. In fact, the applied sciences are much more described than pure sciences such as mathematics. There is clearly an opportunity for historical research in these subjects. Even if there is a trend to place finding aids online, the consultation of catalogs in the library or archives remains mandatory, especially when the extensive work of describing the collection is difficult to put online. If archives do not have a strong public outreach, they may not have a large presence in the institution's Web site and are therefore unlikely to publish their finding aids.

The aim of this chapter is not to list all primary sources available for historians of science, as they are far too numerous and uneven. Primary sources are vital for historians of science, and the reference tools presented in this chapter should aid in the quest. To avoid primary sources is a mistake, and historians of science must discover the key points in the area of their research's subject. This will be scholars' main reason for selecting the most accurate sources for their study.

BIBLIOGRAPHY

Amstrong, J. "An Introduction to Archival Research in Business History." *Business History* 33, no. 1 (1991): pp. 7–34.

Amstrong, J., and S. Jones. *Business Documents: Their Origins, Sources and Uses in Historical Research.* London and New York: Mansell, 1987.

Bedford at St. Martins. "Science: Finding Sources." http://www.bedfordstmartins.com/hacker/resdoc/sciences/general.htm.

Bracke, Marianne Stowell, and Paul J. Bracke. "Science and Technology Resources on the Internet. Selected Web Resources in the History of Science." *Issues in Science and Technology Librarianship,* no. 21, winter (1999).

Brown, Pr. "Good Science/Bad Science. Resources for Research." In EARS, Winter Term 2002. http://www.dartmouth.edu/~krescook/instruct/ES7.W03.html.

Butler, Declan. "Search Engine Metadata Science." *Nature* 405, 11 May 2000, pp. 112–115.

Columbia University. "Archives and Manuscripts Collections." Columbia University Web Site. http://www.columbia.edu/cu/lweb/eguides/specol.html.

Conant, James B. *On Understanding Science.* New Haven, Conn.: Yale University Press, 1947.

Crowe, Michael J. "The History of Science. A Guide for Undergraduates." Homepage of Robert T. Hatch. http://www.clas.ufl.edu/users/rhatch/pages/02-Teaching Resources/crowe/crowe.html.

Direction des Archives de France. *Les archives personnelles des scientifiques,* Paris: Archives Nationales, 1995.

Fordham University. "Internet History of Science Sourcebook." Fordham University Web Site. http://www.fordham.edu/halsall/science/sciencebook.html.

Harvard University. *Sources Books in the History of Science Series.* Cambridge, Mass.: Harvard University Press, 1929.

Highwire. Library of the Science and Medicine. http://highwire.stanford.edu/.

Horus Publications. "Beginner's Guide to Research in the History of Science." Horus Publications Web site. http://www.horuspublications.com/guide/bi103.html.

Hurt, C.D. "Information Sources in Science and Technology." Englewood, Colo.: Libraries Unlimited, 1998.

International Council of Archives (ICA). "Archiving the Records of Contemporary Science." Summary of proceedings of meeting in Liège, 1996. ASAP Web site. http://www.asap.unimelb.edu.au/asa/stama/stama_int/liege96/.

Krige, John, and Dominique Pestre, eds. *Science in the Twentieth Century.* Amsterdam: Harwood Academic Publishers, 1997.

McClung, Patricia. "Access to Primary Sources: During and After the Digital Revolution." Keynote address for the Berkeley Finding Aids Conference, April 1995. Berkeley Digital Library SunSITE. http://sunsite. berkeley.edu/FindingAids/EAD/ucb3.html.

Members of the Clever Project. "Hypersearching the Web." *Scientific American,* June 1999, pp. 54–60. http://www. sciam.com/.

National Digital Archive of Datasets (UK NDAD). "Links and Resources. Links to Other Archives and Information Resources." http://ndad.ulcc.ac.uk/links/other_links.htm.

Olby, R.C. *Companion to the History of Modern Science.* London and New York: Routledge, 1990.

Parker, Sybil P., ed. *The MacGraw Hill Encyclopedia of Science and Technology.* New York: McGraw Hill, 1997.

Porter, R., and M. Ogilvie. *The Biographical Dictionary of Scientists.* Oxford: Oxford University Press, 2000.

Raymond Walters College Library. "Historical Documents Online: Internet Sites for Primary Source Material."

Raymonds Walters College Web site. http://www.rwc. uc.edu/library/pathfinders/primary.html.

Stewart, Doug. "Reference Sources in History of Science and Science Studies." Doug Stewart Web site. http://www.wsulibs.wsu.edu/hist-of-science/.

University of Adelaide Library (Australia). "Science, History, Philosophy and Education." University of Adelaide Web site. http://www.library.adelaide.edu.au/guide/ sci/Generalsci/histsci.html.

University of California, Berkeley. "Library Research Using Primary Sources. Primary Sources on the Web." University of California, Berkeley Web site. http://www.lib.berkeley.edu/TeachingLib/Guides/ PrimarySourcesOnTheWeb.html.

University of Chicago "Special Collections Research Center." University of Chicago Web site. http://www. lib.uchicago.edu/e/spcl/linkwrld.html.

University of Jussieu Library (France). "Ressources Internet. Science et Société." University of Jussieu Web site. http://bleuet.bius.jussieu.fr/intsts.html.

CHAPTER 4
Religious Archives

Alan Delozier

INTRODUCTION

The spirit and substance of religious archival research can be a revelation in many profound respects. This is the case when it comes to seeking an understanding of historical information from both a sacred and temporal viewpoint as the printed word and image found within the realm of theological-based scholarship takes on different meanings depending upon the informational focus of the researcher and the religious discipline represented. The very essence and value of creating and preserving a spiritual record is captured by John Corrigan who wrote the following passage in his book *Archives: The Light of Faith* about archival illumination in this regard: "The historical development of archives in general and those of the church in particular had and still have as their primary function, the preservation of records of the past for informational and scholarly research. Each local church, each religious community and institution in establishing archives can do no less in preserving the history of the church, the people of God, for future generations." (Corrigan, 1980) With this in mind, anything from the actual scripture related to one's faith to commentary on religious practice and the chronicle of rituals performed are just a few of the countless types of informational illumination sought by both the religious archivist and the research community. Therefore, this particular chapter is not designed to be a comprehensive study, but rather an introduction to some of the more prolific denominational archival repositories found throughout the United States. This survey will also attempt to promote initial and more detailed search options related to the field of religious studies in each of its varied and inspirational forms outlined in the text below.

BASIC TYPES OF RECORDS AND STARTING POINTS FOR RESEARCH

The foundation of organized religious thought and doctrine in written form comes in the presence of a holy book which serves as the wellspring of its adherents and respective concept of God whether it be the *Torah* in Judaism, the Christian *Bible,* the *Qur'an* of Islam, or any other source from which archival documentation can directly or indirectly trace as its lineal origin. From this foundation, other key works were created in line with the human concept of theological interpretation through the past several centuries including the *Letters of St. Paul,* Martin Luther's *Thesis of Christianity,* the Jewish *Talmud,* the *Baltimore Catechism,* or the *Dead Sea Scrolls* for instance. The written output of religious-oriented works has proliferated ever since, and countless variations have been preserved for the benefit of all interested adherents and students of religious thought.

In addition to famous primary source documents, there are several other types of texts that were produced in line with a philosophical or functional need of the writer and advocate on a denominational, diocesan, parish/synagogue, or personal level. Records of this nature might include administrative records (including incorporation deeds, financial/business ledgers, seminary books, and so on); clergy papers (such as liturgy and sermon transcripts, correspondence to and between bishops, pastors, parishioners, and so on); and religious community information (which feature church bulletins, anniversary books, appointment ledgers, and so on). Or it can be found in other relevant forms such as prayer books, hymnals, spiritual journals, broadsides, and similar examples.

Consequently, the focus and mission of the religious archivist is capsulized by August Suelflow who wrote in his excellent volume, *Religious Archives: An Introduction,* that "A religious body or organization has the obligation to preserve those records and resources necessary to continue its operations, to meet its legal requirements, and to provide for its historical continuity." (Suelflow, 1980)

Another value of archival resources comes in the cyclical nature of their usage. Books and journals are often used as the guidepost for an idea, and they are also the end product of the research and written odyssey, making it the alpha and omega of religious enlightenment for the professional and the amateur researcher alike. Even with the presence of unique archival resources, the most widely utilized resources in the field of theological scholarship still tend to come from the text of religious lectures relating to the nature of faith and inspiration, teaching notes, or mainstream books, including biographical studies on saints from Aaron to Zynovij and prominent church figures, such as Henry Ward Beecher, Fulton Sheen, John Wesley, and Isaac Mayer Wise.

On a personalized level, the most popular form of religious record research relates to the field of genealogical inquiry. The quest for uncovering family information from a sacred perspective provides a means of learning about the spiritual orientation of ancestors, which often mirrors civil records (which sometimes might contain information about religious affiliation), but mainly through the rites of passage associated with personal beliefs from birth through death. Counted among the most important ceremonies are baptism, christenings, confirmation, bar mitzvahs, marriage vows, and other comparable milestones. Each ceremony is often documented either in a special ledger or a certificate form, but most individuals also record events independently in family bibles or prayer books. Additional citations can be found in newspaper clippings (notably a community events page or obituary section), mass cards, testimonial letters, cemetery records, or other like items which are commonly created and consulted for the sake of divine posterity.

When it comes to setting policy on what a religious research center keeps and maintains is set by a particular governing body on a national level or by a bishop/district leader on a diocesan or sectional scale or by the director of each facility on a daily basis. However, at the present time there are no uniform guidelines for record retention, but rather it varies from denomination to denomination and initiatives devised by those responsible for the ultimate decision-making process. The most prominent advocate of church record preservation is the Church of Jesus Christ Latter-day Saints (Mormons) which by rule is required to microfilm church records regardless of faith, making it a truly universal aid to the archival profession and research community. In other cases, strategies vary in degree from the Reformed Church in America and the Episcopalian Church, which mainly have centralized systems, to the Catholic Church, which is organized primarily on a diocesan level, to the Moravian Church, which is divided by province and region.

Once the basic collecting parameters, mission, and focus is determined, the researcher can perform a more concentrated search for appropriate materials whether it be at a traditional archival repository or via the World Wide Web, which has revolutionized the field of historical scholarship by its convenience and accessibility. Counted among the most powerful search engines and tools devoted to location of the appropriate archive are the National Union Catalog of Manuscripts (NUMC), Research Libraries Information Network (RLIN), and Archives USA. These Web sites are not exclusively religious in focus, but contain substantial amounts of information related to the field at large. Christianity and Judaism are among the most prolific denominations in the United States when it comes to membership numbers, but all religious traditions, regardless of size or value system, have significant resources worth further study. Conversely, various secular-operated archival centers, including the Library of Congress Manuscript Division and the National Archives and Records Administration, are among the best sources in the United States on materials related to Islam, Hinduism, Buddhism, and many other faiths as well. Along with federal repositories, state archives are of prospective benefit especially when it comes to exploring the earliest vestiges of religious settlers in a particular region such as the Society of Friends in Pennsylvania, Catholicism in Maryland, the Lutheran Church in Missouri, Mormon settlement throughout Utah, and so forth.

In tandem with traditional archival sources, the creation and utility of the Internet has been a boon for viewing documents in electronic form or by finding a specific research center via the search engine route. With the presence of convenience, a measure of caution should also be observed and weighed when it comes to testing the validity of any information offered on a public Web site, even those dealing with religious themes. Major denominational homepages proper and those connected to archival endeavors (such as those listed below) are usually on the square and provide detailed, methodical, and genuine data to the viewing public as a matter of course.

Selected sites are featured elsewhere in this chapter, but there are also special Web areas that include general introductory facts on various religious disciplines such as historical outlines and doctrinal texts. Counted among the most detailed Internet research tools currently available is http://www.Adherents.com/, which features more than 41,000 statistics and religious geographical citations on more than 4,200 different sects throughout the world. Another useful resource is the *Material History of American Religion Project,* which provides an individual with insights on the historical nature of religious life in the United States. The *Religious and Sacred Texts* highlights various theological documents from a number of different faith perspectives including many Christian favorites along with such specific articles as the *Bhagavad Gita, Egyptian Book of the Dead, Urantia Book,* and many others. The *American Religion Data Archive* includes maps and reports on the national religious landscape between 1980 and 1990 combined with quantitative data on church administration, membership, professional activities, and group dynamics among other topics. When it comes to specifics on local congregations, family history, and manuscript information Cyndi Howell's *Cyndi's List of Religion & Churches* is an extremely well-detailed and useful Web site that features thousands of entry links that are broken down by category and denominational type. These are just a few examples of how the new technology provides timeless information related to religion in all of its diverse and precious forms.

OVERVIEW OF VARIOUS PRINT AND ELECTRONIC RESOURCES (BY DENOMINATION)

Protestantism

Archival resources related to the development of Christianity in the United States have a long-standing place in the written historical memory of America as evident in the rich tradition of Protestant-centered thought from the seventeenth century to the present day. Denominational branches are typically represented by national governing bodies and organizational structures such as the assembly, diocese, and synod. Archival repositories, which represent the Protestant Church, are broken down by sect, and each has their own unique customs and ceremonies featuring printed documents of various format type and subject matter focus providing enlightenment on these rituals.

There are several different repositories that house Protestant-related materials of note including the Billy Graham Center Archives at Wheaton College, Illinois, founded in 1975. It contains the papers obtained from one of the most influential clerics of the twentieth century. The mission statement of this repository also reflects the professional and generous manner in which most general and religious-oriented history centers typically operate. "The Archives gathers, preserves and makes available for use unpublished documents on the history of North American nondenominational Protestant efforts to spread the Christian Gospel. Although anyone may come and use the collections, these materials are especially intended as a resource for the evangelistic mission of the church." (Billy Graham Center Archives Home Page, 2002)

When searching for information on the Baptist Church, especially in regard to the study of denominational history, there are various prominent centers of note including the American Baptist Historical Society in Pennsylvania (which features manuscript collections and reports tracing the evolution and development of the American Baptist Church), United American Free Will Baptist General Conference, and Danish Baptist General Conference of America. In addition, the Samuel Colgate Historical Library of American Baptist History contains materials related to the historical legacy of the Baptist Church with over 80,000 bound volumes, 500 original church record texts, and 400 manuscript collections including annual reports of associations and conventions amassed from various ministers and other spiritual sources. The Southern Baptist Historical Library and Archives is another research facility with depth in the form of over 71,000 annual reports and relevant newspapers, audio/visual resources, pamphlets, and 16,000 reels of microfilm containing various Baptist-related historical papers among other documentation of note.

The Archives of the Episcopal Church, USA located in Texas is one of the most organized and prolific research centers in the country. This archival Web site is devoted to the collection and maintenance of special materials related to Episcopalianism, including those connected to the General Convention and Missionary Societies (both foreign and domestic), along with the papers of key leaders (both religious and lay) among other relevant record types. Along with a national archive and records management center, the Episcopal Church also encourages record keeping to be done at a local level. Informative manuals, such as the *Records Management for Congregations: Financial and Common Business Records,* along with microfilm, preservation, and proper storage advisement programs have been successfully implemented by church officials and the general public alike. The Episcopal Historical Society is an organization that is devoted to the usage of archival resources and promoting the history of the Church proper within the context of the American society at large.

Archival records representing the Lutheran Church and its different branches are situated in various locations across the country. The Missouri Synod, founded in 1847, had from its very beginning produced important documents that are now housed at the Concordia Historical Institute in St. Louis. Concordia has also been designated as the official archival repository for the denomination and also features a substantial library on the history of Lutheranism in North America from 1959 onward. Traditional types of materials representing the Evangelical Lutheran Church in America (ELCA), founded in 1987, include the personal papers of prominent church leaders, oral history materials, parish records, and various types of genealogical documents.

Wesleyan Theology has a strong archival tradition as found in the presence of the official United Methodist Church General Commission on Archives located at Drew University in New Jersey. For example, this repository contains the records of denominational agencies, personal papers donated by a distinguished array of missionaries and bishops, and annual conference journals dating from 1796 to the present. Representation from different branches of the Methodist Church are also conserved as shown in the contents of papers from those who built and upheld the teachings of such spiritual branches as the Methodist Episcopal Church (1784–1939), Methodist Protestant Church (1828–1939), United Brethren in Christ (1800–1946), United Evangelical Church (1894–1922), and Evangelical Church (1922–1946), among others.

Presbyterianism is another Protestant denomination that has a solid archival program as found in the Presbyterian Historical Society located in Pennsylvania (with a regional office in North Carolina). This department is a part of the Office of the General Assembly and is designed to serve all levels of the Church from

an administrative, legal, and historical standpoint. The society is dedicated to housing materials that date back to the 1600s and contains over 1,500 cubic feet worth of documentation related to the Presbyterian ministry, specific church bodies, and many other prime aspects of the faith and its presence in the United States. Another historical center related to the Presbyterian Church is located in Missouri and is designed to assist researchers on various aspects of the creed and its place in history.

Each of the aforementioned religious traditions has their theological roots in Europe, but arose to prominence through the efforts of their faithful and subsequent search for spiritual freedom and expression in America. Other denominations that followed this path include the Congregational Church, which emphasizes leadership in the form of government as elected by the membership. This particular approach helps to generate a steady stream of administrative paperwork, and the Congregational Library and Archives located in Massachusetts is the main focal point devoted to this religious tradition, especially from nineteenth century onward. The Reformed Church in America Archives located in New Jersey is a centralized repository that houses the records of more than 240 different congregations and records related to the faith in the form of official documents produced by the Church, local parishes, and missionary field from 1630 to the present. Among the oldest archival records related to American religion are found at the Huguenot Historical Society Library and Archives situated in New York. This center contains materials dealing with family genealogies, cemetery lists, bible records, census rolls, and other related information dating from 1582 onward.

Other American religious movements are also well documented through the establishment and operation of denominational archival repositories. The Salvation Army Archives and Research Center located in Virginia collects, preserves, and makes their records (which date back to the start of the religious movement in 1880) available to researchers upon request. The Church of the Brethren Library and Archives (also known as the German Baptist Brethren or Dunkers) founded in 1936 is located in Illinois and contains various congregational records, family history research aids, and various internally-produced manuscript guides including the *Brethren Historical Library* and the *Archives and Guide to Research in Brethren History* among others. Founded in 1970, the United Brethren Historical Center focuses upon the history of the denomination in various traditionally documented forms. The Assemblies of God Flower Pentecostal Heritage Center located in Missouri is a repository that not only devotes its collection focus to the faith and its history but also to the study of Pentecostal, charismatic, and evangelical traditions from the late 1800s to present times.

The Disciples of Christ is a sect that has an active archival presence, and the Historical Society that represents them has a collection of more than 35,000 volumes and 50,000 subject files, including personal and institutional records of note. The Church of Nazarene Archives has a collection with early historical ties to Methodism and contains records of general assemblies, chronicles, and information files on important people of the Church. The Seventh-Day Adventists General Conference Archives found in Maryland features sections devoted to administrative records, personal collections, published records, periodicals, and other types of formats measuring more than 10,000 linear feet in depth. These and several other prolific repositories house important documents related to various branches within the Protestant religious experience.

Church of the Latter-day Saints (Mormons)

The Church of the Latter-day Saints is a unique religious tradition that has its roots in nineteenth-century America, and the work of their followers has been beneficial to the historical community and praised widely by archivists and family historians alike. Within the Mormon faith proper, the LDS Family History Library located in Utah features newspapers, periodicals, temple, membership and missionary records, journals, personal accounts of church history, and the church file, which traces the lineage of the Latter-day Saints from 1840 through 1941.

The Mormon Church is ecumenical when it comes to genealogical outreach as well. As a rule they have established more than 3,400 Family History (or LDS) Centers nationwide from which patrons have a choice of viewing more than two million rolls of microfilm (featuring information on more than two billion people) by special request. Through this endeavor, individuals, regardless of religious orientation, can view sacramental records from a wide-range of denominations, which is part of the LDS mission to save personal information regardless of one's spiritual direction. Included among the most popular personal

data areas utilized are infant blessings, baptisms, confirmations, marriages, and death records. The LDS seeks to preserve printed records and are concerned with the preservation of each individual record through the practice of obtaining authorization to microfilm any available original ledger book, parchment, or associated format for later usage by church officials and the research community at large. Not only are microfilmed sacramental register records available through LDS centers, but extra copies are also available through purchase by an originating parish, diocese, or other entity for their own usage. In addition, within the past two years, the LDS has published many of their family records on the Internet, which features a search engine that can be used by finding matches according to surname making accessibility more convenient for interested users.

Society of Friends (Quakers)

The Religious Society of Friends in America is known for religious tolerance and topnotch scholarship, which has resulted in the maintenance and preservation of records related to the faith from the mid-seventeenth century to the present day. The Quakers have one of the most structured record-keeping systems of any denomination in existence. Personal information is usually included in most Quaker records and typically features birth, marriage, and congregational details. This brings structure to their membership rolls and provides significant data for present ledger-notation system within the Quaker Meeting (a religious service held on a monthly basis) itself, especially when it comes to those who joined either from birth or converted later in life. The proceedings of each Quaker Meeting including statements from those who speak as the spirit moves them are transcribed for future reference and serve as a record for future generations to review. The monthly Meeting features a myriad of information that is recorded along with the minutes and often includes biographical data, birthright particulars, family name, marriage and witness lists, burial, and other relevant particulars such as those who attended non-Quaker services, military enlistment, and other significant acts of note.

Quaker Meeting Houses or specially designated repositories hold the majority of Meeting records and other important documentation related to the development of the Society of Friends. However, institutions of higher learning affiliated with the Society of Friends tend to have the largest and most comprehensive set of records on Quakerism available to the research community. The prominent collections at Haverford and Swarthmore Colleges, both located outside of Philadelphia, Pennsylvania, are also very prolific in the area of Friends records. Swarthmore has one of the most substantial collections of Quaker-related archives in the country and holds the official records for both the Philadelphia and Baltimore Yearly Meetings, which are among the oldest and largest in the country. Haverford has an equally impressive amount of Quaker resources of more than 32,000 printed titles and 250,000 items on the Friends currently available to researchers. The Earlham College Archives has more than 12,000 books and pamphlets along with relevant manuscripts that have been amassed since the 1890s, which help in making the Society of Friends one of the best represented of religious faiths in the United States.

Catholicism

The largest single denomination in the United States is the Roman Catholic Church, which has a tradition of detailed record keeping on the religious passages and spiritual mysteries of life. When it comes to material substance related to the Catholic Church, the printed output usually comes in different forms with sacramental, ecclesiastical, or administrative being the main types found. The sacramental record is one that the family historian is most familiar with, and there are seven different types within the Catholic Church. Most times baptism, marriage, and death records are the most commonly recorded in a designated parish register. In addition, first Communion (Holy Eucharist) and confirmation (official ritual of joining the Church) are also a record of ordination if a relative joins the priesthood (Holy Orders). The amount of data along with the corresponding detail of the entry in a ledger varies by church and the recorder of information, which is usually taken down by the priest performing a particular ceremony. This leaves a permanent record for future generations to reference and reflect upon.

On a more official level, documentation related to the Catholic Church is typically earmarked for protection according to Code 486.2 of Canon Law, which features the necessity of an archive on both the parish and diocesan levels which states in effect that "…there is to be established in a safe place a diocesan archive in which the instruments and writings which refer to both the spiritual and temporal affairs of the diocese properly arranged and diligently secured, are to be safeguarded.…" (Corrigan, 1980). By 1974, documents produced within the Church were the responsibility of each bishop who in turn was strongly encouraged to appoint a diocesan archivist to look over the safeguarding of their permanent records while encouraging parishioners to become more active and glean an appreciation of American Catholic history in the process. The same dedication to preservation technique goes for religious orders such as the Franciscans, Jesuits, and Augustinians who usually have their own archival collections situated within a province or community house represented and separate from diocesan control.

As per archival jurisdiction on the diocesan level, the Catholic Church has several repositories that have thriving programs including the larger archdioceses, such as Baltimore, Boston, and Newark, which had been at the very forefront of American Catholicism during the late eighteenth and nineteenth centuries. Counted among the most prominent is the Archdiocese of Chicago's Joseph Cardinal Bernardin Archives and Records Center, which was founded in 1966 and is very active in terms of collection and storage of business files and spiritual papers. Included in this repository are informational services for genealogy, sacramental records, and other areas of related interest. This center covers more than 8,000 cubic feet, making it one of the largest centers of its class in the world. The Philadelphia Archdiocesan Historical Research Center is another important repository that contains numerous records accumulated by the American Catholic Historical Society including more than 100 manuscript collections and several thousand volume-book collections, which represents one of the largest and oldest Episcopal Sees in the nation.

The other major source of Catholic archival documents comes at the college and university level. The American Catholic History Research Center and University Archives located at the Catholic University of America was established in 1948 and renamed in July 2002. This research center includes the United States Conference of Catholic Bishops and Catholic Charities, USA papers among other important resources. The University of Notre Dame Archives features more than 700 collections concerning the history of the Catholic Church in the United States in the form of manuscript, book, artifact, and audio-visual among others from 1576 to the present. Georgetown University, the first Catholic institution of higher education in the United States, had its university archives set up through a resolution made by the board of directors in 1816, and a modern-day Special Collections model arrived in 1970 to handle the nearly 300 collections related to the Catholic experience found on this campus.

Judaism

As one of the oldest religious traditions on the globe, the archival legacy of Judaism is alive and thriving. Unlike Christianity, the life records associated with Jewry feature written birth and marriage records usually not produced even with the occurrence unique events. However, oral and lineal information can often begin with parents and grandparents who have a wealth of knowledge in regard to family tradition and custom. Marriage in a Jewish Synagogue includes a written document between the couple and a Rabbi called a Ketubah, which is not in the form of a register. For deaths, tombstones have the information of the father of the deceased, and the written notices are sent to the congregation, a record that is not always required. Another group that serves to aid in genealogical terms is the Landsmanshaft Societies, which is "based on towns of ancestry" and produces records on events germane to Jewish ritual and custom.

The Jacob Rader Marcus Center of the American Jewish Archives founded in 1947 is a repository that includes representation on the religious, social, and cultural aspects of the Hebrew experience as shown in the presence of more than 10 million pages of records and 650 major and 14,000 smaller individual collections covering all aspects of Jewish life. The American Jewish Historical Society, founded in 1892, is another key location for documentation on the faith and is oftentimes referred to as the national archives for American Jewish life, which spans the ages from the sixteenth century to contemporary times. The Yivo Archives and Library of Jewish History has more than 22 million documents in its collection and relates to the history and cultural life of Eastern Europe, the Holocaust, Jewish genealogy, and several other related topic areas in document, photographic, audio, and other forms of expression.

INTERNATIONAL RELIGIOUS ARCHIVES

The main focus of this chapter is on American religious archival repositories, but the importance of global perspective should also be kept in mind when contemplating a well-rounded research project. There are thousands of different information centers, church archives, and other unique places across the world that feature religious-oriented documentation of interest to the curious American scholar and genealogist. Perhaps the best place to start is tracing the origin of one's religious faith or the land from which an ancestor emerged when it comes to genealogical study.

Elsewhere in North America, Canada is home to a wide range of well-organized religious archival repositories that represent each major faith and are especially useful for those living in nearby northern U.S. states, such as New England and New York. Europe is another prime location for primary source inquiry. The Vatican Secret Archives is perhaps the most famous home for Catholic records in the world, but others such as the National Archives (and governing church bodies) of France, Ireland, Italy, and Spain are worth investigation. Various Protestant institutions such as the Church of England (Anglicanism), Church of Scotland (Presbyterianism), Netherlands (Dutch Reformed), and Germany and Scandinavia (Lutheranism) also have their own special historical record centers as well.

The Central Archives for the History of the Jewish People located in Jerusalem is another important site, and a major one devoted to Judaic scholarship. Several other religious denominations including those devoted to Buddhism, Islam, and Hinduism situated in Africa, Asia, Central and South America, or Oceania can be found via the Internet as well as through printed source guides and books containing data on a particular nation, language, and spiritual preference.

BIBLIOGRAPHY

Adherents.com. http://www.adherents.com/.

American Baptist Historical Society. http://www.abc-usa. org/abhs/.

American Baptist Historical Society. *Samuel Colgate Library of the American Baptist Historical Society.* http://www.crds.edu/abhs/default.htm.

American Catholic History Research Center & University Archives. *Catholic University of America.* http://libraries.cua.edu/archives.html.

American Jewish Historical Society. http://www.ajhs.org/.

American Religion Data Archive. http://www.theards. com/main_Home.asp.

Archdiocese of Chicago Archives. *Joseph Cardinal Bernardin Archives & Records Center.* http://www. archdiocese-chgo.org/archives/.

Billy Graham Center Archives. *Billy Graham Center Archives of Wheaton College.* http://www.wheaton.edu/ bgc/archives/archhp1.html.

Brandon, Samuel George Frederick, ed. *A Dictionary of Comparative Religion.* New York: Scribner, 1970.

Brethren Historical Library & Archives. *Church of the Brethren Historical Library & Archives.* http://www.brethren.org/genbd/bhla.

Central Archives for the History of the Jewish People. http://sites.huji.ac.il/archives/.

Church of the Nazarene Archives. http://www.nazarene.org/archives/index.html.

Congregational Library & Archives. http://www.14beacon.org/.

Corrigan, John T., C.F.X. "Archives: The Light of Faith." *Catholic Library Association Studies in Librarianship No. 4.* Haverford, Penn.: Catholic Library Association, 1980.

Cyndi's List—Religion & Churches List. http://www.cyndislist.com/religion.htm.

Disciples of Christ Historical Society. http://www.dishistsoc.org.

Episcopal Church, USA Archives. *Archives of the Episcopal Church, USA.* http://episcopalarchives.org/.

Evangelical Lutheran Church in America Archives. http://www.elca.org/os/archives/intro.html.

Family History Library of the Church of the Latter-Day Saints. http://www.familysearch.org/.

Friends Collection & College Archives. *Earlham College Friends Collection & College Archives.* http://www.earlham.edu/%7Elibr/quaker/.

Friends Historical Library. *Swarthmore College Friends Historical Library.* http://www.swarthmore.edu/Library/friends/index.html.

Georgetown University Library, Special Collections Division. http://gulib.lausun.georgetown.edu/dept/speccoll/.

Greenwood, Val D. *The Researchers Guide to American Genealogy.* Baltimore, Md.: Genealogical Publishing Co., Inc., 1977.

Hinnells, John R., ed. *The Penguin Dictionary of Religions.* Middlesex, England: Penguin Books, 1984.

Historical Society of the Episcopal Church. http://www.hsec-usa.org.

Huguenot Historical Society Library & Archives. http://www.hhs-newpaltz.net/index.html.

Jacob Rader Marcus Center of the American Jewish Archives. http://www.americanjewisharchives.org.

Levinson, David. *Religion: A Cross-Cultural Encyclopedia.* Santa Barbara, Calif.: ABC-CLIO, 1996.

Lutheran Church—Missouri Center Archives. http://chi.lcms.org/.

Material History of American Religion Project. *Vanderbilt University Divinity School—American Religion Project.* http://www.materialreligion.org/.

Melton, J. Gordon, ed. *American Religious Creeds.* New York: Triumph Books, 1991.

Philadelphia Archdiocesan Historical Research Center. http://www.rc.net/philadelphia/pahrc/.

Presbyterian Historical Society. http://history.pcusa.org/.

Quaker & Special Collections. *Haverford College Quaker & Special Collections and Friends Historical Association.* http://www.haverford.edu/library/special/.

Reformed Church in America Archives. http://www.rca.org/welcome/history/.

Salvation Army National Archives & Research Center. http://salvationarmyusa.org/www_usn.nsf/vw_sublinks/EC6B8F906C5D268585256B92005517CD?openDocument.

Seventh-Day Adventists Archives. *General Conference of the Seventh-Day Adventists Archives.* http://www.adventistarchives.org.

Southern Baptist Historical Library & Archives. http://www.sbhla.org/.

Suelflow, August R. *Religious Archives: An Introduction.* Chicago, Ill.: Society of American Archivists, 1980.

United Methodist Church Archives. *General Commission on Archives and History of the United Methodist Church.* http://www.gcah.org/.

University of Notre Dame Archives. http://www.nd.edu/~archives/.

Vatican Secret Archives. http://www.vatican.va/library_archives/vat_secret_archives/.

Wiley, David. "Religious & Sacred Texts." http://davidwiley.com/religion.html.

Yivo Institute of Jewish Research. http://www.yivoinstitute.org/archlib/archlib_fr.htm.

CHAPTER 5
Women's History Archives

Wendy Chmielewski

Until the 1960s the study of the history of women in the United States was mainly limited to the story of the women's rights movement from the convention in Seneca Falls, New York, in 1848 to the passage of the Nineteenth Amendment to the Constitution in 1920, which granted all women the right to vote.[1] In addition to this history, there were biographies of some elite public women, especially those who were married to prominent male politicians. A close investigation of the historiography of women's history will note exceptions to this, but for the most part this body of work made little use of archival sources.[2] It was commonly believed that women as a group had had little part or significant influence in the public realm of politics, the economy, or other aspects of civic life in the United States. In the 1960s, with the revitalization of feminism, the expansion of the women's liberation movement, and the advent of the burgeoning scholarly and popular interest in social history—the history of ordinary people, outside of elite institutions and circumstances—the history of women's role in the story of the United States became a topic of enormous interest as well. Historians of women, half the U.S. population, began to question the assumption that women had no influence on the development of the country. Some scholars also examined the accepted periodization of U.S. history, suggesting alternative, and important, markers for change based on the experience of women.[3] Much of this early work focused on the role of white middle-class women.[4] Since that time the field of women's history and the investigation of U.S. history from the point of view of women has broadened in scope and diversity of populations studied and grown in sophistication and influence on the field in general.

As scholars continued to research and write the history of U.S. women, they combed the archives looking for the documents from which to create a broader and deeper interpretation of the role women had played. Before the 1970s it was often difficult to find even the archival resources on women and women's issues that had been collected. Collections of the papers of a few individual women, especially publicly active and elite women, such as Eleanor Roosevelt, or women's organizations like the National American Woman Suffrage Association were sometimes recorded and listed in general archival guides. However, even some well-known women were subsumed under the papers of their family or under their husband's name. This made it extremely difficult to find individual women, even when one knew their names. It was almost impossible to survey archival resources on nonelite women or women as a social group. Institutions such as the Library of Congress, the Arthur and Elizabeth Schlesinger Library on the History of Women in America at Radcliffe College, and the Sophia Smith Collection at Smith College were known for their collections on women.

As archivists, librarians, historians, and women's studies scholars turned their attention to looking for materials on women in archival collections, they discovered that the resources had been deposited over time. New methodologies and new ways of reading the archival resources often revealed vast amounts of information about women and their lives in the public and private areas of American life. Even when researchers suspected the archival resources must be available, there was no systematic way to access them, nor were they easy to find. Archivists and librarians interested in the new field of women's history and women's studies were responsible for creating the first guides and bibliographies to the archival resources. In partnership with scholars and researchers, these professionals work to make sure the archival resources on women are available and accessible.

HISTORY OF WOMEN'S ARCHIVES

In the mid-1930s historian Mary Beard was instrumental in organizing the World Center for Women's Archives (WCWA), an institution that would collect the documents on the history of women, the first of its kind in the United States. Beard, an early scholar of U.S. women's history, recognized that the archival documents were crucial to preserving and understanding the role of women in the history of the United States:

What documents, then, have women? What history?… women may be blotted from the story and the thought about history as completely as if they had never lived.… But what do the women of today know about the women of yesterday to whom they are so closely linked for better or for worse? What are the women of tomorrow to know about the women of today?[5]

"No Documents, No History," was the motto of the WCWA. Beard, with other activist women, such as suffragist Inez Hayes Irwin, held the first meeting of the WCWA in October 1935. An early pamphlet stated their mission:

To make a systematic search for undeposited source materials dealing with women's lives and activities.… To reproduce important materials, already deposited elsewhere, by means of microfilming and other modern processes.… to encourage recognition of women as co-makers of history.[6]

By the middle of the twentieth century women historians, archivists, activists, politicians, and women with public lives recognized the importance of preserving the documents of their own history. For several years Beard and the WCWA board worked to locate and record these materials. Correspondence with archivists such as Ellen Starr Brinton, the curator of the Swarthmore College Peace Collection, reflect both the search for materials and the excitement of this important project to preserve the archival resources of women's history.[7] The idea of collecting and interest in these materials quickly spread. The New Jersey Center for Women's Archives, which began as a branch of the WCWA, actively collected the papers of prominent New Jersey women between 1937 and 1940.[8]

By the end of the decade, the approaching war, lack of funding, and some internal disagreements had all worked to end the WCWA. Mary Beard resigned from the board in 1940. Materials already collected were returned to the original owners or deposited with colleges that had a nascent interest in these materials, such as Smith, Radcliffe, Hunter, and Swarthmore.[9] However, the WCWA project inspired others and convinced other institutions of the importance of women's documents and women's history. For example, Dorothy Porter, representative of the National Council of Negro Women (NCNW) on the WCWA board, served as chairman when the NCNW formed their own archives in 1940. This became the National Archives for Black Women's History in 1979.[10] Other institutions such as the Sophia Smith Collection at Smith College and the Schlesinger Library at Radcliffe College are some of the famous successors to the WCWA. In the present many institutions have discovered that their collections contain important material on the history of women. In many instances they have initiated practices that emphasize women's history topics in their already established collections. Other institutions have begun new collecting practices to include the papers of women and women's organizations. The following sections detail the bibliographic resources available to assist in locating archival materials on women.

PRINTED RESOURCES

Until the mid-1990s and the advent of the World Wide Web, there were few published archival finding aids to collections focused on women. Many bibliographies and specialized resource guides on women covered published materials such as books, magazines, articles, periodicals, and government publications on a wide variety of topic areas related to women all over the world. There were exceptions in the archival field, and this section will survey the printed literature. While the Web has increased access to archival resources on women many thousand-fold, researchers should still consult some of the guides available in paper to make sure the entire subject area has been covered.

In 1972 a group of historians and archivists sponsored a session on the "grand manuscripts search" to help identify "little-known archival sources to support the growing field of women's history" at the annual conference of the Organization of American Historians.[11] Due to the enthusiasm of the audience at that conference, Andrea Hinding and Clarke Chambers of the Social Welfare History Archives at the University of Minnesota, with the support of historians and archivists, decided to survey archival holdings on women at institutions around the United States. They received major funding, first from the Rockefeller Foundation and then the National Endowment for the Humanities and the University of Minnesota, to complete a nationwide survey of more than 11,000 archives and manuscript repositories. This was an immense project conducted by a large and dedicated staff over a four-year period. The result was *Women's History Sources: A Guide to Archives and Manuscript Collections in the United States,* edited by Andrea Hinding and Suzanna Moody, index editor. It contains descriptions of 18,026 collections of papers in more than 1,500 repositories. The guide is divided into two volumes. The first volume contains a descriptive list of manuscript collections on women and women's organizations within specific institutions. The listing of repositories is arranged geographically by state and city. The second volume is an index of names and subject areas that leads to the descriptive listings in volume one. Each listing contains the title, linear feet, dates, and a brief description of a collection of an individual woman's papers or the records of a women's organization. Neither finding aids nor inventories of the individual collections are included. The greatest limitation of this resource is that it does not include archival collections that contain information on women but are not listed under the name of an individual woman or a women's organization. However, more than two decades after its publication, *Women's History Sources* remains *the* most complete guide to U.S. archival repositories and collections on women.

It is now clear that archivists have always collected materials on women and women's activities.[12] However, that material was not as accessible as it should have been. The vast resources on women's collections found and published in *Women's History Sources* far exceeded the expectations of even the most knowledgeable archivists and historians at the time.[13] The editors of *Women's History Sources* correctly assumed that their publication was only "the beginning of a new era of research into women's lives."[14]

Women's Collections: Libraries, Archives, and Conscientiousness, edited by Suzanne Hildenbrand (originally published as *Special Collections* vol. 3, no. 3/4,

spring/summer 1986), includes essays authored by librarians and archivists on the history and development of collections focused on women. Oddly this volume includes no mention of the monumental *Women's History Sources* when describing the development of women's history, the collecting of archival material on women, and the access to those collections. Hildenbrand, the general editor of *Women's Collections,* clearly links the political shifts in the history of feminism in the twentieth century to interest, support, and advancement of these collections. Descriptions of nine different institutions as well as an essay on access issues for material on women and feminism are included. A bibliographic essay on minority and third world women covers a wide range of publications, but most appear to include secondary published resources, rather than archival material. An appendix at the end of the book includes a list of U.S. and international institutions with collections on women.

Biographical Dictionaries

In 1971 a three-volume encyclopedia, *Notable American Women,* was published by Harvard University Press in cooperation with the Arthur and Elizabeth Schlesinger Library on the History of Women in America at Radcliffe College. More than 1,300 scholarly and biographical essays on women who were public, influential figures in U.S. society and who had died before 1950 were included. Whenever possible the authors included information at the end of each essay on where the papers of these women might be found. For example, one learns that the papers of Mary Ware Dennett, an early-twentieth-century sex education advocate, may be found at the Sophia Smith Collection at Princeton University and at the New York State Department of Health.

In 1980 a fourth volume, *Notable American Women, the Modern Period,* was published, edited by Barbara Sicherman, with the same format, for women who died between 1951 and 1975. A fifth volume, edited by Susan Ware, containing essays on notable women who died between January 1, 1976, and January 1, 2000, is currently in process, with an expected publication date of 2004.

Two other notable publications, following a similar format but covering special areas on women, are *Women Building Chicago, 1790–1990: A Biographical Dictionary,* ed. Rima Lunin Schultz et al. (Bloomington and Indianapolis: University of Indiana Press, 2001) and *Black Women in America: An Historical En-*

cyclopedia, ed. Darlene Clark Hine and associate eds. Elsa Barkley Brown and Rosalyn Terborg-Penn (Brooklyn, N.Y.: Carlson Pub., 1993). Both publications followed the *Notable American Women* format of biographical essays with primary and secondary sources noted at the end of each entry when available. *Black Women in America* also includes a "Bibliography of Basic Resources" with a subsection of "Major Research Collections of Primary Materials." Eighteen academic institutions are listed with their mailing addresses and a selection of manuscript collections.

Many other biographical dictionaries on women have been published, but few of them list primary sources or locations of archival collections.

Selected Institutional Publications

Arthur and Elizabeth Schlesinger Library and Sophia Smith Collection

Two major archival repositories on the history of women in the United States, the Schlesinger Library and the Sophia Smith Collection at Smith College, both published inventories of their manuscript collections in the early 1970s. The Schlesinger Library first published *Arthur and Elizabeth Schlesinger Library on the History of Women in America: The Manuscript Inventories and the Catalogs of Manuscripts, Books, and Periodicals,* Radcliffe College, Cambridge, Massachusetts (Boston: G.K. Hall), an inventory of their catalog, in 1973. Volume three of that publication contained information on Schlesinger manuscript collections. A second and enlarged edition was issued in 1984. Both editions contain reproductions of the Schlesinger Library's card catalog, with collection-level descriptions of manuscript collections and cards for some individual documents. Almost all of the information on the holdings in these volumes has been placed in the Harvard University online catalog.

In 1975 the Sophia Smith Collection at Smith College followed suit and published an inventory of their holdings on women: *Smith College. Library Catalogs of the Sophia Smith Collection: Women's History Archive* (Boston: G.K. Hall, 1975). These volumes contain pages of reproduced catalog cards from the Smith Collection. Some individual letters and other items in the Sophia Smith Collection are only listed in the G.K. Hall publication. Neither the Schlesinger Library nor the Sophia Smith Collection have issued further editions of these publications.

The Schlesinger Library also published two other noteworthy sets of guides to their holdings in specific areas:

Hill, Ruth Edmonds, ed. *The Black Women Oral History Project: From the Arthur and Elizabeth Schlesinger Library on the History of Women in America, Radcliffe College.* 10 vols. Westport, Conn.: Meckler, 1991. (This guide includes the oral histories.)

von Salis, Susan, compiler. *Revealing Documents: A Guide to African American Manuscript Sources in the Schlesinger Library and the Radcliffe College Archives.* Boston: G.K. Hall, 1993.

Library of Congress

The Library of Congress has one of the most extensive collections of resources on women in the country, and specialists on staff have produced a magnificent guide to the published and unpublished holdings on women at that institution. *American Women: A Library of Congress Guide for the Study of Women's History and Culture in the United States*, edited by Sheridan Harvey et al., introduction by Susan Ware (Washington, D.C.: Library of Congress, 2001: For sale by the Supt. of Docs., U.S. G.P.O.; Hanover, N.H., distributed by University Press of New England) This guide is jam-packed with information about the holdings in the various divisions of the library. There is a helpful introductory essay by Susan Ware on the historiography of women's studies and women's history and the current state of the field. This guide is divided into 12 chapters, each written by a specialist from the Library of Congress, describing the different holdings of materials on women in their division. Each chapter describes the holdings, subject areas that could be researched, and tools available for using the materials in that division. Special attention is paid to collections of family papers or organizational records or other collections that are not obviously by or about women but in fact do contain significant material on women. Some examples of this include the papers of architect William Thornton, which contain the correspondence of his wife Anna Maria Brodeau Thornton, a major source on nineteenth-century social life in Washington, D.C.; the Armed Forces Radio and Television Services Collection, which includes programs, sound recordings, advertisements, and so forth on the role of women in the military; and the records of the National Association for the Advancement of Colored People

(NAACP), with materials that document the part women played in the formation and ongoing work of that organization and in the twentieth-century civil rights movement.

For each division of the library, there is a concise description of the collection, a list of rules about its use, and access information. Contact information includes mailing address, telephone number, fax number, and Web site address. An effort is made by the general editors to make this information consistent and accessible to researchers of all levels. Detailed as this guide is, users should contact the appropriate division(s) for further information about their research topic. The volume does not include finding aids to individual manuscript collections.

Almost all of the 12 chapters are of interest here as having archival or primary source material on women. Rare Books and Special Collections, Manuscript Division, Prints and Photographs Division, Music Division, Recorded Sound Section, Moving Image Section, American Folklife Center, and the Area Studies Collections have especially strong collections. For example, the Manuscript Division offers the description of the most extensive holdings. Holdings are especially strong on women who were involved in the suffrage and abolition campaigns, the papers of first ladies, women who were pioneers in fields traditionally male dominated, women's reform organizations, and voluntary associations. There are also significant holdings on women's health, women pioneers in the field of psychology, Congressional collections, and other government agencies. This volume demonstrates just how extensive the role of women in U.S. history has been and how well archivists have collected the materials that record it.

Information on the *American Memory* online digital collection from the Library of Congress is described below.

Other Printed Guides—A Selection

Documenting Women's Lives: A User's Guide to Manuscripts at the Virginia Historical Society, Gail S. Terry (Richmond, Va: Virginia Historical Society, 1996).

The Florida State Archives: Collections Pertaining to Women's History and Women's Issues. (Tallahassee, Fla.: Florida Dept. of State, Division of Library and Information Services, Bureau of Archives and Records Management, 1996).

Guide to Collections in the Archives and Special Collections on Women in Medicine at the Medical College of Pennsylvania, Ericka Thickman Miller (Philadelphia: The College, 1987).

Guide to Manuscript Collections Documenting Women in Society: A Descriptive List of Holdings, introduction by Hilary Cummings, ed. Amy Joy Talbot, compiled by Amy Joy Talbot, Sue Wright, and April Minnich (Eugene, Or.: Knight Library, University of Oregon, 1989).

A Guide to Materials on Women in the United Methodist Church Archives, Kristen D. Turner (Madison, N.J.: The Commission, 1995).

Guide to Sources on Women in the Swarthmore College Peace Collection, ed. Wendy E. Chmielewski (Swarthmore, Penn.: Swarthmore College, 1988).

A Guide to the Women's History Archives at Rutgers (New Brunswick, N.J.: Rutgers University Libraries, 1990).

Guide to Women's History Resources in the Delaware Valley Area, ed. Trina Vaux, foreword by Mary Maples Dunn (Philadelphia: City of Philadelphia, 1983).

A Guide to Women's History Resources in the East Carolina Manuscript Collection, Maurice C. York (Greenville, N.C.: East Carolina Manuscript Collection, J. Y. Joyner Library, East Carolina University, 1982).

Selected Nontraditional Repositories

In the 1980s archivists and historians began to look at subject areas and repositories originally thought to contain little material on the history of women. As Glenn Porter, director of the Hagley Museum and Library, noted: "Fields that had long found little place for women's history today give it abundant attention.... The very landscape of evidence from the past has been reexamined and rearranged, revealing its pertinence to women's history."[15] In 1997 Lynn Ann Catanese edited *Women's History: A Guide to Sources at Hagley Museum and Library* (Westport, Conn.: Greenwood Press, 1997). The collections at the Hagley focus on economic history and the history of business and technology, areas in which it was long thought women had little influence. However, Lynn Ann Catanese includes nearly 300 manuscript, archival, and pictorial collections in her guide. These collections contain information on such issues as "gender and the workplace, domesticity, female entrepreneurs,...the culture of consumption, and fashion and technology in the women's clothing industry."[16] The Hagley contains some of the personal papers of the elite du Pont family, with important collections of du Pont women, especially from the eighteenth through twentieth centuries. This guide also includes information on the role of women within nineteenth-century domesticity, religious associations, and politics. The Hagley's artifact collections contain resources useful for material culture studies, especially on household furnishings and decorative arts. Following this tradition, the Harvard Business School (HBS) launched the Web site *Unheard Voices: Women in the Emerging Industrial and Business Age* (http://www.library.hbs.edu/hc/wes.) in January 2001. In the second phase of this project, HBS launched *Women, Enterprise and Society: A Guide to Resources in the Business Manuscripts Collection at Baker Library* (http://www.library.hbs.edu/hc/wes.) to "document women's participation in American business and culture from the eighteenth through the twentieth century."[17]

Guides to Organizations

Some women's organizations have formally established archives run by their own professional library and archival staff. For example, the General Federation of Women's Clubs (GFWC) has a collection, the Women's History and Resource Center Library, at their headquarters in Washington, D.C. This extensive library contains GFWC archives from the 1890s to the present and has a special emphasis on women in volunteerism. *A Guide to the Archives of the General Federation of Women's Clubs* (in print) is available from the organization. Soroptimist International of the Americas, a women's volunteer organization, also maintains its own archives. The Soroptimists have not published a printed guide to their collections, but a description of their archives, collections available, and access information is available on their Web site at http://www.soroptimist.org/archives.htm.

Many organizations have neither deposited their archives or historical documents in an archival institution nor do they have an established archival program of their own. Their resources may continue to reside in organization offices. This may be especially true of currently active or recent groups. The following print publications list some of the many women's organizations and contact information. Only a few of these publications list the location of organizational archives.

Where Women Stand: An International Report on the Status of Women in over 140 Countries, 1997–1998, Naomi Neft and Ann D. Levine (New York: Random House, 1997).

Encyclopedia of Women's Associations Worldwide: A Guide to Over 3,400 National and Multinational Nonprofit Women's and Women-Related Organizations, ed. Jacqueline K. Barrett, and Jane A. Malonis, associate ed. (London, Detroit: Gale Research, 1993).

Women's Movements of the World: An International Directory and Reference Guide, ed. Sally Shreir, contributors F. John Harper et al. (Phoenix, Ariz.; Harlow, Essex, England: Longman, 1988: Distributed in the U.S. and Canada by Oryx Press). This publication includes the addresses of women's groups and in some cases lists the location of their archives.

U.S. Women's Interest Groups: Institutional Profiles, ed. Sarah Slavin (Westport, Conn.: Greenwood Press, 1995).

MICROFORMS

There is no one single resource that lists all of the archival and manuscript collections transferred to microform concerned with individual women, women's organizations, or topics that might be of interest to women's studies researchers. The microfilming of archival materials has been especially helpful in providing access to the actual documents and papers of individual women and women's organizations. By the 1970s publishers of microform realized there was a market for the sale of archival collections. As one such publisher, Primary Source Microfilm, states: "Our purpose has been to provide access to rare, valuable research materials for libraries, scholars, faculty and students."[18] With the increase in popularity of women's history and women's studies, there is a growing demand for access to resources on women. Some major academic institutions with major holdings in women's archival sources undertook filming projects beginning in the 1960s and 1970s. They considered this filming as a preservation and access technique for their most important and/or fragile archival collections. Some microfilm collections have an accompanying printed guide or inventory of material. Researchers should always contact the originating institution to learn if there are additional materials in the collection that are not included in the microfilmed set. The following list includes only a selection of institutions that have microfilmed some of their archival collections. Collections in microform that are available from commercial publishers are listed separately.

Selected Institutional Microform Collections

Women's History Research Center

Examples:

The Women and Health/Mental Health Collection, Women's History Research Center (Berkeley, Calif.: The Center, 1975).

Women and Law, Women's History Research Center (Berkeley, Calif.: The Center, 1975–76).

State Historical Society of North Dakota

Examples:

Congregational Church Records, (1886–1972) series 10414, one roll microfilm. The collection consists of a church record book providing rosters of pastors, deacons, church committees, and membership; minutes of church organizations; baptism, marriage, and death records; worship attendance records; and records of contributions. (Oberon, North Dakota)

University of Missouri/State Historical Society of Missouri, Western Historical Manuscript Collection

Examples:

New Directions for Women, records, 1971–1993
Papers of Sylvia Porter, 1913–1991

National Archives and Records Administration

Examples:

Records of the Bureau of Refugees, Freedmen, and Abandoned Lands (record group 105). The collection contains records of all affairs relating to refugees, freedmen, and freedwomen and correspondence with subordinate officers and teachers in the field concerning funds, buildings, and supplies. Letters to teachers also relayed procedural instructions and occasional reprimands. Many teachers employed by this bureau were women.

Records of Revolutionary War Soldiers (especially "claims for bounty land and pensions"). Applications for these bounty land warrants and pension files may contain a great deal of personal information about a veteran and his family. The files may show the veteran's name, age, and residence at the date of the application; the names of his wife and children; and dates of births, marriages, and deaths within the family.

Other projects have been collaborations between institutions when archival holdings surrounding an organization or person were divided among several places. Some published microfilm products include artificial collections of special subject areas, such as women's studies, with materials originating at several different institutions. The following list includes the major publishers of microfilm with examples of their collections about women currently available on microfilm. Publishers often provide printed guides to the microfilmed collections.

Selected Commercially Published Microform Collections

Pro-Quest (Now Includes Chadwyck-Healey, University Microfilm, Inc., and Bell and Howell)

Chadwyck-Healey, Inc.
Examples:

The Emma Goldman Papers: A Microfilm Edition (Chadwyck-Healey, Inc., 1991) and *Emma Goldman: A Guide to Her Life and Documentary Sources* (Chadwyck-Healey, Inc., 1995).

University Microfilm, Inc.
Examples:

Papers of Jane Addams (Ann Arbor, Mich.: University Microfilms, Inc., 1984). A printed index, *The Jane Addams Papers: A Comprehensive Guide,* eds. Mary Lynn McCree Bryan et al. (Bloomington: Indiana University Press, 1996), is essential to using the papers of Jane Addams.

Smith-Townsend Family Papers, 1670–1892 (Ann Arbor, Mich.: University Microfilm, Inc., 1977). There are numerous letters of Abigail (Smith) Adams, wife of President John Adams, in this collection.

American Association of University Women: Archives, 1831–1976; A Guide to the Microfilm Edition, ed. Barbara A. Sokolosky (Ann Arbor, Mich. University Microfilm, Inc., 1980).

Bell and Howell
Examples:

Papers of the Association of Southern Women for the Prevention of Lynching, 1930–1942 (Bell & Howell Information and Learning, 1983).

Scholarly Resources, Inc.
Examples:

National Association of Colored Graduate Nurses Records, 1908–1951 (Wilmington, Del.: Scholarly Resources, Inc., n.d.)

Women's International League for Peace and Freedom, U.S. Section, 1919–1959 (Wilmington, Del.: Scholarly Resources, Inc.. 1988)

The Papers of Emily Greene Balch, 1875–1961 (Wilmington, Del.: Scholarly Resources, Inc., 1988).

FBI File on Eleanor Roosevelt (Wilmington, Del.: Scholarly Resources, Inc., 1996).

Primary Source Microfilm
Examples:

Women's Trade Union League and Its Leaders (Woodbridge, Conn.: Primary Source Microfilm, n.d.).

University Publications of America
Examples:

Records of the National Association of Colored Women's Clubs, 1895–1992 (Bethesda, Md.: University Publications of America, 1993).

Women's City Club of New York, 1916–1980 (Bethesda, Md.: University Publications of America, 1989).

Readex
Example:

American Women's Diaries (Readex, a Division of Newsbank, Inc.). Includes diaries from New England women, Southern women, and Western women from the colonial period through the turn of the twentieth century.

WEB SITES, DIGITAL COLLECTIONS, AND OTHER ONLINE RESOURCES

With the advent of the Internet and the World Wide Web, resources available for finding archival information on women have exploded. This has been driven by three developments: the technology of electronic resources, the desire of archival professionals to highlight the materials on women in their institutions, and the continued work of scholars with interest in women. Archival professionals and scholars interested in women have created and expanded new methodologies of scholarship that have illuminated the resources on women in the archives. It is the work and interest of these professionals and scholars that has created the voluminous amount of information now available on women's archival sources.

In the 1980s librarians, especially those working with special collections, and archivists together began to create standardized catalog records for archival materials. These catalog records were included in the two major national utilities—OCLC and RLIN—and the information about these formerly not easily accessible collections became available to researchers through public and institutional libraries. Along with many other subject areas, collections containing resources on women could be searched through these electronic resources. These catalog records remain a major online resource, even with the advent of the World Wide Web. Catalog records usually contain pertinent information about a collection, such as author, title, amount of material, date(s) of the collection, subject headings, and sometimes an abstract or description of the archival materials. However, researchers should be aware that these might not contain information about individual women or about women's issues, even when there are important resources in the collection described. In large collections of material, women's studies topics may form a minor area and thus cannot be described in the brief catalog record. In addition, the archivist cataloging the collection must be aware of the major issues in women's history and women's studies to consider noting this in the catalog record. Examples of collections with substantial information about women, but with little or no information in their catalogs, are given below.

Institutions that do not have a Web site, or that have only a minimal presence on the Web, might very well have created catalog records for their archival collections. These records are located in institutional databases that are usually accessible over the World Wide Web, but these records are not included in the searches performed by the main search engines, such as Google or Yahoo. For example, a search for the papers of Zelda Fitzgerald on Google receives 369 hits. Very quickly the searcher learns that there is a collection of papers under her name in the Special Collections Department in the Firestone Library at Princeton University. The papers of her husband, F. Scott Fitzgerald, also at Princeton, contain materials on Zelda as well. However, the searcher will not find mention in this search of the Web of a third collection at Princeton, "John Biggs collection of F. Scott Fitzgerald estate papers, 1936–1978," which also contains letters by Zelda

Fitzgerald. The Biggs collection may be found under "Fitzgerald, Zelda" through a direct search in the library catalog at Princeton.

The following section includes an overview of major resources available in electronic format, especially those on the World Wide Web. Resources on women over the Web still tend to be bibliographical, rather than documentary. In other words, the records, finding aids, and inventories describing archival collections on women and women's issues are more likely to be available, while the original materials themselves are not as readily accessible. There are some exceptions to this, and this section does contain an overview of Web sites that contain actual documents or primary resources. Even these sites often contain only examples or small portions of a whole collection. In general, visual images such as photographs and graphic materials are more available than electronic forms of manuscript documents.

Types of Archival Resources Available on the World Wide Web or in Other Digital Formats

Online Finding Aids to Archival and Primary Resources

National utilities
Megasites—lists of links to other World Wide Web sites
Individual institutions

Digital Collections

Commercial Collections (subscription-based collections)
Collections available online on the World Wide Web (single institution)
Collections available online on the World Wide Web (multi-institution)

National Utilities

ArchivesUSA

ArchivesUSA is a subscription-based directory with records of more than 5,400 repositories and with finding aids for more than 124,400 collections of primary source material across the United States. Information on repositories and specific manuscript collections in those repositories is included in the ArchivesUSA site on the World Wide Web. Records from the National Union Catalog of Manuscript Collections (NUCMC) and links to more than 4,300 col-

lection finding aids are also available. ArchivesUSA also produces microfiche of thousands of finding aids not yet available in electronic format. Searches may be done by repository or by collection name.

Example:

A search on ArchivesUSA on Susan B. Anthony, one of the leaders of the nineteenth-century woman's rights movement in the United States, leads to the manuscript collection for the Blackwell family, many of whom were also leaders in the movement. The record includes a description of the repository holding the collection, in this case the Library of Congress, Manuscript Division. There is a description of the collection on the Blackwell family. This includes the type of material in the collection, the dates, and the amount of material in the collection. From the description of the collection it can be noted that Susan B. Anthony is one of the major correspondents. The record does not reveal the type or how much material in this collection concerns Anthony. There is a notation that a finding aid for the collection is available from the holding institution.

Research Libraries Information Network (RLIN)

RLIN is an information system used by many academic research libraries and major archival repositories to catalog primary and secondary resources. It is only available through online systems of libraries by subscription. Many smaller academic libraries may link to the database to view the catalog, but they do not contribute records of the holdings at their own institutions. The RLG Union Catalog (RLIN) is a comprehensive database that serves as a major union catalog for everything from books and serials to archives, manuscripts, maps, music scores, sound recordings, films, photographs, posters, computer files, and more. As archivists and librarians have become more aware of resources on women in their collections, they have included more references in their catalog records to lead to that material. Information on RLIN is supplied by the institution holding the original material. Researchers who have access to RLIN, WorldCat, and ArchivesUSA should perform their searches through all three utilities as the same resources may not appear in all the databases.

RLIN may be searched by title, author, subject, or keywords. Searches may be limited to primary resources, such as archival materials or visual materials. It is also possible to limit searches for computer files.

Information on RLIN may be incomplete. There are no direct links from the catalog record to online forms of the archival finding aid for a collection. Many of the new digital collections have not been cataloged on RLIN and are not accessible through that database.

Example:

By searching the subject heading "women in advertising" on RLIN the researcher will find many listings and sublistings by geographical location for primary and secondary sources. One collection, the records of a feminist group active through the 1980s, Women Against Violence Against Women (WAVAW), is listed on RLIN as being part of the Women's Educational Center, Women's Movement Archives (Cambridge, Mass.). Information about the content, dates of the material, and amount of material is given in the RLIN record. It should be noted that this record is not up to date. The Women's Educational Center is listed as the holding institution. However, the WAVAW records and the rest of the collections from the Women's Educational Center are now housed at Northeastern University. A further keyword search of "women in advertising" limited by visual materials finds several primary source collections including a slide collection of advertisements at Stanford University and a collection of nineteenth-century advertising cards at the Library Company, Philadelphia. There is no way to limit a search on visual materials to primary or archival materials only, so many of the records found were for published video recordings on this subject. A keyword search on "women in advertising" limited to computer files failed to locate any records, even though there are several digital collections now available, most notably the Ad*Access collection at Duke University, http://scriptorium.lib.duke.edu/.

WorldCat (Online Computer Library Center-OCLC FirstSearch Service)

WorldCat is described as a "catalog of books, web resources and materials worldwide." Public and academic libraries in the United States and other countries around the world contribute records about the archival holdings of their institutions. WorldCat and other OCLC products are subscription based and available through academic and major public libraries. Many smaller public libraries contribute records through OCLC and provide access to the utility to their staff, but cannot afford to provide FirstSearch services to their patrons. Under these circumstances

researchers should enlist the assistance of public service staff at local libraries.

On WorldCat it is possible to limit searches by a list title, author, subject, or keywords. Searches may also be limited by format criteria, such as books, serials, archival materials, and electronic or digital collections. Several criteria may be selected at one time, so the researcher could limit the search to digital collections of primary resources on a particular person or subject area. MARC records include basic information about a collection, such as author, title, date, size, major subject areas, and holding institution. There may be a link to the detailed finding aid and the inventory of the collection.

Example:

In searching for the papers of twentieth-century philosopher Hannah Arendt, a record indicates that the Library of Congress holds a collection of her papers. The record includes information about the size, range, and content of the collection at the Library of Congress, the primary language of the collection, and a link to a World Wide Web site at the Library of Congress about this collection of papers. At the Web site there is a link to portions of the finding aid, some of which is available online, and the information that the full digitized collection of Arendt's papers is only available at New School University in New York City and the Hannah Arendt Center at the University of Oldenburg, Germany. Parts of the collection and the finding aid are available for public access on the Internet.

Megasites on the World Wide Web

American Women's History: A Research Guide, created and maintained by Ken Middleton, Middle Tennessee State University Library. http://www.mtsu.edu/~kmiddlet/history/women.html

This is one of the most complete sites for print, microforms, and electronic resources of archival and secondary sources on women. The site is well maintained and kept up to date by Ken Middleton, reference/microforms librarian at Middle Tennessee University Library. There are more than eighteen hundred links to other Web sites and resource guides. More than three hundred digital collections that contain some information about the history of women are also listed. A subject index links the researcher to more than seventy subfields. There is also a list of links arranged state by state. This site does not contain, in itself, finding aids to specific collections or collections of actual documents. Rather the researcher will find links to other institutions that have created digital finding aids. There are links to digital collections of archival materials as well. The site includes sections on archives and manuscript collections, lists of some microfilmed collections, and links to institutions with Web sites of archival materials on women and women's organizations. There is so much information on this site that the user could get lost, even though it is well designed. It may be easiest to use this site through a particular subject area, as each topic then offers links to institutions holding different types of primary sources—for example, archival collections; commercial and noncommercial digital collections; microform collections; and selected books of documents, periodicals of women's organizations, statistics, media, and oral histories.

Archives for Research on Women and Gender Project—A Geographic Guide to Uncovering Women's History in Archival Collections, prepared and maintained by staff at the Center for the Study of Women and Gender, University of Texas, San Antonio. http://www.lib.utsa.edu/Archives/links.htm

This site contains links to academic libraries, a few women's organizations, and historical societies. It is organized alphabetically by state. There is a list of links to important sites outside of the United States, with most of these located in Great Britain and Australia. There is a short description of the holdings of each library or collection. It is unclear if this geographic guide has continued to be maintained after the year 2000.

Genesis: Developing Access to Women's History Resources in the British Isles, a project of the Research Support Libraries Programme (Great Britain). http://www.genesis.ac.uk/index.html

Although most resources listed in this chapter cover collections and materials in the United States, the Genesis project is included here because of its innovation and broad coverage. The Genesis home page describes the project: "to identify and develop access to women's history sources in the British Isles. The database holds descriptions of women's history collections from libraries, archives and museums from around the British Isles." Forty-six institutions participate in this project and have created standardized records for the database. Researchers may conduct a simple or advanced search for archival materials and manuscript collections across the 46 institutions that contribute to this database.

Besides access to the database, Genesis links to international resources. There are two valuable lists for researchers: a list of British and international "links to

directories, gateways, portals and information resources relevant to the study of women's and gender history" and links to the Web sites of institutions and collections that hold material on women. The links are mostly geared to European, British, and U.S. institutions.[19]

H-Women Archival and Manuscript Collections, maintained by the staff of H-Women, a listserv of *H-Net, Humanities & Social Sciences OnLine.* http://www2.h-net.msu.edu/~women/manuscripts/

This site lists approximately fifty links mostly to the Web sites of special collections in the libraries of academic institutions in the United States and Great Britain with significant holdings on women. There are a few sites listed here that are not found in the other bibliographies. However, as of 2002 about one-third of the links at this site were not functioning.

Information Resources for Women's Studies, created and maintained by Sherri Barnes, University of California, Santa Barbara Library. http://library.ucsb.edu/subj/women.html.

This site contains links to both primary and secondary online resources on women. The links are divided into categories such as reference and archival resources, women of color, labor studies/labor and work, lesbian studies, sports, and publishers and booksellers. There is a short description of each site. The information on the links to Web sites for women's organizations and women's businesses listed on this site is especially helpful.

Matilda Joslyn Gage Website Links to Websites on Women in the 19th Century, created and maintained by supporters of a Matilda Joslyn Gage Foundation, P.O. Box 192, Fayetteville, NY 13066. http://www.pinn.net/~sunshine/gage/features/gage_lnk.html#arch3

This site has links to a mixture of primary and secondary Web sites and information on women in the nineteenth-century United States. There is an alphabetical list at the top of the site that leads to the rest of the site. Researchers might find such material as a digital collection of eighteenth- and nineteenth-century floral drawings by women artists, an online copy of Sarah Grimke's *Letters on the Equality of the Sexes,* and three lectures by feminist Caroline Dall from 1870.

Women's Archives Mapping Project, created and maintained by staff at the Archives of the Ann Ida Gannon, Sisters of Charity of the Blessed Virgin Mary, Center for Women and Leadership, Loyola University.

http://www.luc.edu/orgs/gannon/archives/donordirectory.html

The editors of this Web site have created a database with information about and links to approximately 55 academic institutions and women's organizations with significant archival collections on women. The collections may also be searched by state, city, or keyword. Information on each collection includes name of the collection, contact information—telephone, fax, email, and name of contact person—Web site URL, materials solicited by each institution or collection, and a brief description of holdings. An online form allows the staff from additional institutions to enter information about their collection.

Women's History Resources, created and maintained by the University of Wisconsin System Women's Studies Librarian, Phyllis Holman Weisbard. http://www.library.wisc.edu/libraries/Womens Studies/hist.htm

This site contains examples of institutions and collections with primary and archival sources on women. The links are organized by subject area.

WSSLINKS Archival Sites for Women's Studies, maintained by the Women's Studies Section of the Association of College and Research Libraries. http://gwis2.circ.gwu.edu/~mfpankin/archwss.htm

This site contains links to the Web sites of academic institutions, public libraries, some government agencies, and historical societies with significant collections on women. There are also links to women's organizations that maintain their own Web pages and archives. The site is divided first geographically by region of the United States and then alphabetically by name of institution or organization. A list of important sites outside the United States is also included. There is a brief description for all links, including additional search instructions where needed, so users can navigate large and complicated sites. A list of links to women's volunteer organizations and other important women's sites is included as well. The WSSLinks site is straightforward, well organized, and easy to use.

Selected Individual Institutions (With No Documents Online)

Jewish Women's Archive
http://www.jwa.org/main.htm

The Jewish Women's Archive is a virtual finding aid rather than an online archives. This site includes infor-

mation about primary resource collections on Jewish women available at institutions in the United States. The Jewish Women's Archive Web site can be searched by personal name, subject, or occupation. A search leads to information on archival resources about an individual person or organization, with further information on the institution holding the materials. Contact information for the institution is included.

Louise Noun—Mary Louise Smith Iowa Women's Archives
http://www.lib.uiowa.edu/iwa/

The Iowa Women's Archives collects primary source materials on the women and women's organizations of Iowa. Finding aids for more than 150 manuscript collections are included at this site. The collections are listed alphabetically by the name of the individual or organization. It is not clear if there is additional material or collections available that do not yet have finding aids available online.

Schlesinger Library
http://www.radcliffe.edu/schles/index.html

The Schlesinger Library has one of the largest collections on the history of women in the United States. The collection has hundreds of manuscript collections and the library Web site generally describes the strengths of the library. There are links at this site to online finding aids for less than 100 of these manuscript collections. None of the documents from these collections are directly available over the Internet. The primary material the Schlesinger has made available over the World Wide Web includes 11,000 plus photographs, as part of the Visual Information Access (VIA) system at Harvard University. VIA may be accessed through the Schlesinger Web site. Further information about the manuscript collections located at the Schlesinger Library may be found through searching HOLLIS, the online catalog of Harvard University.

Sophia Smith Collection
http://www.smith.edu/libraries/libs/ssc/home.html

The Sophia Smith Collection located at Smith College has extensive holdings on the history of women. The collection Web site contains more than 300 collections on women and women's organizations, including documents, photographs, scrapbooks, and lists of collections. The description of each collection consists of the date and the amount of material available, but no abstract or description of each collection or a link to finding aids for these collections is available. The archival collections are also listed by subject area, so a researcher may search for materials on journalism, women's diaries, labor history, social work, the woman suffrage movement, and other areas of interest.

See also:

Smith College Archives
http://www.smith.edu/libraries/libs/archives/info.htm#collections

The Woman's Collection of the Blagg-Huey Library, Texas Women's University
http://www.twu.edu/library/collections.htm

The Woman's Collection includes a manuscript collection that provides rich research materials on the history of women's education in Texas. The collection is divided into three major areas. There is a manuscript collection of individual women and women's organizations. Holdings are especially strong in the history of Anglo women in Texas, education, women in politics, suffrage, and women's rights. An international cookbook collection contains mostly published materials, but also includes some primary materials on women cookbook and recipe collectors. The records of the Women Air Force Service Pilots collection form a third area of the Woman's Collection. The Web site includes an abstract of each collection and a brief description of each woman or organization.

Digital Collections

There are several hundred projects at institutions around the United States to make historical materials available on CD-ROM, DVD, or over the World Wide Web. Many of these projects include materials on women and women's issues. At present the process of digitizing materials is expensive, time consuming, and needs considerable expertise. Most institutions recognize that the goal for digitizing their materials is one of access. With the continual demand for resources on women, collections dealing with women or women's issues have been primary candidates for digitization. Primary resources such as photographs, diaries, letters, posters, advertisements, oral interviews, government reports, and audio files, are among the materials now available. Photographs and other visual images are the most popular type of digital collections. In general, most digital collections are selections from the institution, rather than complete collections or holdings. The user should be aware of this and contact the institution for further information.

Other digital projects include materials from several institutions, gathered to illustrate the sources available on a particular topic or subject area. Again, re-

searchers should be aware that often the materials are only representative of the full holdings from each institution or on each topic.

Commercial digitized products are also available for purchase. The cost of these collections usually limits them to academic institutions or large public libraries. The list below covers only a selected number of the digital collections with information on women that are now available.

Commercial Digital Collections

North American Women's Letters and Diaries (Alexandria, Va.: Alexander Street Press, 2001–). http://www.alexanderstreet2.com/nwldlive.

This collection includes letters or diaries from 107 women of North America. The researcher may search the collection by name of author, sources, historical events, or the texts themselves. Biographical information about each author includes all forms of the author's name, place of birth and death, birth and death dates, race, marriage, religion, occupation, and so on. A link leads the researcher to a list of the diaries, and letters may be viewed chronologically. These documents may also be accessed by the "Personal Events" table of contents so that the researcher could find all the letters and diary entries on childbirth or increase of income. These personal events include: attending school; birthday; death of parent; inheritance; physical illness; starting job; sale of slave; travel. There are 36 categories in all. A similar sort of search of the documents can be conducted on the "Historical Events" table of contents, with important dates stretching from 1754 to 1867. The ability to conduct simple word or phrase searches as well as advanced multifield searches is also possible. The original letters and diaries in this digital collection all come from published sources, usually books and magazines. There is no information listed on which institutions hold the original versions of the letters and diaries.

Access to Women's Studies: CIS History Universe (Congressional Information Service: Washington, D.C., 2000–). http://www.lexisnexis.com/academic/1univ/hwomen/w11.htm (The URL is for a tour of site.)

This digital collection includes transcriptions of selected letters, reports from such organizations as the League of Women Voters on their political crusade for child welfare in the 1920s, some items from manuscript collections of key activists (e.g., Elizabeth Cady Stanton) in the battle for woman suffrage, and the records of government agencies, such the Women's

Bureau of the U.S. Department of Labor. A complete list of collections is available. Each item in this digital product is defined as a primary or secondary resource. There is complete bibliographic data with each document, including author, title, date, name of collection, series, folder, length of document, institution where original document may be found, and whether or not the collection is available on microfilm. The documents in this digital collection are retrieved as PDF files and are fully searchable. Keyword or controlled subject searching is also available. Images of the original documents do not seem to be included in this collection.

Selected Institutional Digital Collections

The collections and Web sites included in this section are only a selection of the ever-growing number of resources available over the World Wide Web. There are some sites devoted to collections of primary sources specifically on women. Other Web sites included here cover broader subject areas, but they include significant amounts of material on women, women's organizations, or topics of interest to researchers on women. The examples in this section were selected to illustrate a range of the kinds of electronic resources available from single institutions.

African-American Women On-line Archival Collections
Special Collections Library, Duke University
http://scriptorium.lib.duke.edu/collections/
african-american-women.html

This site includes three collections of primary documents from the writings of African American women. These collections contain rare nineteenth-century and early-twentieth-century writings of slave women and a woman born to former slaves. This site provides links to descriptions of other manuscript collections of African American women's organizations at Duke University. These collections represent only a portion of the archival holdings on African American and Anglo women in the Special Collections Library at Duke University.

American Memory
(Washington, D.C.: Library of Congress, National Digital Library Program, 1994–)
http://memory.loc.gov/

This enormous Web site is a gateway to access seven million digitized items from more than one hundred historical collections at the Library of Congress. It is easy to use, and researchers may search across all collections at once. Searches may be limited to documents, maps, motion pictures, photographs and prints, or sound recordings. Alternatively, a search may be performed on a specific historic collection, under such general headings as Geography, Politic Science and Law, or Recreation and Sports. The collections themselves include "Born in Slavery," "American Variety Stage: Vaudeville and Popular Entertainment," "American Life Histories: Manuscripts from the Federal Writer's Project."

At the home page for the *American Memory* Web site a search limited to manuscripts on the word "women" elicited five hundred hits. These included photographs, letters, writings by and about women, and other items. Records of each document include an image of the original item, a transcription, links to other items of similar interest, and links to the online collection at the Library of Congress, which sponsors the original document. In some cases a link to a catalog record is available. For example, an early draft of *The Woman's Bible* by Elizabeth Cady Stanton may be found through the American Memory site. A link to the catalog record for the entire collection of Elizabeth Cady Stanton papers eventually leads to a finding aid for that manuscript collection. Within the Stanton papers finding aid, links are provided to specific documents available online through the *American Memory* project, thus returning the researcher back the starting Web site. The extensive printed guide, *American Women: A Library of Congress Guide for the Study of Women's History and Culture in the United States,* described earlier in this chapter, provides a broader view of the collections available at the Library of Congress.

Dickinson Electronic Archives
http://www.iath.virginia.edu/dickinson/index.html

This extensive Web site was designed and continues to be maintained by staff at the University of Virginia. The site, in its entirety, includes primary documents by and about Emily Dickinson, other members of the Dickinson family, and connected friends and colleagues. Much of the archival material about Emily Dickinson is restricted to the sources connected to the University of Virginia. Primary materials, mostly letters and writings, from other members of the Dickinson family are available over the World Wide Web.

Emergence of Advertising in America (online)
Durham, N.C.: Digital Scriptorium, Rare Book, Manuscript, and Special Collections Library, Duke University, 2000 (cited June 26, 2001).
http://scriptorium.lib.duke.edu/eaa/

This database presents more than 9,000 images, with information, relating to the early history of advertising in the United States. There are no documents in the database. A researcher may perform a keyword search across all the collections included on this site. Images of women were often included in advertisements whether companies were directing their products towards women or not. A search on this database on the topic of tobacco advertising found 285 images, with only 9 of them listed as containing women. However, in searching through the images, all 23 advertisements listed for just the tobacco company Watson and McGill contain images of women. Not all of the records, which accompany the images in this whole site, had the word *woman* or *women* noted, even where women appear in the image.

Emma Goldman
http://sunsite.berkeley.edu/Goldman/

This Web site describes the Emma Goldman Papers Project based at the University of California at Berkeley. The larger project has published two microfilm collections of Goldman materials: *The Emma Goldman Papers: A Microfilm Edition* (Chadwyck-Healey Inc., 1991) and *Emma Goldman: A Guide to Her Life and Documentary Sources* (Chadwyck-Healey Inc., 1995) The Web site contains descriptions of the microfilm and print project and also sample documents on Goldman and radical contemporaries, on anarchism, antiwar work, socialism, an online exhibit of photographs and documents with explanatory text, and a section of curriculum to aid middle and high school students. This site also includes the *Open Road,* a newsletter about the Goldman Papers Project. Portions of some of Goldman's writings are available as well.

National Archives and Records Administration (NARA) and *National Archive Information Locator* (NAIL)
http://www.archives.gov/research_room/nail/index.html

The National Archives and Records Administration (NARA) is the agency that archives all federal records. National Archive Information Locator (NAIL) is NARA's current online catalog of holdings in Washington, D.C., the regional records services facilities, and the presidential libraries. A new catalog, the Archival Research Catalog (ARC), is planned as a replacement. NAIL currently contains descriptions of more than 607,000 archival holdings descriptions and 124,000 digital copies; it represents only a portion of NARA's vast holdings.

Researchers may use the basic or advanced search form to locate records of the physical holdings information for motion picture films and sound and video recordings of NARA's Motion Picture, Sound, and Video Branch. Searches may be limited by media type, specific titles, title keywords, control number, and/or specific description level identifiers. A portion of the NARA holdings listed in NAIL has digital images. A search may be limited to those records with digital images of the original items. A link in the record leads the researcher to the image of the document. No transcriptions of the documents are available.

A keyword search on the word *women* retrieved more than 6,000 records. Only 600 of these records had digital representations of the original documents or images. Nevertheless, information on women and women's history occurs throughout the NAIL database if researchers are aware of what sorts of documentation to search. For example, before gaining the right to vote in 1920, women used petitions as a political tool to make their voices heard in the courts and in Congress. Hundreds of petitions were signed by groups of women on such public issues as slavery and antislavery, rights of Native Americans, women's rights, polygamy, child labor, and disarmament. Women also petitioned the federal government as individuals in attempts to address personal concerns. Even where women are the only signers of a petition or the majority of signers, in most of the NAIL records for these petitions the word *women* does not appear, so the original keyword search (finding more than 6,000 records) did not include this material. Creative use of these materials will yield substantial amounts of archival resources for the study of women.

Suffrage Oral History Project
The Bancroft Library, University of California at Berkeley
http://sunsite.berkeley.edu:2020/dynaweb/teiproj/oh/suffragists/

The Suffragists Oral History Project was originally conducted in the mid- to late-1970s. Historians interviewed a small number of 11 suffrage leaders, including Alice Paul and Jeannette Rankin. The taped interviews were transcribed and published by the Bancroft Library. The interviews document their activities in behalf of passage of the Nineteenth Amendment and their continuing careers as leaders of movements for welfare and labor reform, world peace, and the passage of the Equal Rights Amendment. The transcribed interviews are now available online. There is a subject index to each interview and a researcher may perform a keyword search across all of the transcriptions.

Triangle Factory Fire
Created by the Kheel Center for Labor-Management Documentation and Archives, Cornell University/ILR
http://www.ilr.cornell.edu/trianglefire/

This site includes primary and secondary sources on the workers and events at the Triangle Shirtwaist Company Factory in New York, New York, 1911. Most of the employees at the company were women; women were leaders and participants in the strikes and union activity surrounding this event. The site documents a significant event in the history of working women. Included is a history of the event, lists of witnesses, victims, and a bibliography. Digitized documents include testimonials, reports, newspaper clippings, oral histories of survivors, photographs, and illustrations. This site contains almost all of the primary documents on the Triangle Factory Fire held by the Kheel Center. There is also a list of primary and secondary resources held at other institutions. There are photographs and illustrations, but no images of original documents, only the transcriptions.

Women in Journalism
Washington Press Club Foundation
http://npc.press.org/wpforal/ohhome.htm

The Washington Press Club Foundation initiated their oral history project in 1986. The project includes nearly 60 interviews with women journalists whose careers span most of the twentieth century. Transcriptions of 42 of these interviews are available online at this Web site. The journalists were chosen to reflect cultural diversity, importance to the field of journalism, and impact on the careers of other women and on the wider community. Tapes and transcripts of all the interviews are available at Columbia University and the National Press Club Library in Washington, D.C. Transcripts of the tapes are available at academic institutions around the United States. A list of holding institutions is included on this Web site.

Women's Studies Collection
Schoenberg Center For Electronic Text and Image, University of Pennsylvania
http://www.dewey.library.upenn.edu/sceti/.

This site contains the complete text of several unpublished nineteenth- and twentieth-century women's diaries and two cookbooks. These documents are available as large images only, with no transcriptions of the pages.

See also at the University of Pennsylvania, the *Marian Anderson Collection of Photographs, 1898–1992,* Annenberg Rare Book and Manuscript Library.

Selected Sites with Digital Collections from Multiple Institutions

DoHistory Created by the Film Study Center at Harvard University in 2000
http://www.dohistory.org/

This award-winning site is a multifunctional tool to teach history and use of primary sources, rather than solely a guide to archival sources or the gateway to a digital collection. The editors state at the top of the opening page that this is "A site that shows you how to piece together the past from the fragments that have survived. Our case study: Martha Ballard."[20] The diaries of Maine resident and midwife Martha Ballard (1785–1812) have thrilled scholars, students, and independent historians. The diaries have been the source of at least two books and a historical film. This site includes portions of the book edited and published by historian Laurel Ulrich Thatcher, transcriptions of the diaries by Robert R. McCausland and Cynthia MacAlman McCausland, and portions of a film on Martha Ballard written and produced by Laurie Kahn-Leavitt. Information about the video, clips from the film, and an essay from Kahn-Leavitt about the process of making a historical film are included on the site.

The digital collection portion of the site includes images and transcriptions of each page of the Ballard diary, as well as images and transcriptions of the original primary and secondary sources used as background material for the site. As the diaries are often difficult to read, information to assist in decoding them is also included on the site. Researchers may view such items as 19 pages from the official records of the town of Hallowell, Maine. Both the diaries and the background documents may be viewed as images of the original pages or as transcribed versions. A database accompanies the documents and diaries, which may be searched by text, a list of keywords, or date range. The location of each original primary resource is listed with the image or text.

Internet Women's History Sourcebook
Created and maintained by Paul Halsall at Fordham University
http://www.fordham.edu/halsall/women/womensbook.html

The editor of this site has provided links to a selection of primary and secondary sources on women in the ancient, medieval, and modern world. Sections on

Ancient Egypt, Mesopotamia, Greece, Rome, Medieval Europe, North America, Latin America, Europe, Asia, Africa, and the Islamic World are subdivided into topics pertinent to the study of women. These include: General, Great Women, Women's Oppression, The Structure of Women's Lives, Women's Agency, and Gender Construction. Links from the site's table of contents take the researcher to a brief title and link. In some cases the resources are located at other sites; in others the historical resources have been transcribed by this site's editor and included on the site itself. Resources located at the Internet Women's History Sourcebook site are transcribed and there are no images of the original documents.

The Margaret Sanger Papers Project
http://www.nyu.edu/projects/sanger/project.htm

This Web site describes the historical editing project on the papers of Margaret Sanger sponsored by the History Department at New York University. There are links to detailed descriptions of the two microfilmed collections: *Margaret Sanger Microfilm Edition: Smith College Series* and the *Margaret Sanger Microfilm Edition: Collected Documents Series*. Both collections are published by ProQuest. A careful search reveals a link at this Web site to primary documents on Sanger through the Web site of the Model Editions Partnership (see below).

The Margaret Sanger Papers Project Electronic Edition
(Model Edition Project)
http://adh.sc.edu/

The Model Editions Partnership is a project sponsored by the University of South Carolina and "explore[s] ways of creating editions of historical documents which meet the standards scholars traditionally use in preparing printed editions. Equally important is our goal of making these materials more widely available via the Web."[21] Documents from the Margaret Sanger Papers Project are included in the Model Editions Project. The documents were selected by the editors of the Sanger Project and include unsearchable digital images of more than 60 archival documents. There are no transcriptions of these documents. Explanatory reference notes and links are available for each document, setting it into the context of Sanger's life and the other documents on the Web site.

Salem Witch Trials
Created under the supervision of Benjamin C. Ray,
University of Virginia
http://etext.virginia.edu/salem/witchcraft/

The Salem Witch Trials Documentary Archive and Transcription project is an electronic collection of primary source materials, including court records, contemporary books, maps, images, and literary works, relating to the Salem witch trials of 1692. Many of the documents included on the site concern the role of women in the trials and in Salem in the late seventeenth century. Court documents and other pertinent materials from archival collections in Massachusetts, Maine, and New York may be found on the site. There are images of the original documents. A separate section of the site contains copies of transcriptions of the court documents produced in 1938. Further transcriptions are planned.

Women and Social Movements in the United States, 1830–1930 (online) 1997–
Created and Maintained by Thomas Dublin and Kathryn Kish Sklar, Center for the Historical Study of Women and Gender at the State University of New York at Binghamton
http://womhist.binghamton.edu/index.html

This site is "Organized around the history of women in social movements between 1830 and 1940, [and] makes the insights of women's history accessible to teachers at universities, colleges, and high schools." Currently the documents on this site are all selected from 24 published microfilm collections of primary sources on the history of women. As of 2003 there are projects underway that will incorporate archival or primary documents from numerous institutions into the site.

This site includes transcriptions of more than 750 documents but only a few images of the original documents. Documents may be searched by date or general subject area. Keyword searching is available. There are also 200 historical photographs, graphics, and other visual items. The site also includes a description of the microfilm collections from which the documents are drawn.

CONCLUSION

Archival collections focused on women and issues specifically concerning women are available at many locations. There are several institutions across the United States, such as the Schlesinger Library, which collect exclusively on women, women's organizations, and women's issues. Almost all archival collections have some information about women, even when the focus of the institution seems directed toward other topics.

A few printed guides to these resources have been published through the second half of the twentieth century, but these publications covered only a tiny portion of the enormous amount of archival resources actually available. Archivists, librarians, and scholars interested in women's history and women's studies have turned with enthusiasm to the World Wide Web as the principle method to disseminate information about the vast amounts of material on women already available in collections. These professionals and scholars have utilized the special capabilities of the Web to increase the information about the location of archival resources on women. However, even with this great increase since the advent of the Web, there remains a great deal of work to be done in exposing the materials available on women.

In cooperation with these professionals and scholars, publishers of archival collections and designers of new electronic resources will also play a significant role in making archival materials on women more easily accessible to researchers. The established partnerships between information professionals and scholars already interested in women's studies will have to be extended to include publishers and Web designers. Archival resources on women are not yet directly available in microform or electronically in proportion to the amount located on paper within institutions.

Those researchers interested in locating archival resources on women now have far more, and far better, guides to collections than they did before the middle of the 1990s. The availability of paper and electronic guides are thanks to the work of archivists and librarians specializing in women's studies and women's history. However, even with the growing number of printed and electronic guides becoming increasingly accessible, it still requires thought, persistence, and creative methodologies on the part of researchers to unearth archival resources on women and their history. The long-established partnerships between archival professionals, librarians, women's studies scholars, and historians will continue to be a necessary component to the development of bibliographical resources to archival resources on women.

NOTES

1. Eleanor Flexner's book *Century of Struggle: The Woman's Rights Movement in the United States* (Cambridge: Harvard University Press, Belknap Press, 1959) and *The Ideas of the Woman Suffrage Movement, 1890–1920,* by Aileen S. Kraditor (New York: Columbia University Press, 1965) are excellent examples of this history.

2. Two books published by historian Mary Ritter Beard were the most famous exceptions to this: Mary Ritter Beard, ed., *America through Women's Eyes* (New York: Macmillan, 1933); and Mary Ritter Beard, *Woman as Force in History: A Study in Traditions and Realities* (New York : Macmillan, 1946).

3. Early examples of this historiographical writing: Barbara Welter, "The Cult of True Womanhood," *American Quarterly* 18, no. 2, part 1 (Summer 1966): pp. 151–75; Kathryn Kish Sklar, *Catharine Beecher; A Study in American Domesticity* (New Haven, Conn.: Yale University Press, 1973); Mary P. Ryan, *Womanhood in America, from Colonial Times to the Present* (New York: New Viewpoints, 1975).

4. A notable exception to this was Gerda Lerner, ed., *Black Women in White America* (New York: Vintage Books, 1973). Lerner used excerpts of previously published primary documents to demonstrate the rich history of African American women.

5. World Center for Women's Archives (WCWA) Pamphlet, ca. 1939, Margaret Sanger Papers, Library of Congress, quoted in "The World Center for Women's Archives: A Look Back at a Novel Idea," *Margaret Sanger Papers Project Newsletter*, no. 7, (spring 1994), http://www.nyu.edu/projects/sanger/wcwa.htm.

6. "World Center for Women's Archives," Correspondence with Mary Beard, 1935–1945, Swarthmore College Peace Collection Official Records.

7. Mary Ritter Beard to Ellen Starr Brinton, 14 August 1939, Correspondence with Mary Beard, 1935–1945, Swarthmore College Peace Collection Official Records.

8. New Jersey Historical Society, "Federal Writers Project. New Jersey," New Jersey Historical Society, http://www.jerseyhistory.org/findingaid.php?aid=0830summary.

9. Mary Ritter Beard to Ellen Starr Brinton, Correspondence with Mary Beard, 1935–1945, Swarthmore College Peace Collection Official Records.

10. Mary McLeon Bethune Council House, "Collections," National Archives for Black Women's History, http://www.nps.gov/mamc/bethune/archives/collect.htm.

11. Andrea Hinding, ed., *Women's History Sources: A Guide to Archives and Manuscript Collections in the United States* (New York: Bowker, 1979), p. ix.

12. Suzanne Hildenbrand makes this same point in the introduction to *Women's Collections: Libraries,*

Archives, and Consciousness (New York: Haworth Press, 1986), p. 1.

13. Ibid., p. xi.

14. Ibid., p. xi.

15. Glenn Porter, "Forward," in *Women's History: A Guide to Sources at Hagley Museum and Library,* by Lynn Ann Catanese (Westport, Conn.: Greenwood Press, 1997), p. 1.

16. Ibid., p. iv.

17. Harvard Business School, "Women, Enterprise and Society: A Guide to Resources in the Business Manuscripts Collection at Baker Library: Introduction," http://www.library.hbs.edu/hc/wes/intro/.

18. Gale Group Inc., Primary Source Microfilm, http://www.galegroup.com/psm/about.htm.

19. All quotations in this section are from Research Support Libraries Programme, "Project Information," http://www.genesis.ac.uk/projectinfo.html.

20. Film Study Center, Harvard University, "Martha Ballard's Diary Online," DoHistory, http://www.dohistory.org/diary/aboutonlinediary.html.

21. University of South Carolina, Division of Libraries and Information Systems, "Model Editions Partnership: Historical Editions in the Digital Age," http://mep.cla.sc.edu/.

CHAPTER 6
Moving Image and Sound Archives

Dwight Swanson

While significant and serious research of film and television history can be done at a first-rate video rental store or through a library's film and video collection, to truly grasp the breadth of the world of moving images, a researcher will eventually have to seek out the resources of a film and video archive. It is only in an archive that one can view prints of films that may never be available commercially, including not only feature films, but such genres as newsreels, home movies, outtakes, and industrial and educational films. Furthermore, moving image archives are not just a resource for the study of film or media history, but for all types of history, since moving images exist at a crossroads of art, entertainment, and documentation. Likewise, some sound recordings, such as radio shows, were only intended as ephemeral broadcasts and only through serendipity do they still exist today in archival collections. Oral history recordings, however, are intentionally created to permanently capture the passage of time through the words of its participants. While recorded words can be transcribed, no textual translation can truly capture the same feeling and meaning of hearing the original voices and the original sounds.

MOVING IMAGE ARCHIVES

Researchers approaching moving image archives for the first time may find a difficult series of obstacles keeping them from actually gaining access to the materials they are searching for. A tradition of secrecy among film archives has thankfully been abandoned, writes Penelope Houston, and "access is the watchword, one might say the talisman, for the modern film archive. They talk about it all the time, practise it, worry about the ways in which they can make themselves and their services available to the public." (Houston 1994, 75) According to film archivist Paolo Cherchi-Usai, in keeping with this new sense of openness, "those which don't or can't provide access now pretend that they do, and feel guilty about it" (Houston 1994, 97).

Two recommended starting points for archival research are the books *Keepers of the Frame* by Penelope Houston and Anthony Slide's *Nitrate Won't Wait.* Both books examine the history of film archives and the politics and philosophies of film preservation, Houston from a primarily European viewpoint and Slide from an American one. Film archives, in their earliest incarnations, were seen as being on the fringes of legality since it was feared that the motion picture companies that owned the copyrights on the films would step up and demand their prints back. Luckily this rarely happened, so gradually this fear was abandoned and archives developed working relationships with film studios.

As archives adopted more traditional library-science approaches to cataloging and access, there still remained impediments to usage. First, are the copyright issues associated with commercial film prints. Especially in the case of commercial films, copyright owners stand at the center of most archival transactions, as rights must be cleared and fees negotiated. This is rarely a problem for on-site viewing of prints or tapes but does become an issue for any type of duplication or exhibition. A more pressing problem is the technical one because unlike almost any other type of archival media, films, videotapes, and audiotapes require machinery in order to be able to make any use of them;

and this machinery is frequently very expensive, fragile, and potentially damaging to the artifacts. Most of the preeminent moving image archives are intimately involved in the preservation process, so will be unwilling to put their original materials at risk. Different archives have different policies about access to master materials, but it is not uncommon for archives to disallow viewing of film prints or tapes that have not been preserved, leaving many titles off-limits to researchers. Film archives, perhaps more than any other type of archive, require advance warning by potential researchers, since film is frequently kept either off-site or in climate-controlled vaults, which demand lengthy staging times before the materials can be used.

Researchers looking into specific topics should of course contact archives such as the ones in other chapters of this book because very frequently manuscript collections end up with media materials, though these often get lost in the back shelves of storage areas. Even the largest, most established media archives, however, have a difficult time keeping up with the bewildering array of different types of film, video, and audio formats, each one with its own idiosyncrasies and each one more expensive than the next. 16mm film, for example, became the standard format for educational, news, and documentary film, whereas 35mm has been the format of choice for most theatrical films for more than 100 years. Maintaining equipment for even these two formats can be a huge financial burden for small archives, which is to say nothing of 8mm, super 8, 9.5mm, 28mm, 70mm and so on. And even though the Video Home System (VHS) has lasted as the standard video access format for several decades, its future is very much in doubt in this digital age. Because of these issues and the costs involved, viewing and listening facilities vary by archive. Larger film archives will have flatbed viewers (such as Steenbecks) for viewing 16mm and 35mm film prints, preferably in separate study rooms. Flatbeds allow for the viewing of prints on small monitor-sized screens, but their mechanisms are gentler on film than traditional projectors. In smaller archives, however, it is more likely that a researcher will be viewing a VHS copy of a film on a VCR in a study carrel.

Paolo Cherchi-Usai, in his book *Silent Cinema: An Introduction,* includes a useful chapter on the relationship between researchers and archives. He begins with the etiquette involved (by both parties), as summarized by his rule: "Both must ensure that the act of consulting to a better knowledge of the work and to its material preservation" (Cherchi-Usai 2000, 124)" Beyond this, however, he offers some key pointers on the processes and tools of archival film research that are well worth reading for the first-time film researcher in order to get the most possible information out of the archival visit.

Given all of these caveats, is archival moving image and sound research a lost cause? Certainly not. In fact, every year the opportunities for access to primary sources grow as the volume of material (including the preserved titles) in archives accumulates. Additionally, the amount of information about media materials is growing exponentially with the development of both centralized databases and noncentralized ones available via the Internet.

The largest American collections are the national collections at the Library of Congress and the National Archives and Records Administration. Beyond these are the cinema collections associated either with Hollywood film production or classic cinema, both American and foreign. The first large-scale association of film archives was the International Federation of Film Archives (FIAF), which was founded in 1938, Web site at http://www.fiafnet.org/. There are currently 11 American FIAF members, including the largest of the American film archives. In recent years, the Association of Moving Image Archivists (AMIA) has had a burgeoning membership both in North America and around the world. One of the most helpful resources in the film preservation and film research world is AMIA-L, the Listserv sponsored by the AMIA.

Archival researchers seeking moving image materials beyond the cinema of the silver screen should seek out the wealth of resources found in regional and specialized collections. Regional moving image archives are frequently found in state or local historical societies or as parts of university libraries. These collections are usually limited only by geography, and have as their mandates the preservation of the moving images created in a particular location. They, therefore, tend to be strongest in nonfiction categories, such as home movies, local television, and documentaries, at the same time frequently including fiction films such as independent films and feature films shot in the region.

Specialized archives are those that build their collections around a specific topic. In some cases, the focus may be on a particular category of film, such as educational films or East German films, but more commonly these archives collect all types of media related to a single research topic, such as baseball or Japanese American life.

Bibliographies and Catalogs

In 1983, Frank Hodsoll, the chairman of the National Endowment for the Arts, wrote "informed decisions about preservation priorities will continue to be difficult to make until the contents and physical condition of films in major collections across the country are listed in one database" (Slide 1992, 147). In 1994, the National Moving Image Database (NAMID) project was established with the support of the American Film Institute to try to centralize and standardize moving image holdings from across the country. Despite its good intentions, by the late 1990s the project had largely stalled, and some of the leading archives still continue to use private and proprietary databases. The closest thing to a single large database of film titles remains the Online Computer Library Center (OCLC), but this tends to be used primarily by university collections, and even then only rarely. Locating a particular film title unfortunately remains a fairly complicated process. In 2002, however, the Association of Moving Image Archivists (AMIA) and the Library of Congress received funding from the National Science Digital Library to begin implementation of the Moving Image Collections (MIC) portal. MIC (http://gondolin. rutgers.edu/MIC) is an ambitious Web-based system to coordinate information about archival moving image collections. The project will eventually include a worldwide directory of moving image archives, cataloging facilities for participating institutions, a union catalog of publicly held film and video titles, and an outreach and education component with links to information on cataloging and preserving moving image materials.

The first publicly available list of titles of films held in the archives of the FIAF was the *Treasures from the Film Archives: A Catalog of Short Silent Fiction Films Held by the FIAF Archives,* which was compiled and edited by Ronald S. Magliozzi (Metuchen, N.J.: Scarecrow Press, 1988). As its subtitle implies, this list is fairly limited in scope, but is still one of the most important sources for early cinema research. This was usurped by *The International Film Archive CD-ROM,* which contains a 1995 update of the silent film list, as well as volumes (1972 to the present) of the *International Index to Film Periodicals,* plus records from its TV-related companion, the FIAF thesaurus and a directory of film and TV documentation collections.

While archives have almost completely abandoned printed catalogs and finding aids in favor of Web sites, there are still several older publications by larger archives, the Library of Congress in particular, which are useful for film study. These include:

Motion Pictures from the Library of Congress Paper Print Collection, 1894–1912, compiled by Kemp R. Niver and edited by Bebe Bergsten (Berkeley: University of California Press, 1967).

The George Kleine Collection of Early Motion Pictures in the Library of Congress: A Catalog, prepared by Rita Horwitz and Harriet Harrison with the assistance of Wendy White (Washington D.C.: Library of Congress, Motion Picture, Broadcasting, and Recorded Sound Division, 1980).

Catalog of Holdings, the American Film Institute Collection and the United Artists Collection at the Library of Congress (Los Angeles, Calif.: American Film Institute, 1978).

The Film Catalog: A List of Holdings in the Museum of Modern Art, edited by Jon Gartenberg with Lee Amazonas (Boston, Mass.: G.K. Hall, 1985).

Three of the largest film and television collections in the country (the Library of Congress, the National Archives and Records Administration, and UCLA) have their catalogues available online, and in all three cases, detailed records give information about the availability of on-site viewing copies. The Library of Congress includes motion picture and videotape records in its general "Library of Congress Online Catalog" at http://catalog.loc.gov/. As of 2002, the National Archives' Archival Research Catalog database at http://www.archives.gov/research_room/arc/ contains records for nearly 100,000 films and videos and 40,000 sound recordings. UCLA's film and television collection is found as part of the university's ORION2 database at http://orion2.library.ucla.edu/. From the main screen select the "Film and Television Archive" database.

Directories

In order to locate a particular film or video title, then, a researcher must first locate the appropriate archive. The most comprehensive published directory of American archival sources is *Footage: The Worldwide Moving Image Sourcebook* (New York: Second Line Search, 1997 [updates earlier 1989 and 1991 versions]). This hefty book is widely available and lists not only publicly held collections, but also collections from private libraries, production companies, and stock footage houses as well. There are 1,860 listings for the United States and Canada, with an additional 934 international sources. Entries include contact information, as well as information about access policies, cataloging, rights, and descriptions of holdings (frequently quite lengthy). In addition to the listings, there are geographic and subject indexes, a directory of related services, and essays about moving image archives, and stock footage.

Although *Footage: The Worldwide Moving Image Sourcebook* does include listings outside of North America, a more comprehensive European directory is *Film and Television Collections in Europe,* edited by Daniela Kirchner; produced by MAP-TV, an initiative of the MEDIA Programme of the European Union (London: Blueprint, 1995). It includes directory information as well as brief nation-by-nation essays about moving image collections. Additional recent international directories include *Film Researcher's Handbook: A Guide to Sources in North America, South America, Asia, Australasia and Africa,* compiled by Jenny Morgan (New York: Routledge, 1996); *International Directory of Film and TV Documentation Centres,*, 3rd ed., edited by Frances Thorpe (Chicago, Ill.: St. James Press, 1988); and *World Directory of Moving Image and Sound Archives,* edited by Wolfgang Klaue (München, Germany: K.G. Saur, 1993).

As expected, perhaps, there are several online directories of moving image collections. The National Film Preservation Board maintains the most comprehensive list at the Library of Congress Web site at http://lcweb.loc.gov/film/arch.html. This is an international list of links to archives' own sites with no additional collections information. The National Film Preservation Foundation maintains its own list in "Community of Archives" at http://www.film preservation.org/community.html. This list includes only the archives that have been awarded NFPF preservation grants, but as such includes most of the preeminent archives in the country. The list is searchable by region, archive name, grant date, grant program, or film title and includes a summary of each archive's holdings. Finally, the Media Resources Center at UC-Berkeley publishes a list of links to television news archives and stock footage libraries in "Stockfootage and News Footage: A Short List of Web Resources" at http://www. lib.berkeley.edu/MRC/stockfootage.html.

AMERICAN FIAF ARCHIVES

Academy of Motion Picture Arts and Sciences Academy Film Archive
1313 North Vine St.
Hollywood, CA 90028
310-247-3000
fax: 310-859-9531
http://www3.oscars.org/filmarchive/index.html
ampas@oscars.org

This collection covers a broad history of American and world cinema, including the silent era and classic Hollywood. Highlights include Academy Award nominees and copies of ceremonies, as well as the personal film collections of Alfred Hitchcock and other prominent directors and actors.

American Film Institute National Center for Film and Video Preservation
John F. Kennedy Center
Washington, D.C. 20566
202-252-3120
fax: 202-252-3126

also:

2021 North Western Ave.
Los Angeles, CA 90027
323-856-7708
fax: 323-856-7616
http://www.afi.com/
AFIFEST@AFI.com

The AFI collection is housed at the Library of Congress and includes features, shorts, newsreels, documentaries, and television programs. Among the collections are those of Hal Roach Studios, Columbia Pictures, Paramount Studios, and Radio Keith Orpheum (RKO).

Anthology Film Archives
32 Second Ave.
New York, NY 10003
212-505-5181
fax: 212-477-2714
http://www.anthologyfilmarchives.org/

This institution is dedicated to the preservation, study, and exhibition of independent and avant-garde film. It includes an active film program in its two theaters, and the Essential Cinema Repertory Collection, a collection of classic independent and experimental films.

Human Studies Film Archives (Smithsonian Institution)
Smithsonian Institution Museum Support Center
4210 Silver Hill Road

Suitland, MD 20746
301-238-2875
fax: 301-238-2883
http://www.nmnh.si.edu/naa/
naa@nmnh.si.edu

Now a part of the National Anthropological Archives, the HSFA is devoted to collecting, preserving, documenting, and disseminating a broad range of ethnographic and anthropological moving image materials from around the world.

International Museum of Photography and Film at George Eastman House
900 East Ave.
Rochester, NY 14607
716-271-3361
716-271-3970
http://www.eastman.org/
film@geh.org

A general cinema collection, highlights include one of the largest collections of silent films in the world, classic American film, and early German and French cinema collections, as well as Warner Brothers motion picture stills.

Library of Congress, Motion Picture, Broadcasting and Recorded Sound Division
Motion Picture and Television Reading Room
LM336
101 Independence Ave. S.E.
Washington, D.C. 20540-4690
202-707-8572 (Reading Room)
fax: 202-707-2371
http://lcweb.loc.gov/rr/mopic/
mbrs@loc.gov

This institution houses the largest and most diverse moving image and sound collection in the United States. The Library acquires materials in part through copyright deposits, therefore giving it unique access to all possible types of acquisitions. Major collections include the Copyright collection (including the Paper Print collection of films from 1894–1914), the American Film Institute Collection, Captured Foreign Collections (German, Italian, and Japanese), the George Kleine Collection (European Cinema), United Artists preprint materials, and numerous other film and television collections. Finding aids for many collections can be found at http://lcweb.loc.gov/rr/mopic/mpfind.html.

Museum of Modern Art Dept. of Film and Video
11 West 53rd St.
New York, NY 10019-5486
212-708-9400

fax: 212-333-1173
http://moma.org/collection/depts/film_media/index.html

MOMA houses a collection of representative American and international cinema, including all periods and genres. Special collections include those of D. W. Griffith, Twentieth Century-Fox, David O. Selznick, and Douglas Fairbanks.

National Archives and Records Administration, Motion Picture, Sound and Video Branch
8601 Adelphi Rd.
College Park, MD 20740-6001
301-713-7050 (Research Room)
fax: 301-713-6904
http://www.archives.gov/

The NARA collection includes a vast range of U.S. government productions as well as the Donated Film Collection, which includes newsreels from Paramount, Fox Movietone, News of the Day, Universal, the March of Time, and television news broadcasts.

Pacific Film Archive
University of California, Berkeley Art Museum
2625 Durant Ave. #2250
Berkeley, CA 94720-2250
510-642-1437 (Library)
fax: 510-642-4889
htp://www.bampfa.berkeley.edu/
uampfaweb@uclink2.berkeley.edu

The PFA collection includes international and U.S. films with special strengths of the collection being Japanese features, Soviet silent cinema, West Coast avant-garde, and California historical footage.

UCLA Film and Television Archive
1015 North Cahuenga Blvd.
Hollywood, CA 90038
213-462-4921 (General offices)
fax: 213-462-4921
http://www.cinema.ucla.edu/

The collection is strongest in classic Hollywood film with collections from Paramount, Twentieth Century-Fox, Warner Bros., and Columbia studios, as well as Hearst Metrotone Newsreels.

Wisconsin Center for Film and Theater Research
Wisconsin Historical Society
816 State St.
Madison, WI 53706
608-264-6466
fax: 608-264-6472
http://www.wisconsinhistory.org/wcftr/

A major archives of research materials relating to the entertainment industry including manuscript collections and stills, as well as the United Artists Collection (1931–49), films by independent filmmakers, and dramatic and documentary television.

REGIONAL FILM COLLECTIONS

Alaska
Alaska Film Archives
Elmer E. Rasmuson Library
Univ. of Alaska, Fairbanks
P.O. Box 756800
Fairbanks, AK 99775-6808
907-474-5357
fax: 907-474-6365
http://image.elmer.uaf.edu/

Collection includes raw footage and edited films on subjects such as early mining, military activity during World War II and the Cold War, shifting transportation patterns, construction of the Trans-Alaska Pipeline, and Alaska's native peoples.

Alaska Moving Image Preservation Association
1325 Primrose St.
Anchorage, AK 99508
907-279-8433
fax: 907-276-0450
http://www.amipa.org/
amipa@alaska.net

A statewide media collection with special strengths that include the collections of independent film and video production companies and broadcasters in Alaska.

Florida
Louis Wolfson II Florida Moving Image Archive
Miami-Dade Public Library
101 West Flagler St.
Miami, FL 33130
305-375-1505
fax: 305-375-4436
http://www.fmia.org/
info@fmia.org

This institution's holdings cover the Miami metropolitan area as well as the state of Florida with special strengths in television news and home movies.

Hawaii
Bishop Museum Archives
1525 Bernice St.
Honolulu, HI 96817-0916
808-848-4148
fax: 808-847-8241
http://www.bishopmuseum.org/
archives@bishopmuseum.org

This archive has a collection of more than 700 titles of films relating to Hawaii and the Pacific, including home movies, television programs, and promotional and anthropological films.

Idaho
Idaho Film Collection
Hemingway Western Studies Center
1910 University Dr.
Boise, ID 83725
208-426-1999
http://www.boisestate.edu/hemingway/film.htm

Collection contains films, audio and videotapes, photographs, scripts, documents, news stories, articles and correspondences, and ephemera relating to silent and talkie feature films made in Idaho.

Kansas
Kansas State Historical Society: Audio-Visual Collection
Kansas History Center
6425 SW 6th Ave.
Topeka, KS 66615-1099
785-272-8681, ext. 303
fax:785-272-8682
http://www.kshs.org/research/collections/documents/
audiovisual/index.htm

Significant collections include the Atchison, Topeka, and Santa Fe film archives, John R. Brinkley films and audio recordings, KSNT news film collection, and WIBW news film collection, as well as large holdings of audio and visual media relating to agriculture, railroads, public health, and hygiene.

Kentucky
University of Kentucky Audio-Visual Archives
111 King Library North
Lexington, KY 40506-0039
606-257-8611
fax: 606-257-8379
http://www.uky.edu/Libraries/Special/av/

Collections cover the history and culture of Kentucky, including university-related educational and public affairs programming, as well as athletics-related film and video, collections of local television and radio programming, Kentucky-related independent filmmakers, and a wide variety of still photographic images.

Minnesota
Minnesota Historical Society
Moving Image Collection
345 Kellogg Blvd. West
St. Paul, MN 55102-1906

651-296-6126
http://www.mnhs.org/library/collections/movingimages/movingimages.html
collections@mnhs.org

Holdings include documentary, educational, amateur, and artistic films and videotapes, travelogues, home movies, television news, and the Intermedia Arts videotape collection, which showcases Minnesota's independent video producers from 1972 to 1989.

Mississippi and the South
Southern Media Archive, Center for Study of Southern Culture
University of Mississippi
307 Hill Hall
University, MS 38677
601-232-7811
fax: 601-232-7842
http://www.olemiss.edu/depts/general_library/files/archives/viscoll/

Collection of historical and cultural media of the twentieth-century mid-South, including still photographs, moving picture footage, videotape, and audio field recordings.

Nebraska
Nebraska State Historical Society
P.O. Box 82554
1500 R St.
Lincoln, NE 68501
402-471-4750
fax: 402-471-3100
http://www.nebraskahistory.org/

Collections relate to the history and culture of Nebraska and the Great Plains region, including home movies, public service films, local TV news footage, advertisements, newsreels, and Nebraska-produced local talent films.

New Mexico
New Mexico State Records Center and Archives: Archives and Historical Services Division
404 Montezuma Ave.
Santa Fe, NM 87501
505-827-7334
fax: 505-827-7331
http://www.nmcpr.state.nm.us/

Historical films from New Mexico and the Southwest including state-produced films, newsreels, home movies, and tourist, documentary and educational films.

North Dakota
State Historical Society of North Dakota, State Archives and Historical Research Library
North Dakota Heritage Center
612 East Boulevard Ave.
Bismarck, ND 58505-0179
701-328-2668
fax: 701-328-3710
http://www.state.nd.us/hist/infcoll.htm

Audiovisual materials include motion picture film and videotape, and oral history interviews, including the North Dakota Television Newsfilm Collection and several individual and family collections.

Northern New England
Northeast Historic Film
P.O. Box 900
85 Main St.
Bucksport, ME 04416
207-469-0924
fax: 207-469-7875
http://www.oldfilm.org/
oldfilm@aol.com

Archive houses film and video collections from Maine, New Hampshire, Vermont, and Massachusetts. Collections include one of the largest home movie collections in the country as well as television news, independent productions, and feature films.

Ohio
Ohio Historical Society
Audiovisual Archives
1982 Velma Ave.
Columbus, OH 43211
614-297-2544
fax: 614-297-2654
http://www.ohiohistory.org/resource/audiovis/index.html
audiovisual@ohiohistory.org

Ohio-related collection includes newsreels, television news, state-produced films, industrial and educational films.

Oregon and the Pacific Northwest
Oregon Historical Society, Moving Images
1200 Southwest Park Ave.
Portland, OR 97205-2483
503-306-5256
fax: 503-221-2035
http://www.ohs.org/collections/index.cfm/
orhist@ohs.org

Holdings include more than 15,000 titles on diverse subjects, including early newsreels, family movies, commercial and industrial films, scenic and wildlife, and a host of segments and outtakes, silent theatrical films, and exploration and wildlife collections.

Tennessee and Appalachia
East Tennessee State University, Archives of Appalachia
P.O. Box 70295
Johnson City, TN 37614-0138
423-439-4338
http://cass.etsu.edu/archives/

Collection contains an oral history and folklore collection with sound and moving image recordings relating to the cultural, economic, historic, political, and social life of Appalachia.

Utah and the West
University of Utah, Marriott Library,
Audio-Visual Department
Marriott Library
Salt Lake City, UT 84112
801-585-3073
fax: 801-585-3464
http://www.lib.utah.edu/spc/photo/aboutAV.html

Collections cover the visual and aural history of Utah and the Intermountain West. Holdings are strong in Utah pioneer history, the arts, skiing and outdoor recreation, the environment, Native Americans and immigrants, and politics.

West Virginia
West Virginia Division of Culture and History,
Archives Section
The Cultural Center
Capitol Complex
1900 Kanawha Blvd. East
Charleston, WV 25305-0300
304-558-0220
fax: 304-558-2779
http://www.wvculture.org/agency/index.html

Materials include documentaries, home movies, and industrial films relating to West Virginia, as well as several television news collections.

Wisconsin
State Historical Society of Wisconsin, Visual Materials Section
816 State St.
Madison, WI 53706
608-264-6470
fax: 608-264-6472
http://www.shsw.wisc.edu/archives/vismat/index.html
vismat@ccmail.adp.wisc.edu

Holdings relate to the regional social, economic, and political history of Wisconsin and the upper Midwest. Topics of national interest include nineteenth-century expeditionary photography, Native American images, mass communication, and social action movements.

SELECTED SPECIALIZED MOVING IMAGE COLLECTIONS

Andy Warhol Museum: Film and Video Collection
Andy Warhol Museum
117 Sandusky St.
Pittsburgh, PA 15212-5890
412-237-8300
fax: 412-237-8340
http://www.warhol.org/collections/film_video.html

Films and videotapes produced by Andy Warhol.

Black Film Center/Archive Home Page (Indiana University)
Smith Research Center, Suite 180
2805 East 10th St.
Indiana University
Bloomington, Indiana 47408
812-855-6041
fax: 812-856-5832
http://www.indiana.edu/~bfca/
bfca@indiana.edu

Films and related materials by and about African Americans.

DEFA Film Library
University of Massachusetts Amherst, Department of Germanic Languages and Literatures
504 Herter Hall
Box 33925
Amherst, MA 01003-3925
413-545-6681
fax: 413-577-3808
http://www.umass.edu/defa/
defa@german.umass.edu

East German cinema.

Duke University, Special Collections and John Hartman Center for Sales, Advertising, and Marketing History
Rare Book, Manuscript, and Special Collections Library
103 Perkins Library
Durham, NC 27708-0185
919-660-5822
fax: 919-660-5934
http://scriptorium.lib.duke.edu/hartman/
special-collections@duke.edu

History of advertising, including the J. Walter Thompson Company Collection.

Japanese American National Museum
369 East First St.
Los Angeles, CA 90012
213-625-0414
fax: 213-625-1770
http://www.janm.org/

Japanese American life.

Mystic Seaport Museum
75 Greenmanville Ave.
Mystic, CT 06355-0990
860-572-5379
fax: 860-572-5328
http://www.mysticseaport.org/research/nf-index.cfm/

Maritime subjects, scenes, and events.

NASA Johnson Space Center
2101 NASA Rd.
AP42
Houston, TX 77058-3696
281-483-4231
fax: 281-483-2848
http://www.jsc.nasa.gov/

NASA research and development; aeronautics and the human space flight program.

Smithsonian Institution, National Air and Space Museum
Archives Division
MRC-322
NASM
Washington, D.C. 20560
202-357-4721
fax: 202-786-2835
http://www.nasm.edu/nasm/arch/info/filmarchives.htm

Materials relating to aviation and space history.

National Baseball Hall of Fame: Film, Video, and Recorded Sound Department
P.O. Box 590
25 Main St.
Cooperstown, NY 13326-0590
607-547-0333
fax: 607-547-4094
http://www.baseballhalloffame.org/library/fvrs.htm

Hall of Fame induction ceremonies, game broadcasts, documentary productions, and interviews.

The National Center for Jewish Film
Lown Building, Room 102
Waltham, MA 02254
617-899-7044
fax: 617-736-2070
http://www.brandeis.edu/jewishfilm/index.html

Films and videos relating to the Jewish experience.

National Library of Medicine, History of Medicine Division
Building 38, Room 1E-21
8600 Rockville Pike
Bethesda, MD 20894
301-496-5405
fax: 301-496-2809
http://www.nlm.nih.gov/hmd/hmd.html

Films and videotapes regarding medicine, public health, clinical and medical teaching, psychiatry, and mental institutions.

Smithsonian Institution, National Museum of American History Archives Center
AHB C340 MRC 601
12th St. and Constitution Ave. NW
Washington, D.C. 20560
202-357-3270
fax: 202-786-2453
http://americanhistory.si.edu/archives/home.htm
acnmah@sivm.si.edu

Diverse collections including advertising history, the Groucho Marx Collection, World's Fairs, Western Union Collection.

National Museum of the American Indian: Film and Video Center
One Bowling Green
New York, NY 10004
212-825-6894
fax: 212-825-8180
http://www.nmai.si.edu/fv/index.html
fvc@ic.si.edu

Films, video, radio, and electronic media by and about indigenous peoples of North, Central, and South America and Hawaii.

New York Public Library for the Performing Arts
40 Lincoln Center Plaza
New York, NY 10023-7498
212-870-1641
fax: 212-787-1769
http://www.nypl.org/research/lpa/lpa.html
theatrediv@nypl.org

Collection includes Billy Rose Theatre Collection and Theatre on Film and Tape Archives.

New York Public Library, Dance Division
40 Lincoln Center Plaza
New York, NY 10023-7498
212-870-1659
fax: 212-799-7975
http://www.nypl.org/research/lpa/dan/dan.html

Documentation of dance in all forms.

U.S. Holocaust Memorial Museum Film and Video Archive
10 Raoul Wallenberg Place SW, 5th Floor
Washington, D.C. 20024
202-488-6106
fax: 202-488-2690
http://www.ushmm.org/research/collections/filmvideo/
right.htm
research@ushmm.org

Audiovisual records pertaining to the Holocaust and related aspects of World War II.

University of South Carolina, The Newsfilm Archive
1139 Wheat St.
Columbia, SC 29208
803-777-6841
fax: 803-777-4756
http://www.sc.edu/newsfilm/

20th Century Fox Movietone newsreels and outtakes (1919–34).

Schomburg Center for Research in Black Culture, Moving Image and Recorded Sound Division
New York Public Library
515 Malcolm X Boulevard
New York, NY 10037-1801
212-491-2200
fax: 212-491-6761
http://www.nypl.org/research/sc/scl/mirs.html

African American, Caribbean and African popular and traditional music genres; public-affairs television programs.

University of Southern California, Moving Image Archive
University Park
Los Angeles, CA 90089-2211
213-740-3182
fax: 213-740-2920
http://cinema-tv.usc.edu/archives/index.html
filmrequest@cntv.usc.edu

Films and videotapes produced by USC students.

Wayne State University, Walter P. Reuther Library
5401 Cass Ave.
Detroit, MI 48202
313-577-2658
fax: 313-577-8019
http://www.reuther.wayne.edu/AV/av.html

North American Labor, trade unionism, and work life.

ONLINE ARCHIVE

Internet Moving Images Archive
P.O. Box 29244

Presidio of San Francisco
San Francisco, CA 94129-0244
415-561-6767
fax: 415-840-0391
http://www.archive.org/movies/
info@archive.com

Online archive of downloadable film clips.

FILM-RELATED MANUSCRIPT COLLECTIONS

The following collections contain nonfilm materials that are related to the American motion picture industry.

Academy of Motion Picture Arts and Sciences, Margaret Herrick Library
http://www.oscars.org/mhl/

Books, periodicals, screenplays, collection files, posters, photographs, special collections, and oral histories relating to the film industry.

American Film Institute, Louis B. Mayer Library
http://www.afi.com/

Collections include scripts, oral history transcripts, and collections of individuals associated with the film industry.

American Museum of the Moving Image
http://www.ammi.org/

Movie artifacts, props, equipment, sets, ephemera, and costumes.

Brigham Young University, L. Tom Perry Special Collections Library, Arts and Communications Archives
http://sc.lib.byu.edu/

Significant personal manuscript collections including those of directors Cecil B. DeMille and Howard Hawks.

Columbia University, Oral History Research Office
http://www.columbia.edu/cu/lweb/indiv/oral/

Collection includes a series entitled *Hollywood Film Industry,* which contains interviews with actors, directors, cameramen, and technicians recorded in 1971.

Indiana University, Black Film Center/Archive
http://www.indiana.edu/~bfca/

A repository of films and film-related materials by and about African Americans; The collection includes interviews, photos, screenplays, press releases, film advertisements, posters, and newspaper clippings.

Indiana University, Lilly Library
http://www.indiana.edu/~liblilly/overview/film.shtml

Film, radio, and television collections include scripts, lobby cards, press books, and publicity stills.

International Museum of Photography and Film at George Eastman House
http://www.eastman.org/10_colmp/10_index.html

Collection includes posters, star portraits, correspondence, music cue sheets, lobby cards, scripts, precinema materials, and other paper documents.

Library of Congress Manuscript Division
http://www.loc.gov/rr/mss/

Manuscript Division holds records of individuals associated with the film industry, including actors Lillian Gish, Hume Cronyn, and Jessica Tandy.

Museum of Modern Art (MOMA; New York City), Celeste Bartos International Film Study Center & Film Stills Archive
http://www.moma.org/collection/depts/film_media/bartos/index.html

Collections include screenplays and dialogue continuities; extensive files of reviews, articles, and program notes, and film indexes.

New York Public Library for the Performing Arts, Billy Rose Theatre Collection
http://www.nypl.org/research/lpa/the/the.html

Collections include production photographs, publicity portraits, prints, movie stills, film posters, sets, costume and lighting designs, and personal records of individuals involved in the film industry.

University of California Los Angeles, Film and Television Archive
http://www.cinema.ucla.edu/

Records include professional papers of individuals and organizations, lobby cards, scripts, posters, stills, and photographs.

University of Southern California, Cinema-Television Library
http://artscenter.usc.edu/cinematv/index.html

Papers, scripts, and production materials of film industry notables.

TELEVISION ARCHIVES

Television was for many years a poor relation in the field of film preservation, but as television has emerged as a significant field of study, so too have television archives. Distinctions between film, video, and television are becoming less distinct each year, meaning that most film archives have become instead moving image archives, collecting regardless of for-mat or medium. While the majority of the previously listed film archives have selective television programs in their collections, there are a number of American archives that specialize in television programming.

The sources for collections of television programming include networks, local stations, production companies, and on a few occasions, shows are taped off-air by the archives themselves. In some cases this means that virtually the entire output of a network is available, but frequently only selective representative episodes of series are kept. Early television broadcasts are especially rare commodities, as so many of the shows were produced live and not recorded aside from occasional kinescope (film) prints.

In North America, many television archives are members of Association of Moving Image Archivists (AMIA), but the overseeing international organization for television archives is the FIAT/IFTA, the International Federation of Television Archives, Web site at http://fiatifta.org/index.html. FIAT membership is not limited to archives, but also includes television networks and commercial vendors.

Television Collections

The Cable Center
Barco Library
2000 Buchtel Blvd.
Denver, CO 80210
303-871-4885
http://www.cablecenter.org/
libraryinfo@cablecenter.org

At present, the collections do not include significant amounts of programming, but do contain materials relating to cable television and telecommunications through manuscript collections, oral histories, documents, photographs, and equipment.

Library of Congress
See Motion Pictures entry for contact information.
http://lcweb.loc.gov/rr/mopic/tvcoll.html

Collections include the National Broadcasting Company (NBC) television collection (1948–77), National Educational Television Programs (NET), Public Broadcasting Service (PBS) collection, television news, as well as off-air taping and copyright deposits.

Publications include *Three Decades of Television: A Catalog of Television Programs Acquired by the Library of Congress, 1949–79*, compiled by Sarah Rouse and Katherine Loughney in 1989 (Washington, D.C.: Library of Congress, 1989, now out of print). The catalog is a complete list of holdings through

1979, excluding commercials and news programs. The nearly 20,000 entries provide synopses of fiction and nonfiction programs, genre and broad subject terms, cast and production credits, and copyright and telecast information.

Chicago Cultural Center, Museum of Broadcast Communications
78 East Washington St.
Chicago, IL 60602
312-629-6000
fax: 312-629-6009
http://www.Museum.TV/
archives@museum.tv

The museum contains a collection of more than 13,000 television programs, 4,000 radio programs, 11,000 television commercials, and 4,500 newscasts that is open to the public. The collection has a searchable database on its Web site.

Museum of Television and Radio
25 West 52nd St.
New York, NY 10019-6101
212-621-6800
fax: 212-621-6700
  also:

465 North Beverly Drive
Beverly Hills, CA 90210
310-786-1000
http://www.mtr.org/

Visitors to the museum may search its collections of television and radio shows using its programming database and view or listen to shows in a separate console room. In addition, researchers may search the museum's microfiche clippings file and collection of television and radio programs in the Scholars' Room in both New York and Los Angeles locations. These research facilities have carrels equipped with an audio/visual monitor for viewing and listening to the museum's collection of programs and a computer that accesses the library's card catalog.

National Jewish Archive of Broadcasting
1109 Fifth Ave.
New York, NY 10023
212-399-3382
fax: 212-410-3855
http://www.jewishmuseum.org/Pages/Programs_Media/progmedia_broadcast.html

Museum holds television and radio programs pertaining to the Jewish culture.

University of Oklahoma, Julian P. Canter Political Commercial Archive
Department of Communication, Room 113
610 Elm Ave.
Norman, OK 73019
405-325-3114
fax: 405-325-1566
http://www.ou.edu/pccenter/

Facility provides a comprehensive collection of U.S. political television commercials from 1950 to the present.

Purdue University, Public Affairs Video Archives (C-SPAN)
1000 Liberal Arts and Education Building
West Lafayette, IN 47907-1000
317-494-5000
fax: 317-494-3421
http://pava.purdue.edu
info@pava.purdue.edu

Archive records are of complete broadcasts of C-SPAN and C-SPAN 2 off-air.

San Francisco State University, San Francisco Bay Area Television Archives
1630 Holloway Ave.
San Francisco, CA 94132
415-338-1856
fax: 415-338-1504
http://www.library.sfsu.edu/special/sfbata.html

Archive houses local news and documentaries from the Bay Area.

University of Georgia, Media Archive and Peabody Award Collection
Main Library
Athens, GA 30602
706-542-1971
fax: 706-542-4144
http://www.libs.uga.edu/media/mediarch.html

Collection archives annual Peabody Awards entries.

Vanderbilt University, Television News Archive
110 21st Ave. South
Suite 704
Nashville, TN 37203
615-322-2927
fax: 615-343-8250
http://tvnews.vanderbilt.edu/
tvnews@tvnews.vanderbilt.edu

A collection of network evening news broadcasts taped off-air since 1968.

University of Maryland, Library of American Broadcasting and National Public Broadcasting Archives

Hornbake Library
College Park, MD 20742
301-405-9255
301-405-9160
fax: 301-314-2634
http://www.lib.umd.edu/NPBA/ (National Public Broadcasting Archives)

http://www.lib.umd.edu/LAB/ (Library of American Broadcasting)

The Library of American Broadcasting collection includes audio and video recordings, publications, personal collections, oral histories, photographs, scripts, and vertical files related to the history of broadcasting. The National Public Broadcasting Archives contains records of American noncommercial broadcasting organizations as well as selected audio and video programming from national networks (NAEB, NPR, CPB/Annenberg) and Washington-area stations (WETA, WAMU-FM, and Maryland Public Television). Also available are oral history tapes and transcripts from the NPR Oral History Project.

RECORDED SOUND ARCHIVES

Recorded sound is a hybrid category of several genres of media. Music collections will not be considered here, but frequently sound collections such as spoken-word recordings are subcategories contained within larger musical archives. Radio shows are also frequently attached to television under the larger category of broadcasting.

The primary North American professional organization for recorded sound archives is the Association for Recorded Sound Collections (ARSC), Web site at http://www.arsc-audio.org/. ARSC runs a recorded-sound discussion list at http://www.arsc-audio.org/arsclist.html. Internationally, the leading organization is the International Association of Sound and Audiovisual Archives (IASA), Web site at http://www.iasa-web.org/.

Recorded Sound Collections

Syracuse University, Belfer Audio Laboratory & Archive
Syracuse University Library
Syracuse, NY 13244
315-443-3477
fax: 315-443-2697
http://libwww.syr.edu/information/belfer/index.html

Collections include more than 300,000 recordings in all formats, including cylinders, discs, and magnetic tapes. Primarily a musical collection, the archive also includes early radio broadcasts and spoken-word recordings by luminaries such as Amelia Earhart, Thomas Edison, Albert Einstein, Lenin, and Oscar Wilde.

Library of Congress, Recorded Sound Reference Center
LM113
101 Independence Ave. SE
Washington, D.C. 20540-4690
202-707-7833
http://lcweb.loc.gov/rr/record/
rsrc@loc.gov

Collections include:

- National Broadcasting Company (NBC) Radio Collection. 150,000 16-inch lacquer discs from the 1930s through the 1980s, including tens of thousands of broadcasts related to World War II
- Armed Forces Radio and Television Service (AFRTS). 300,000 12- and 16-inch discs from1942 to 1998
- Office of War Information (OWI). More than 50,000 instantaneous lacquer discs from 1942 to 1945
- National Public Radio (NPR). The cultural programming portions of NPR broadcasts, 27,000 tapes from 1971 to 1992
- Voice of America (VOA). More than 50,000 discs and tapes of musical-event broadcasts dating from 1946 to 1988
- WOR-AM Collection. Flagship station of the Mutual Broadcasting Network located in New York City; includes several thousand 16-inch instantaneous transcription discs, the paper archives of WOR, as well as an outstanding group of materials relating to the radio career of Phillips H. Lord
- Archive of Recorded Poetry and Literature. Several thousand recordings of notable authors reading their own works in the recording studios and Coolidge Auditorium of the Library of Congress

University of Missouri-Kansas City, Marr Sound Archives
Miller Nichols Library
5100 Rockhill Rd.
Kansas City, MO 64110
816-235-1534
fax: 816-333-5584
http://www.umkc.edu/lib/spec-col/marr.html

The archives holds nearly 250,000 sound recordings including LPs, 78s, 45s, cylinders, transcription discs, instantaneous cut discs, and open-reel tapes. Holdings include historic voices, radio programs, and authors reading their own works.

National Archives
See contact info in Moving Image section.
http://www.archives.gov/research_room/media_formats/fil
m_sound_video.html
http://mopix@nara.gov/ (Motion Picture, Sound, and
Video unit reference staff)

Collections include 90,000 spoken-word recordings, primarily from agencies of the U.S. government but also from private, commercial, and foreign sources. Collections date from 1896 and include recordings of performances of the Federal Theater and Music Projects of the Works Progress Administration, press conferences, panel discussions, interviews, and speeches promoting and explaining policies and programs of some 75 federal agencies. Additional recordings include World War II propaganda broadcasts in German, Japanese, and Italian and American propaganda broadcasts and news coverage of war campaigns. Other recordings include oral arguments before the U.S. Supreme Court during the 1955–74 sessions, entertainment broadcasts, documentaries and dramas relating to U.S. history, proceedings of political conventions, campaign speeches, and extensive news coverage.

Online Finding Aids and Indexes

Captured German Sound Recordings
Finding aid at: http://www.archives.gov/research_room/
research_topics/captured_german_sound_recordings.html

Voices of World War II, 1937–45
Finding aid at: http://www.archives.gov/research_room/
research_topics/voices_of_world_war_2.html

The Crucial Decade: Voices of the Postwar Era,1945–54
Finding aid at: http://www.archives.gov/research_room/
research_topics/voices_of_postwar.html

Nixon White House Tapes
http://www.archives.gov/nixon/tapes/tapes.html

Stanford University, Stanford Archive of Recorded Sound
Braun Music Center
Stanford, CA 94305-3076
650-723-9312
fax: 650-725-1145
http://garamond.stanford.edu/depts/ars/

Recordings include the speeches of Churchill, Kennedy, and Paderewski, the Pryor Collection of late 1930s and early 1940s radio broadcasts, Project South (interviews with participants in the Civil Rights movement of the 1960s), the Djerassi Foundation tape archives, and the C. E. Morse (One Man's Family) archives.

Michigan State University, Vincent Voice Library
100 Library
East Lansing, MI 48824
517-355-5122
http://www.lib.msu.edu/vincent/

Currently in progress is the online National Gallery of the Spoken Word, a collection of twentieth-century recordings including a variety of interests and topics such as Thomas Edison's first cylinder recordings, the voices of Babe Ruth and Florence Nightingale, and Studs Terkel's timeless interviews.

ORAL HISTORY

One of the most common types of sound recordings held in archival collections is the oral history interview. In the vast majority of cases, oral history tapes are held by oral history divisions or departments of universities or other institutions. It creates a unique situation in which the archive is also the primary producer of the archival holdings.

While databases such as RLIN and NUCMC do include some oral history collections, as with most endeavors, oral history research is increasingly Internet-oriented. The last published directory was 1990's *Oral History Index : An International Directory of Oral History Interviews,* compiled by Ellen S. Wasserman (Westport, Conn.: Meckler Media Corp., 1990). Interviews here are listed alphabetically by interviewee's name. There is no subject index, but the book does contain a directory of oral history collections. Previous to that was the *Directory of Oral History Collections* by Allen Smith (Phoenix, Ariz.: Oryx Press, 1988). This helpful, though dated, directory includes listings for 476 U.S. collections including a subject index, contact information, collection size, conditions of access, catalog, and purpose. This in turn superseded *Oral History Collections,* which was compiled and edited by Alan M. Meckler and Ruth McMullin (New York: R. R. Bowker, 1975).

The central worldwide professional association for oral historians is the International Oral History Association, Web site at http://www.ioha.fgv.br/. In the United States, however, the leading organization is the Oral History Association, Web site at http://www. dickinson.edu/oha/. In addition to this national association, there are numerous regional groups, including the Michigan Oral History Association (MOHA), the New England Association of Oral History (NEAOH), the Northwest Oral History Association (NOHA), the Southwest Oral History Association (SOHA), and the Texas Oral History Association (TOHA). The Oral History Association's Journal, *Oral History Review* (Berkeley: University of California Press), is another source for locating oral history projects.

Another especially useful resource is the OHA's H-Oralhist listserv. This list's homepage at http://www2.h-net.msu.edu/~oralhist/ includes an annotated list of links to oral history centers and collections, as well as an index of sites arranged by subject and a list of online oral history projects with downloadable sound files.

Oral History Archives

Baylor University, Institute for Oral History
Carroll Library, Suite 306
P.O. Box 97271
Waco, TX 76798-7271
254-710-3437
fax: 254-710-1571
http://www3.baylor.edu/Oral_History/

Topics include rural life, Texas Baptists, the economic history of Texas.

California State University, Oral History Program
Long Beach History Department
FO2-113
1250 Bellflower Blvd.
Long Beach, CA 90840
562-985-5428
fax: 562-985-5431
http://www.csulb.edu/depts/history/relprm/oral03.html

Collections include arts in southern California, Asian and Asian American history, and Chicano and Mexican American history.

Center for Documentary Studies
Duke University
1317 W. Pettigrew St.
Durham, NC 27707
919-660-3651
fax: 919-681-7600
http://cds.aas.duke.edu/

Behind the Veil: Documenting African American Life in the Jim Crow South. This collection includes more than 1,200 oral history interviews.

Claremont Graduate University, History Department
Oral History Program
710 North College Avenue
Claremont, CA 91711
909-621-8172

fax: 909-621-8609
http://www.cgu.edu/hum/his/oralhis/index.htm

Special collections include missionaries in China, Pomona College Oriental Study Expedition, and women's educational politics.

Columbia University, Oral History Research Office
801 Butler Library, Box 20
535 W. 114th St., MC 1129
New York, NY 10027
212-854-7083
fax: 212-854-9099
http://www.columbia.edu/cu/lweb/indiv/oral/
oralhist@libraries.cul.columbia.edu

Special interests include American craftspeople, Argentina, African American journalists, Chinese oral history, the Eisenhower administration, U.S. Marine Corps, Naval history, physicians and AIDS, social security, and student movements of the 1960s.

Yale University, Fortunoff Video Archive for Holocaust Testimonies
Sterling Memorial Libraries
P.O. Box 208240
120 High St., Room 331C
New Haven, CT 06520-8240
203-432-1879
fax: 203-432-1879
http://www.library.yale.edu/testimonies/

A collection of more than 4,200 videotaped interviews of Holocaust witnesses and survivors (1979–81).

Indiana University, The Center for the Study of History and Memory
Ashton-Aley 264
Bloomington, IN 47405
(812) 855-2856
http://www.indiana.edu/~ohrc/
ohrc@indiana.edu

Collections include Indiana history, American foundations, Studebaker Company, village mothers.

Institute of Oral History at the University of Texas at El Paso
Liberal Arts Building, Room 334
El Paso, TX 79968-0532
915-747-7052
fax: 915-747-5948
http://dmc.utep.edu/oralh/OralHistory.html

Special projects include the Mexican Revolution of 1910, Big Bend National Park, United States and Mexico border history

Smithsonian Institution, National Air and Space Museum
Oral History Project
Archives Division
National Air and Space Museum
MRC 322
7th and Independence Ave. SW
Washington, DC 20560
202-357-3133
fax: 202-786-2835
http://www.nasm.edu/nasm/dsh/oralhistory.html
reference.desk@nasm.si.edu (note: contact by E-mail first
for current mailing address and phone number)

Development of aeronautics, NASA, and the space
sciences.

Northeast Archives of Folklore and Oral History
Maine Folklife Center
5773 South Stevens Hall
University of Maine
Orono, ME 04469-5773
207-581-1891
fax: 207-581-1823
http://www.umaine.edu/folklife/
folklife@maine.edu

Folklife in Maine and eastern Canada.

Oral History American Music
Yale School of Music and Library
P.O. Box 208246
New Haven, CT 06520-8246
203-432-1988
fax: 203-432-1989
http://www.yale.edu/oham/

Collections of major figures in American music.

Smithsonian Institution, Oral History Collection
Institutional History Division
Smithsonian Institution Archives
P.O. Box 37012
Arts and Industries Building, Room 2135, MRC 414
Washington, D.C. 20013-7012
202-357-1420
fax: 202-357-2395
http://www.si.edu/archives/ihd/ihda.htm
SIHistory@osia.si.edu

Current and retired Smithsonian staff and others who
have made significant contributions to the institution.

University of North Carolina, Southern Oral History Program
CB# 3195
406 Hamilton Hall
University of North Carolina
Chapel Hill, NC 27599-3195
919-962-0455

fax: 919-962-1403
http://www.sohp.org/
sohp_info@sohp.org

Special projects include southern politics, rural
electrification, southern women, Piedmont industrial-
ization, southern communities, African American
high school principals, foundation history, the press
and the Civil Rights movement, African American life
and culture.

Survivors of the Shoah Visual History Foundation
Coordinator, Archival Access
P.O. Box 3168
Los Angeles, CA 90078-3168
818.777.7802
fax: 818-733-0312
http://www.vhf.org/

Videotapes of 50,000 testimonies of Holocaust survivors and witnesses

Louisiana State University, The T. Harry Williams Center
for Oral History
Agnes Morris House
Baton Rouge, LA 70803
225-578-7439
http://www.lib.lsu.edu/special/williams/

Collections include Louisiana storytelling, Acadian
Handicraft Project Series, Americans in Vietnam, civil
rights, history of education.

UCLA Oral History Program
A253 Bunche Hall
Box 951575
Los Angeles, CA 90095-1575
310-825-4932
fax: 310-206-2796
http://www.library.ucla.edu/libraries/special/ohp/
ohpindex.htm
oral-history@library.ucla.edu

A complete listing of interviews is contained in *The
UCLA Oral History Program: Catalog of the Collec-
tion*, 3rd ed., compiled by Teresa Barnett (Los Ange-
les, Calif.: Oral History Program, Department of
Special Collections, 1999). Collections include
African American artists and leaders of Los Angeles,
Frank Lloyd Wright, Los Angeles art community, bio-
medical scientists, California state government.

United States Holocaust Memorial Museum
Oral History
100 Raoul Wallenberg Place, SW
Washington, D.C. 20024-2126
202-488-6103

http://www.ushmm.org/
oralhistory@ushmm.org

7,000 audio and video interviews of Holocaust survivors and witnesses.

University of California at Berkeley,
Regional Oral History Office
486 The Bancroft Library #6000
Berkeley, CA 94720-6000
510-642-7395
fax: 510-642-7589
http://bancroft.berkeley.edu/ROHO/
roho@library.berkeley.edu

Research material includes twentieth-century Western mining, the California wine industry, women political leaders of California, California's political history, suffragists, the AIDS epidemic in San Francisco, earthquake engineering, health maintenance organizations, California's legal history, the Sierra Club, water resources, sanitary engineering, disability rights and independent living movements.

University of Connecticut at Storrs, Center for
Oral History
Thomas J. Dodd Center
405 Babbidge Road, Unit 1205
Storrs, CT 06269-1205
860-486-5245
fax: 860-486-4582
http://www.oralhistory.uconn.edu/

Connecticut history, World War II, African National Congress, and the Nuremberg war crimes trials.

University of Florida Libraries, Samuel Proctor Oral History Program
P.O. Box 115215
4103 Turlington Hall
Gainesville, FL 32611-5215
352-392-7168
fax: 352-846-1983
http://www.history.ufl.edu/oral/

Native Americans, civil rights activities in St. Augustine, women in Florida, pioneer settlers, Florida's education system, and the citrus industry.

University of Hawai'i, Center for Oral History
Social Science Research Institute
University of Hawai'i at Manoa
2424 Maile Way
Saunders Hall 724
Honolulu, HI 96822
808-956-6259
fax: 808-956-2884
http://www.oralhistory.hawaii.edu/

Collections include Hawaiian history and ethnic groups.

University of Kentucky, Oral History Program
Special Collections and Archives
University of Kentucky Libraries
Lexington, KY 40506
606-257-2651
606-257-8634
http://www.uky.edu/Libraries/Special/oral_history/

Collections include Frontier Nursing Service, Robert Penn Warren, and Appalachia.

University of South Dakota, South Dakota Oral History Center
Institute of American Indian Studies
414 East Clark St.
Vermillion, SD 57069
605-677-5011
877-COYOTES
http://www.usd.edu/iais/oralhist/index.html
iais@usd.edu

Collections include Native American history and South Dakota history.

University of Southern Mississippi, Center for Oral History & Cultural Heritage
College Hall, Room 112
Box 5715
Hattiesburg, MS 39406-5175
601-266-4574
fax: 601-266-6217
http://www.dept.usm.edu/~ocach/

Collections include Mississippi's history, Hurricane Camille, gay and lesbian life, Gulf Coast history, prisoners of war.

BIBLIOGRAPHY

Cherchi-Usai, Paolo. *Silent Cinema: An Introduction.* London: British Film Institute, 2000.

Footage: The Worldwide Moving Image Sourcebook. New York: Second Line Search, 1997.

Houston, Penelope. *Keepers of the Frame.* London: British Film Institute, 1994.

Kirchner, Daniela, ed. *Film and Television Collections in Europe.* London: Blueprint, 1995.

Klaue, Wolfgang, ed. *World Directory of Moving Image and Sound Archives.* München, Germany: K. G. Saur, 1993.

Meckler, Alan M., comp., and Ruth McMullin, ed. *Oral History Collections.* New York: R. R. Bowker, 1975.

Morgan, Jenny, comp. *Film Researcher's Handbook: A Guide to Sources in North America, South America, Asia, Australasia and Africa.* New York: Routledge, 1996.

Slide, Anthony. *Nitrate Won't Wait: A History of Film Preservation in the United States.* Jefferson, N.C.: McFarland & Company, 1992.

Smith, Allen. *Directory of Oral History Collections.* Phoenix, Ariz.: Oryx Press, 1988.

Thorpe, Frances, ed. *International Directory of Film and TV Documentation Centres.* 3rd edition. Chicago, Ill.: St. James Press, 1988.

Wasserman Ellen S., comp. *Oral History Index: An International Directory of Oral History Interviews.* Westport, Conn.: Meckler Media Corp., 1990.

CHAPTER 7
Fine Arts Archives
Tammi Moe

INTRODUCTION

Scholarly pursuits in the field of fine arts are undertaken for various reasons. The common thread is the interest in the creative, imaginative, and aesthetic impulses manifested by human beings. Discovering relationships and securing relevant meaning between the various forms of fine art crosses disciplines and cultural boundaries. The resources available are sometimes so large that the researcher is lost in the possibilities. To add to the complexity, the locations of those resources are widespread and not always easily accessible. The fine art object extends beyond a specific institutional boundary and can be housed in library special collections, museum archives, academic archives, cultural institutions, and research centers. There are many ways to access different types of information using bibliographies, periodical and newspaper indexes, exhibition catalogs, collections of art criticism, auction records, museum directories, monographic studies, publications on wartime activities of dealers and collectors, art schools, artists' cooperatives, and art organizations. The Library of Congress classifies private art collections under N 5200—5299. The level of research being conducted will dictate the appropriate avenues to pursue. Inherent in the world of fine arts is the decentralized location of individual pieces of artwork, so comprehensive coverage is not always possible and requires the use of two or more collections. This can also be problematic when it comes to locating primary sources. The historical organization of Western art is commonly arranged into five periods: antiquity, the Middle Ages, Renaissance, baroque, modern, and post-modern. Eastern art movements are generally organized by dynasty, philosophy,

and religion. Each era is then subdivided into more specific classifications reflecting geography, politics, and common aesthetics. The organization of this chapter will reflect these determinants. While the chapter in no way represents a complete list of primary source material, it is a guide to the most prominent and accessible archival collections. Larger collections, such as the Archives of American Art, will appear in multiple places according to subject. This will help guide the researcher to the appropriate collection when there are hundreds available.

COMPREHENSIVE COLLECTIONS
The Archives of American Art

The Archives of American Art houses the world's largest collection of primary source documentation of the visual arts in America with 5,000 collections and approximately 14 million items. The largest collection is the Carnegie Institute Museum of Art records, which contain international correspondence and exhibition documentation of contemporary paintings traveling through the Pittsburgh museum. The archive also collects the records of the American Art Association, Art Students League, American Academy in Rome, Pennsylvania Academy of Fine Arts, National Academy of Design, National Arts Club, Print Council of America, National Watercolor Society, and several auction houses in the United States. The documentation dates span a period of time from the mid-eighteenth century to the present.

Notable artists within the collection include Ansel Adams, Dankmar Adler, Abbott Handerson Thayer, Joseph Albers, Keith Haring, David Hockney, Alexander Lieberman, Jackson Pollock, Gifford Beal, Thomas Pollock Anshutz, Edward Hicks, Winslow Homer, Georgia O'Keeffe, Mark Rothko, Robert Motherwell, George Mueller, Erwin Panofsky, Maxfield Parrish, Lilla Cabot Perry, Alexander Calder, Mary Cassatt, George Catlin, Salvador Dali, Marcel Duchamp, and thousands of others. *(Adapted from the Archives of American Art Web site, 2002.)*

The collections are indexed alphabetically and can be accessed online at http://archivesofamericanart. si.edu/collectn.htm. Copies of the archive's finding aids can be requested from the AAA reference staff at http://archivesofamericanart.si.edu/askus.htm.

The Research Library Group Union Catalog for cultural materials also contains the AAA finding aids but requires a subscription to the site. The Smithsonian Institution Research Information System provides access to all available online resources at http://www. siris.si.edu/.

Archives of American Art, Washington, D.C.
750 9th St. N.W.
Suite 2200
Washington, D.C.
Mailing: Reference Services /ILL
Archives of American Art
Smithsonian Institution
P.O. Box 37012
Victor Building, Room 2200, MRC 937
Washington, D.C. 20013-7012
(202) 275-1961
Access: Microfilm Reference Room does not require an appointment. Monday through Friday 9:00 A.M. to 5:00 P.M. Use of oral history tapes and transcripts requires an appointment. Manuscript Reading Room requires an appointment. Monday through Friday 9:30 A.M. to 12:00 P.M. and 1:00 to 4:30.

Archives of American Art, New York City
1285 Avenue of the Americas (Located between 51st and 52nd Streets.)
Lobby Level
New York, NY 10019
(212) 399-5015
Fax: (212) 307-4501
Access: No appointment required, but calling ahead recommended. Monday through Friday 9:30 A.M. to 5:00 P.M.
yeckleyk@aaany.si.edu

Archives of American Art, California
Huntington Library
1151 Oxford Rd.
San Marino, CA 91108
(626) 583-7847
Fax: (626) 583-7207
Access: Appointment required. Monday through Friday 9:00 to 12:00 and 1:00 to 5:00 P.M.
aaawcrc@aaa.si.edu
http://archivesofamericanart.si.edu/

Bibliothèque nationale de France

The Prints and Photograph collections contain over 15 million items. Artists of note are Rembrandt, Toulouse-Lautrec, and Clouet, plus 40,000 prints by over 3,000 artists. The photo archive contains Nadar, Eugene Atger, Reutligen, and Victor Hugo. *(Adapted from the French National Library, 2002.)*

Richelieu site—Prints Department
58, Rue de Richelieu
75002 Paris
33(0)1 53 79 59 59
Access: http://www.bnf.fr/pages/zNavigat/frame/pratic.htm
http://www.bnf.fr/
http://www.bnf.fr/site_bnf_eng/index.html (English version)

The British Library

Extensive collections include all world languages and cover all disciplines. The collection dates from 1753 forward. The music collection holds over a million discs, 185,000 tapes, and other music-related elements from around the world that span the entire history of recorded sound. *(Adapted from the British Library Web site, 2002.)*

Rare Books and Music Reading Room
96 Euston Road
London NW1 2DB
+44 (0)20 7412 7676 (Rare Books)
+44 (0)20 7412 7772 (Music)
Fax: +44 (0)20 7412 7609
Access: Limited to approved researchers. Appointment required. Monday 10:00 to 4:00. Tuesday through Thursday 9:30 to 8:00. Friday through Saturday 9:30 to 5:00.
Online Manuscript Catalog http://molcat.bl.uk/
rare-books@bl.uk
music-collections@bl.uk
http://www.bl.uk/services/reading/collection.html

Columbia University

Rare Book and Manuscript Library
Columbia University

Contains oral histories of prominent figures in twentieth-century art, such as Tibor De Nagy and David M. Solinger; art collectors; and historians. Emphasis is on the Arts and Crafts movement, with several artisans involved in metal work, textiles, glass, ceramics, and wood. Also houses collections for research into music and theater in the late nineteenth and early twentieth centuries. Notable artists within the collection: David Tisdale, Will Barnet, Max Weber, George Segal, Louise Nevelson, Kenyon Cox, William Zorach, Louis Corinth, Rockwell Kent, Alfred Stieglitz, Pablo Picasso, Diego Rivera, Paul Guillaume, Marius de Zayas, Andre Racz, Alice Neel, Ben Shahn, Edwin Walter Dickinson, Jack Levine, Leon Krull, Robert Indiana, William Zorach, and Roland Rood. *(Adapted from the Columbia University Web site, 2002.)*

Comprehensive list of Columbia Libraries
http://www.columbia.edu/cu/lweb/indiv/locations.html

Access: Reading Room use requires an appointment.
Hours for the different libraries vary.
rarebooks@libraries.cul.columbia.edu
http://www.columbia.edu/cu/lweb/indiv/rare/guides/

Butler Library, 6th Floor East
535 W. 114th Street
New York, NY 10027
(212) 854-5153
Fax: (212) 854-1365

Avery Architectural and Fine Arts Library
300 Avery
1172 Amsterdam Ave.
New York, NY 10027
(212) 854-3501
Avery@libraries.cul.columbia.edu

The Getty Research Institute

The Getty Research Institute states that the goals and mission of the institution are to promote scholarship in the arts by providing both on-site and remote access to an extensive collection of primary and secondary source material in the arts. The special collection houses rare and unique materials that enable scholars and other advanced researchers to conduct primary research in all fields relevant to the visual arts. The finding aids are available online and provide detailed access to archival papers, collections of rare photographs, prints, and architectural drawings.

Getty Fine Arts Databases

The Getty Provenance Index Online Searchable Databases consist of several databases regarding the history and provenance of individual works of art.

The focus is predominantly European paintings between the sixteenth and nineteenth centuries. The Archival Documents database offers descriptive information about archival documents inventorying French, Netherlandish, and Spanish art collections. The Inventory Contents contains item level description of individual works of art in the Archival Documentation database. The Sale Catalogues contain information from auction records of nineteenth-century Belgian, British, French, and Netherlandish art sales and seventeenth- and eighteenth-century German art sales. The Sales Contents database provides item level description of paintings from the auction catalogs database. The Public Collections database contains information about individual paintings from a selection of American and British public collections. The Provenance of Paintings contains the provenance of a portion of the paintings in the Public Collections database. The Vocabulary Databases contain the Art and Architecture Thesaurus, the Union List of Artists Names, and the Getty Thesaurus of Geographic Names.

Getty Special Collection Finding Aids

The collections are extensive, and providing individual reference to each piece would require a much larger publication. Some of the more notable collections within the research center cover areas related to experiments in art and technology, prominent art galleries and art collectors in the nineteenth and twentieth centuries, British museums and art institutes, Phaidon publishing, writings of prominent art historians and art critics, Medieval art, the Bauhaus, Russian Constructivism, the Dadaist movement, Lettrism, Surrealism, Futurism, the Avant-garde movement in Germany, Abstract Expressionism, Minimal and Conceptual art, Mail art, Concrete and Sound Poetry, and Mexican religious engraving. Artists within the collection include but are not limited to: Douglas Cooper, Boccioni, Della Bella, Marcel Duchamp, Hans Richter, Josef Franz Maria Hoffmann, Rauschenberg, Gavarni and Grandville, Max Ernst, Bontempelli, Ian Hamilton Finlay, Malvina Hoffman, Romeyn De Hooghe, Robert Irwin, Philip Johnson, Wassily Kandinsky, Allan Kaprow, Jean Le Pautre, Filippo Thomaso Marinetti, Benedetta Cappa Marinetti, Jean Pillement, the Gentili family, Jose Guadalupe Posada, Man Ray, and Frank Lloyd Wright. *(Adapted from the Getty Research Center Web site, 2002.)*

1200 Getty Center Drive, Suite 1100
Los Angeles, CA. 90049-1688
(310) 440-7390
Access: The Reading Room is available by appointment only Monday through Saturday 9:00 A.M. to 6:00 P.M. Finding aids for most collections are available. The institute is closed all major U.S. holidays. The Getty Integrated Catalog (GIC) provides online access to all the research libraries' resources, including the special collection's finding aids, at http://www.getty.edu/research/tools/gic/.
http://www.getty.edu/research/library/reference_form.html
www.getty.edu/research/library/

Harvard—Special Collections

For a comprehensive list of all Harvard libraries and archives, refer to the Hollis catalog at http://lib.harvard.edu/libraries/listings_alpha.html. The Houghton Library houses collections that focus on the study of Western civilization. The Rare Books department has 500,000 printed books, including nearly 2,600 books from the fifteenth century with several different subjects, including music. The Manuscripts department administers a diverse collection of over 10 million manuscripts dating from 3000 B.C.E. to the present. Collections subjects include illuminated manuscripts; music; Arabic, Persian, and Syriac manuscripts; photographs; drawings; and paintings. *(Adapted from the Houghton Library Web site, 2002.)*

Houghton Library of the Harvard College Library
Harvard University
Cambridge, MA 02138
(617) 495-2441
(617) 495-2449 (Department of Manuscripts)
Fax: (617) 495-1376
Access: Access to rare books and manuscripts is predominantly handled in the Harvard Reading Rooms. A limited number of archival holdings have been cataloged into HOLLIS, the Harvard online catalog. The Houghton Library is open to everyone regardless of academic affiliation Monday through Friday 9:00 A.M. to 5:00 P.M. and Saturday 9:00 A.M. to 1:00 P.M. A growing number of finding aids are available online using the Online Archival Search Information System, at http://oasis.harvard.edu/.
houghref@fas.harvard.edu
Houghton_Manuscripts@harvard.edu
http://hcl.harvard.edu/houghton/

The Fine Arts Library—Harvard

The Fine Arts Library has a comprehensive collection of both Western and non-Western art and archi-tecture spanning antiquity to the present. The library contains extensive holdings in the fields of master drawings, Italian primitives, Romanesque sculpture, Renaissance painting, French Impressionism, German Expressionism, and Islamic and Asian art. A major collection of auction-sale catalogs, large holdings of exhibition catalogs, the literature of conservation and technical study of works of art, history of photography, Russian and East European art history, and Islamic art and architecture adds to the strength of the library's resources. *(Adapted from the Fine Arts Library Web site, 2002.)*

Fine Arts Library
Harvard University
32 Quincy Street
Cambridge, MA 02138
(617) 495-3374
Fax: (617) 496-4889
Access: Access to the collections is granted through an application process. The hours change with the academic semesters. During active Sessions: Monday through Thursday 9:00 A.M. to 10:00 P.M. Friday 9:00 A.M. to 6:00 P.M. Saturday 10:00 A.M. to 5:00 P.M. Sunday 1:00 P.M. to 6:00 P.M. Intersessions: Monday through Friday 9:00 A.M. to 5:00 P.M. Closed Saturday and Sunday.
mailto:falibref@fas.harvard.edu
http://hcl.harvard.edu/finearts/

The Ruebel Asiatic Research Collection—Harvard

The Ruebel collection is one of the leading unified collections of Asian Art within the United States. The collection focuses on the art of East Asia, Central Asia, Southeast Asia, and India. The holdings include books, periodicals, offprints of rare and important articles, maps, rubbings of inscriptions from stone monuments, reproductions of Chinese and Japanese scroll paintings, auction and exhibit catalogs, and manuscripts. Strengths of the collection are Chinese ritual bronzes, Buddhist arts, Chinese and Japanese painting, Japanese woodblock prints, and East Asian ceramics. Languages include Chinese, Japanese, Korean, English, and Western European languages. *(Adapted from the Fine Arts Library Web site, 2002.)*

The Harvard University Art Museums
32 Quincy Street
Cambridge, MA 02138 (Within the Sackler Museum at the Corner of Quincy and Broadway.)
(617) 495-0570

Access: Monday through Thursday 9:00 A.M. to 10:00 P.M. Friday 9:00 A.M. to 6:00 P.M. Saturday 10:00 A.M. to 5:00 P.M. Closed Sunday.

Intersession: Monday through Friday 9:00 A.M. to 5:00 P.M. The entire Asiatic collection can be searched online via Hollis, at http://hcl.harvard.edu/ois/services/pubs/ils/hrefguide.html.
mailto:rubelcol@fas.harvard.edu
http://hcl.harvard.edu/finearts/rubel.html

The Harvard Semitic Museum Photographic Archives—Harvard

Developed between 1891 and 1992, this is one of the world's most important collections of historical Middle Eastern photographs. The archive's contents number approximately 38,000 images in a wide range of formats. Several archives with extensive visual documentation of Middle Eastern culture, architecture, and art exist within the photographic archive. The Edgar J. Fisher Archive documents Istanbul in the late nineteenth and early twentieth century. The Karl S. Twitchell Archive documents Yemen and Saudi Arabia in the early twentieth century. Baroness Marie-Thérèse Ullens de Schooten Archive documents ancient sites, Islamic architecture, and the landscape and ethnography of Iran and the Sufis. The Abdul Hamid Albums document the Ottoman Empire. *(Adapted from the Fine Arts Library Web site, 2002.)*

Harvard University
32 Quincy Street
Cambridge, MA 02138
(617) 495-3372
Fax: (617) 496-4889
Access: Resides within a locked space in the visual collection and is accessible to anyone with scholarly interests. Primary access is through an inventory report with accompanying photographer and country indexes. Several surrogate records allow preview access before consulting the primary visual sources.
spur@fas.harvard.edu
http://hcl.harvard.edu/finearts/semitic_photo.html
Visual Information Access is a union catalog of visual resources at Harvard
http://via.harvard.edu:748/html/VIA.html.

Huntington Library, Art Collections, and Botanical Gardens

The Huntington Library supports the study of British art, Continental European art of the seventeenth and eighteenth centuries, and American art from the sixteenth century to the present. The book, manuscript, and photographic resources at the Hunt-

ington are extensive. The catalog photo study collection on British seventeenth- and eighteenth-century painting and sculpture is the largest outside of London. Archives include the Esdaile Archive of British sculpture and the C. H. Collins Baker Archive of exhibition catalogs and newspaper clippings on artists of all nationalities who exhibited in London between 1900 and 1920. *(Adapted from the Huntington Library Web site, 2002.)*

The Huntington
1151 Oxford Road
San Marino, CA 91108
(626) 405-2228
Fax: (626) 449-5720
Access: Scholars must apply for reading privileges before coming to the library. Reading Rooms are accessible to qualified applicants Monday through Saturday from 8:30 A.M. to 5:00 P.M. Closed on all major holidays. Printed guides to both the British and American manuscript collections are available. The southern California offices of the Archives of American Art, housed at the Huntington, contain microfilms of the complete holdings. The Huntington library collection can be searched online, at http://catalog.huntington.org/.
http://www.huntington.org/index.html

Metropolitan Museum of Art

Thomas J. Watson Library—Metropolitan

The Thomas J. Watson Library has been developing its holdings for over 120 years and is one of the largest primary source research collections in the world. The collection strengths are predominantly European and American art, with substantial holdings in Near Eastern, Egyptian, Greek, Roman, Asian, and Islamic art.

Artists of importance within the rare book and manuscript collection are Albrecht Dürer, Michelangelo, Tintoretto (Giacopo Robusti), Sebastiano Serlio, Andrea Palladio, Leonardo da Vinci, Giovanni Paolo Lomazzo, Thomas Chippendale, Josiah Wedgewood, Sir Richard Westmacott, Athanasius Kirchner, Michele Todini, Filippo Bonanni, Louis Haghe, Theodore Henry Adolphus Fielding, Samual P. Avery, William Harnett, and Aubrey Beardsley. Important subject matter documented in the rare book and manuscript collection includes Le Descriptions de l'Egypte, from Napoleon Bonaparte's invasion in 1798; documentation of all the paintings, sculptures, epitaphs, and inscriptions found in the churches of Venice in 1684; a catalog of Brescian art in private and public collections in 1760; detailed account of techniques in British marbling; privately produced catalog of the J. Pierpont

Morgan collection; the handmade papers of Japan; decorative motifs in the Art Nouveau and Art Deco styles; and the VVV Surrealism publication. *(Adapted from the Metropolitan Museum Web site, 2002.)*

The Henry R. Luce Center for the Study of American Art—Metropolitan

The Henry R. Luce Center for the Study of American Art makes available for inspection American fine art and decorative art objects not currently on view within the museum. Objects are arranged by material and then subcategorized by form and chronology. All of the objects within the Department are cataloged for computerized access.

The Metropolitan Museum of Art
1000 Fifth Avenue at 82nd Street
New York, NY 10028-0198
Thomas J. Watson (212) 650-2225
Henry R. Luce (212) 570-3903
Fax: Thomas J. Watson (212) 570-3847
Access: Reading Room use is open to qualified researchers, appointment highly recommended. The Central Catalog is open to all visitors by appointment. Hours for individual libraries vary. Hours: Thomas J. Watson Library is open Tuesday through Friday 10:00 A.M. to 4:40 P.M. The Luce Center is open Friday and Saturday 9:30 to 8:45 P.M., Sunday and Tuesday through Thursday 9:30 A.M. to 5:15 P.M. The Metropolitan Museum's libraries and archival collections can be accessed online, at http://www.metmuseum.org/education/er_online_resourc.asp#watsonline.
Watson.library@metmuseum.org
http://www.metmuseum.org/home.asp/

MAKE—the Organization for Women in the Arts

The MAKE research center offers a comprehensive collection of contemporary and historical women artists.

107–109 Charing Cross Road
London WC2H 0DU
00 44 (0)20 7514 8860
Fax: 00 44 (0)20 7514 8864
Access: Access to the collection is on-site. Email reference available.
http://web.ukonline.co.uk/womensart.lib/

The Morgan Library—Reading Room

The collection includes over 10,000 drawings and prints spanning the fourteenth through the twentieth centuries. Works include: Mantenga, Dürer, G. B. Tiepolo, Blake, Rembrandt, Watteau, Degas, Pollock, Pontormo, and Rubens. The Medieval and Renaissance Manuscripts collection spans ten centuries of Western illumination with over 1,300 manuscripts, including the Hours of Catherine of Cleves, the Lindau Gospel, and the Hours of Cardinal Alessandro Farnese. The library houses a comprehensive collection of bookbindings from the seventh century to the present. The Ancient Near Eastern Seals and Tablets collection houses artifacts from ancient Mesopotamia dating from the fifth millennium B.C. to the Persian Empire in the fifth century B.C. The Music Manuscripts and Books collection is the largest in the United States, encompassing handwritten works by Beethoven, Mozart, Brahms, Schubert, Stravinsky, and Gilbert and Sullivan. The Literary and Historical collection highlights Charles Dickens, Henry David Thoreau, Thomas Jefferson, Jane Austen, Charlotte Brontë, Albert Einstein, Abraham Lincoln, John Steinbeck, and Voltaire. *(Adapted from the Morgan Library Web site, 2002.)*

The Morgan Library
29 East 36th Street
New York, NY 10016-3403
(212) 590-0315
Fax: (212) 685-4740
Access: The reading room is available by appointment Monday through Friday 9:30 A.M. to 4:00 P.M. Applications must be submitted in writing with an accompanying letter of reference from a scholar or educational institution.
readingroom@morganlibrary.org
http://www.morganlibrary.org/research/html/index.html

National Gallery Archive—London

The London National Gallery's permanent collection spans the period from 1250 to 1900 and consists of Western European paintings. The archive contains Gallery records and private papers of art collectors associated with the institution. The Gallery records are useful for determining provenance of the art objects and documenting correspondence with artists such as Edwin Landseer, Barbara Hepworth, and Henry Moore. *(Adapted from the National Gallery Archive—London Web site, 2002.)*

The National Gallery
Trafalgar Square
London WC2N 5DN
020 7747 2831
Fax: 020 7747 2892
Access: Appointment required. Daily 9:30 A.M. to 5:30 P.M. Closed January 1. Finding aids are available for most collections and can be used within the reading rooms.

lad@ng-london.org.uk
http://www.nationalgallery.org.uk/about/history/archive/default.htm

National Gallery of Art—Curatorial Records

The department of Curatorial Records maintains files on all paintings, sculptures, and works of decorative art in the permanent collection of the National Gallery of Art. Files include all documentation and records of provenance, correspondence, exhibition history, and other materials. Bibliographies and biographies of collection artists, donors, previous owners, and portrait sitters are available. (*Adapted from the National Gallery of Art Web site, 2002*)

Department of Curatorial Records
National Gallery of Art
Washington, D.C. 20565
(202) 737-4215
Access: Appointment required. 10:00 to 5:00 Monday through Friday, closed on federal holidays. Types of access available: http://www.nga.gov/resources/resource.htm
curatorial-records@nga.gov
http://www.nga.gov/resources/dcrfdesc.htm

National Museum of the American Indian

This collection originally belonged to the Museum of the American Indian, which the Heye Foundation assembled at the turn of the twentieth century under the direction of George Gustav Heye. Now part of the Smithsonian Institution, the collection contains thousands of masterworks, including wood and stone carvings and masks from the northwest coast of North America. Works on paper and canvas include Plains ledger drawings and contemporary prints and paintings. The museum's collections also include a substantial array of materials from the Caribbean, Mexico, Central America, and South America, including a wide representation of artifacts from the Caribbean; ceramics from Costa Rica, central Mexico, and Peru; beautifully carved jade from the Olmec and Maya peoples; textiles and gold from the Andean cultures; and elaborate featherwork from the peoples of Amazonia.

The museum's photographic archive holds approximately 90,000 images, including 47,000 negatives; 30,000 vintage prints; and 13,500 transparencies, lantern slides, and glass-plate negatives. While the collection ranges from mid-nineteenth-century daguerreotypes to color slides that record contemporary Native American artists and events, its reputation is built upon field photography from the early twentieth century. It is considered one of the world's most significant collections of images documenting Native American peoples of the Western Hemisphere. (*Adapted from the National Museum of the American Indian web site.*)

Access: "The National Museum of the American Indian has Resource Centers in two of its facilities—the George Gustav Heye Center (GGHC) in New York, and the Cultural Resources Center (CRC) in Suitland, Maryland. There will also be a Resource Center in the National Museum of the American Indian on the National Mall in Washington, D.C., opening in 2004. At that time, all three Resource Centers will be digitally connected, and information will flow from New York to D.C. to Maryland." (*From the NMAI Web site.*)

New York

Resource Center
George Gustav Heye Center
National Museum of the American Indian
Smithsonian Institution
One Bowling Green
New York, NY 10004
(212) 514-3799
Fax: (212) 514-3792
nin@ic.si.edu
http://www.nmai.si.edu/research/index.html

Maryland

Resource Center
Cultural Resources Center
National Museum of the American Indian
Smithsonian Institution
4220 Silver Hill Road
Suitland, MD 20746
(301) 238-6624
Fax: (301) 238-3200
nin@ic.si.edu

Royal Commission on Historical Manuscripts

The Artists' Papers Register

The Artists' Papers Register is an online database of the papers and primary sources of artists, designers, and craftsmen held in publicly accessible collections in the United Kingdom. Nationality and status are not criteria for inclusion. Approximately 1,150 national, regional, and local repositories were surveyed, including archives, records offices, libraries, museums, galleries, universities, and historic houses. The Royal Commission on Historical Manuscripts maintains the database. *(Adapted from the APR Web site, 2002.)*

Artists' Papers Register
Royal Commission on Historical Manuscripts
Quality House, Quality Court
Chancery Lane
London WC2A 1HP
0113-233-5518
Access: Online only.
artists@hmc.gov.uk
d.tomkins@leeds.ac.uk
http://www.hmc.gov.uk/artists/

Stanford University

The university houses collections with small collections of letters by or about artists, catalogs, and examples of their works. Painters, sculptors, architects, and photographers are included. Artists include Ansel Adams, Malvina Hoffman, Rockwell Kent, and Henri Matisse. Stanford also houses an East German art collection, German Artist Correspondence from the late nineteenth and early twentieth centuries, medieval manuscripts, and North American Indian Art, including Canada, Great Plains, Eastern U.S., Western U.S., and New Southwest. *(Adapted from the Stanford University Web site, 2002.)*

Department of Special Collections
Green Library
557 Escondido Mall
Stanford, CA 94305
(605) 725-1022
Fax: (605) 723-8690
Access: Closed stacks. Reading Room use only by approved requests. Requests must be submitted by 5:00 P.M. for a return of 11:30 the following morning. Closes at 5:00.
http://www-sul.stanford.edu/depts/spc/ask.html
http://www-sul.stanford.edu/depts/spc/

COLLECTIONS ARRANGED BY PERIOD

Modern and Post-Modern

George Eastman House International Museum of Photography and Film

"The Richard and Ronay Menschel Library at George Eastman House is internationally recognized as a significant resource for research in the history of photography and cinema. The scope of the library reflects the Museum's extensive resources in the photography, motion picture, and technology collections. The library collects and preserves books, periodicals, manuscript collections, audiotapes, and ephemera that illuminate the history of more than 160 years of photography and a century of film. The collection traces a multifaceted history of both mediums, including technological developments, scientific research, the photographic and motion picture industries, artistic endeavors, the work of professional photographers, amateur efforts, film directors' contributions, the interests of film fans, as well as the birth and accumulated history of the two disciplines.

"The library houses more than 51,000 volumes on photography and film. The comprehensive periodical collection numbers more than 2,500 titles. Two hundred and sixty-six linear feet of manuscript materials, the papers of photographers, studios, scientists, and others connected to the field are an important sub-collection. Nine hundred and seventy audiotapes document the lives of photographers and more than fifty years of programs at the Museum." *(Taken from the George Eastman House Museum Web site.)*

900 East Avenue
Rochester, NY 14607
(716) 271-3361
Fax: (716) 271-3970
Access: The Museum's photography, motion picture, technology, and George Eastman collections are open to supervised research for any visitor. Appointments are required. Some of the collection is accessible on microfilm. The Richard and Ronay Menschel Library is open Tuesday through Friday, 10 A.M. to 12 P.M. and 1:00 P.M. to 4:30 P.M. Contact the education department at extension 217.
http://www.eastman.org/14_libcoll/refquestion.html
http://www.eastman.org/14_libcoll/libpage.html

International Dada Archive

The International Dada Archive supports scholarly research of the Dadaist movement. The purpose of the archive is to preserve and disseminate written documentation of the Dada movement. The collection is especially strong in manuscripts of Hans Arp, Johannes Baader, Hugo Ball, George Grosz, Raoul Hausmann, John Hartfield, Hannah Höch, Richard Huelsenbeck, Hans Richter, Kurt Schwitters, and Christof Spengemann. The collection is housed throughout the University of Iowa Libraries. The collection includes microfilmed manuscript collections, video and sound recordings, books and articles, and some computer files.

100 Main Library
University of Iowa
Iowa City, IA 52242-1420
(319) 335-5824
Access: Appointment required. The collection is accessible through an indexed card catalog, available on-site, containing 47,000 titles and an online catalog with 42,000 titles, at http://www.lib.uiowa.edu/dada/oasis.html.
timothy-shipe@uiowa.edu
http://www.lib.uiowa.edu/dada/index.html

The Museum of Modern Art, New York

This collection supports the scholarly research of twentieth-century American art. Holdings include exhibition catalogs, art show ephemera, oral history project, correspondence, twentieth-century manuscripts, museum papers, video recordings, research material, lectures, and departmental and program records. Significant twentieth-century artists within the collection include Chuck Close, Marcel Duchamp, Gertrude Stein, Umberto Boccioni, Constantin Brancusi, Vladimir Isdebsky, Wassily Kandinsky, Frederick J. Kiesler, Paul Klee, Hellmut Lehmann-Haupt, Ant Farm, Image Bank, J. B. Neumann, Elie Nadelman, Morgan Russell, Jasper Johns, and Sol Le Witt. Also available is a collection of letters from major artists in the cubist movement. *(Adapted from the Museum of Modern Art Web site, 2002.)*

Museum of Modern Art
Museums Archive and Research Center
11 W. 53rd Street
New York, NY 10019-5401
(212) 708-9617
Fax: (212) 333-1122
Access: Reading Rooms require an appointment Monday, Tuesday, Thursday, and Friday from 10:00 A.M. to 5:00 P.M. Primary access to archival resources is through the finding aids, entries in the RLIN database and the Museum's online catalog, or research resources at http://library.moma.org/. A comprehensive list of archival holdings can be viewed online, at http://www.moma.org/research/archives/holdings.html#twentieth/.
archives@moma.org
http://www.moma.org/

Georgia O'Keeffe Museum and Research Center

Has Georgia O'Keeffe's papers.

217 Johnson Street
Santa Fe, NM 87501

(505) 946-1000
contact@okeeffemuseum.org
http://www.okeeffemuseum.org/center/index.html

National Museum of Women in the Arts, Library and Research Center

Supports scholarly research on women's contributions to the arts. Contains over 16,000 files with resumes, bibliographies, representative contacts, artist statements, periodicals, exhibition catalogs and ephemera, and reproductions.

National Museum of Women in the Arts
Library and Research Center
1250 New York Avenue N.W. (Corner of New York Avenue and 13th Street)
Washington, D.C. 20005-3920
(202) 783-7365
Access: Reading Rooms use by appointment only Monday through Friday 10:00 A.M. to 5:00 P.M.
http://www.nmwa.org/library/libindex.htm

The Oakland Museum of California

Houses a comprehensive collection on twentieth-century photographer Dorothea Lange.

1000 Oak Street
Oakland, CA 94607
(510) 238-2200
Fax: (510) 238-6579
museumca@museumca.org
http://www.museumca.org/

The Robert Gore Rifkind Center for German Expressionist Studies

Dedicated to the study of the German Expressionist movement during the early twentieth century. Contains a collection of approximately 5,000 prints and drawings, over 6,000 volumes, 2,000 rare books (predominantly in German), and documentary sources such as monographs, exhibition catalogs, oeuvre catalogs, almanacs, anthologies, contemporaneous books, 8 monographic series, and runs of 111 periodicals. Original graphics by more than 150 different artists are represented, including those of Max Ernst, Max Beckmann, Ernst Ludwig Kirchner, Max Oppenheimer, and Otto Schubert. *(Adapted from the Los Angeles County Museum Web site, 2002.)*

Los Angeles County Museum of Art
5905 Wilshire Blvd.
Los Angeles, CA 90036

(213) 857-6165
Fax: (323) 857-4752
Access: Reading Room available by appointment only
Monday, Tuesday, and Thursday from 12:00 P.M. to 9:00
P.M. and Saturday and Sunday from 11:00 A.M. to 8:00 P.M.
rifkind@lacma.org
http://www.lacma.org/lacma.asp/

The Tate Archive Collection

A collection of archival material relating to British
art and artists, collectors, critics, writers, galleries,
and institutions from the beginning of the twentieth
century.

Hyman Kreitman Research Center
Tate Britain, Millbank
London SW1P 4RG
020 7887 8838
Access: Appointment required for approved researchers.
Monday through Wednesday from 10:00 to 5:00.
Research.Center@tate.org.uk
http://www.tate.org.uk/researchservices/researchcentre/
archive.htm

The Andy Warhol Museum

"The archives are a part of the artist's life work and
the greatest single collection of ephemera documenting
the diverse worlds in which Warhol was active. The collection currently consists of over 8,000 cubic feet of material, and functions as an integral part of the Andy
Warhol Museum, along with his paintings, films, video
work, sculpture and graphic art. The collection includes
scrapbooks of press clippings related to Warhol's work
and his private and public life; art supplies and materials
used by Warhol; posters publicizing his exhibitions and
films; over 4,000 audio tapes featuring interviews and
conversations between Warhol and his friends and associates; thousands of documentary photographs; an entire
run of *Interview* magazine, which Warhol founded in
1969; his extensive library of books and periodicals;
hundreds of decorative art objects; many personal items
such as clothing and over thirty of the silver-white wigs
that became one of Warhol's defining physical features."
(Taken from the Warhol Museum Web site.)

117 Sandusky Street
Pittsburgh, PA 15212-5890
(412) 237-8300
Fax: (412) 237-8340
Access: Reading room available by appointment only. Sunday 10:00 A.M. to 5:00 P.M. Monday—closed. Tuesday
through Thursday 10:00 A.M. to 5:00 P.M. Friday 10:00 A.M.

to 10:00 P.M. Saturday 10:00 A.M. to 5:00 P.M. Hours are
subject to change to accommodate special events or holidays.
wrbicanm@warhol.org
http://www.warhol.org/collections/index.html

Nineteenth Century

The Rossetti Hypermedia Archive

The Rossetti Hypermedia Archive presents the
complete writings and pictures of Gabriel Rossetti.

The Institute for Advanced Technology in the Humanities
Alderman Library
University of Virginia
P.O. Box 400115
Charlottesville, VA 22904-4115
(804) 924-4527
Fax: (804) 982-2363
Access: Online.
iath@virginia.edu
http://jefferson.village.virginia.edu/rossetti/index.html

Medieval

The Cloisters Library and Archive

The Cloisters Library and Archive contains materials specifically for the study of medieval art. The collection of over 13,000 volumes addresses medieval
architecture, paintings, tapestries, illuminated manuscripts, and sculpture. The archive contains the papers
of Sumner McKnight and Harry Bober, two prominent historians of medieval art, and other research collections. *(Adapted from the Cloisters Library and
Archive Web site, 2002.)*

The Cloisters
Fort Tryon Park
New York, NY 10040
(212) 396-5319
Fax: (212) 795-3640
Access: The Reading Rooms are available for approved researchers by appointment only Tuesday through Friday
10:00 A.M. to 4:30 P.M.
http://www.metmuseum.org/events/ev_cloisters.asp/

Middle Ages

The Women Artists Archive

This archive is a special collection in the University
Library at Sonoma State University. It contains mate-
rials concerning over 1,400 women artists from the
Middle Ages forward.

Special Collections/University Archives
University Library
Sonoma State University
1801 E. Cotati Ave.
Rohnert Park, CA 94928
(707) 664-2861
Access: The Women Artists Archive Database is available online and lists all the artists within the collection.
Lisa.Strawter@Sonoma.edu
http://libweb.sonoma.edu/special.html

COLLECTIONS ARRANGED BY REGION

Western Hemisphere

British Columbia Archive—Visual Collection—Canada

The archive contains over 110,000 photographic items and approximately 10,000 paintings, drawings, and prints relating to British Columbia's history and culture. Unique collections represent the work of early British Columbia photographers, including Frederick Dally, F. G. Claudet, Richard and Hannah Maynard, Edward Dossetter, J. Howard A. Chapman, Savannah and Ernest William Albert Crocker. The paintings and drawings collection includes works by Emily Carr. All collections can be searched by geographic region, subject, and artist. *(Adapted from the British Columbia Archive Web site.)*

655 Belleville Street
Victoria, B.C.
Canada
(250) 387-1952
Fax: (250) 387-2072
Access: Research using primary sources by appointment only. Call slips may be submitted during full service hours, 9:30–11:45 and 1:00–4:00 Monday through Friday, January 2nd through August 13th. Research facilities are closed on Wednesdays, August 14th through December 31st. Retrieval not available between 11:45 and 1:00. Some material may take 24 hours or longer to access.
access@www.bcarchives.gov.bc.ca
http://www.bcarchives.gov.bc.ca/

Europe—Italy

The Institute of Art History in Florence

Collection contains Italian art and artists of the twentieth century.

Kunsthistorisches Institute in Florenz
Via Giuseppe Giusti 44
I-50121 Firenze
Italia
0039-055-249-11-1

Fax: 0039-055-249-11-55
Access: Appointment required. Monday, Tuesday, Thursday, and Friday 9:00 to 10:00, Wednesday 2:00 to 5:00. The collection is cataloged and available to qualified researchers. Inquiries into the collection can be made by phone.
http://www.kubikat.org/

Medici Archive Collection

"The archive of the Medici Grand Dukes is one of the greatest yet least known Medici monuments. Established by Grand Duke Cosimo I in 1569, it offers the most complete record of any princely regime in Renaissance and Baroque Europe. Since this Archive consists mostly of letters (nearly three million filling a full kilometer of shelf-space), it offers an incomparable panorama of two-hundred years of human history, as told in the words of the people most immediately involved. However, this unique documentary resource has never been cataloged and indexed, nor microfilmed and accessed by electronic means. Only now, with The Medici Archive Project, is it fulfilling its potential to revolutionize our understanding of the past. The archive provides resources for the arts and humanities to a broad international public for the first time, by way of the Internet. With the custom database system, it is now possible to track all references to people, places and topics and then combine them freely in sophisticated search functions. When work is complete, *Documentary Sources* will be available as a searchable database on the Internet. Meanwhile, sample data is available at Medici Archive Project Access Sites in selected scholarly institutions around the world and on the Internet." *(Taken directly from the Medici Archive Project Web site.)*

Access: The Medici Web site does not yet offer direct access to the custom database, but its goal is to do so within the next few years. The research staff has transferred a series of preformatted reports, one set organized chronologically, the other according to 39 predefined topic categories. The report pages can be browsed or searched online. The report totals several thousand pages and offers scholars access to documentary material from the Medici Granducal Archive.
info@medici.org
http://www.medici.org/

Europe—Scotland

Glasgow School of Arts Archive

Collections include the papers of William Hardie, an acknowledged authority on Scottish painting and reputable art dealer, records from the Glasgow Dilettante Society, fine arts society from 1777–1843, John Ruskin's letters, the Royal Society of Painters in Watercolors, and Barlow's studies of Dante and European art during the nineteenth century. *(Adapted from the Glasgow School of Art Web site, 2002.)*

Glasgow School of Art
167 Renfrew Street
Glasgow G3 6RQ
0141 353 4592
Fax: 0141 353 4670
Access: Reading Room use by appointment only Monday through Friday 9:30 A.M. to 12:00 P.M. and 2:00 P.M. to 5:00 P.M.
archives@gsa.ac.uk
http://www.gsa.ac.uk/library/archives/index.html

Europe—United Kingdom

National Art Library Archive

The Victoria and Albert Museum Archive is comprised of three sections. The Archive of Art and Design provides research material on individuals, associations, and companies involved in art and design. The collection strength is twentieth-century British design. The Beatrix Potter Collection contains correspondence, drawings, watercolors, photographs, and literary manuscripts. The Linder Collection is also housed in the Beatrix Potter archive and has over 280 drawings. The V & A Archive houses the institutional documentation of several million pieces of artwork within the museum. *(Adapted from the National Art Library at the Victoria and Albert Museum Web site, 2002.)*

Blythe House
Archive of Art and Design
23 Blythe Road
London W14 OQF
+44 (0)20 7603 1514
The Beatrix Potter Archive: +44 (0)20 7602 0281 ext. 212
The V & A Archive: +44 (0)20 7602 8832
Fax: 020 7602 0980
Access: The Reading Room is available by appointment only. Tuesday through Thursday 10:00 A.M. to 4:30 P.M. Finding aids for each collection can be consulted on-site. The archive is closed for three weeks during late August and early September.
Archive@vam.ac.uk
http://www.nal.vam.ac.uk/archives.html

Yale Center for British Art

The Center houses a collection of over 20,000 rare volumes. The emphasis is on visual art and cultural life in the United Kingdom and former British Empire from the seventeenth century through the nineteenth century.

The collection also contains Rupert Gunnis's *Dictionary of British Sculptors.* Techniques covered in the collection range from the eighteenth-century revival of chiaroscuro, woodcuts, aquatint, and the development of chromolithography in the mid-nineteenth century. The collection includes hundreds of artists' manuals dating from 1600 to 1900. Artists include John Ruskin, Thomas Bewick, Thomas Gainsborough, David Roberts, James Ward, A.W.N. Pugnin, and Dante Gabriel Rossetti. The collection also contains 1,300 individual leaves from illustrated incunables. *(Adapted from the Yale Center for British Arts, 2002.)*

1080 Chapel Street
New Haven, CT 06520-8280
(203) 432-2814
Fax: (203) 432-9613
Access: Reading Rooms are the principal means of access. Open Tuesday through Friday 10:00 A.M. to 4:30 P.M. Records for the collection can be accessed online through the ORBIS search engine.
elisabeth.fairman@yale.edu
http://www.yale.edu/ycba/collection/index.htm

Europe—Wales

The National Library of Wales

The Library archive contains images relating to Wales and the other Celtic nations; this online catalog reflects that emphasis, with the majority of pictures illustrating some aspect of Welsh life, places in Wales, or people associated with this country. Artists of note within the collection are J.M.W. Turner, Richard Wilson, Thomas Gainsborough, Paul Sandby, and James Ward. Also included are artists who reflect the native Welsh artistic tradition, such as William Roos, Hugh Hughes and the Reverend Evan Williams, Sir Kyffin Williams, Will Roberts, and Evan Walters. The library also houses over 1,000 items in the architecture of Wales collections and has several scholar/collector collections that provide a broad base for visual studies. *(Adapted from the National Library of Wales Digital Mirror site.)*

National Library of Wales
Aberystwyth
Ceredigion
Wales SY23 3BU
+44 (0)1970 632 800
Fax: +44 (0)1970 615 709
Access: Reading room access is granted through application for long- and short-term reading tickets. Entrance Hall exhibitions are open Monday through Friday 9:30 A.M. to 6:00 P.M. Saturday 9:30 A.M. to 5:00 P.M. Pictures and Maps Reading Room open Monday through Friday 9:30 A.M. to

6:00 P.M. Saturday 9:30 A.M. to 5:00 P.M. The Library is closed on Sundays and public holidays and throughout the first full week in October every year.
http://www.llgc.org.uk/ymholiadau.htm
http://www.llgc.org.uk/drych/index_s.htm

North America

The Heard Museum's Billie Jane Baguley Library and Archives Collection

The collection's focus is on Native American art and culture with an emphasis on contemporary Native American fine art and Native American writings. The archive houses a Native American artists resource collection with broad scope and depth. Also included in the collections are indigenous arts of Oceania, Africa, Asia, and the Americas. *(Adapted from the Heard Museum Web site, 2002.)*

The Heard Museum
P.O. Box 210026
Tucson, AZ 85721-0026
Phone inquiries not accepted.
Access: Appointment is required. Monday through Friday 10:00 to 4:45. The collection finding aids are available on-line, at http://www.heard.org/research/archives/index.html.
archives@heard.org
http://www.heard.org/

Pacific—Hawaii

Bishop Museum Archives Special Collection

The earliest pieces in the museum's documentary art collection are drawings by artists who accompanied European expeditions in the eighteenth century. The art collection provides early visual documents of the changes that have occurred in Hawaii and the Pacific. The collection is indexed by artist and subject.

(808) 848-4182
Fax: (808) 847-8241
Access: Hours 12:00 to 3:00 Tuesday through Friday and 9:00 to 12:00 on Saturday. Online index.
archives@bishopmusem.org
http://www.bishopmuseum.org/research/cultstud/libarch/

EASTERN HEMISPHERE

National Palace Museum—Ch'ing Archive

The National Palace Museum Archive houses a collection of rare books, Ch'ing dynasty archives, documents, and noncirculating books and periodicals on Chinese art and culture. The Museum owns over 650,000 objects, including ceramics, paintings, ritual bronzes, carvings, embroidery, jade, and calligraphy. *(Adapted from the National Palace Museum Web site.)*

Located in the Building for Documents and Library.
+886-2-2881-2021
Fax: +886-2-2881-4138
Access: Appointment required. Library hours are 9:00 A.M. to 5:00 P.M. Monday through Saturday.
service01@npm.gov.tw
http://www.npm.gov.tw/english/library/library.htm

OTHER RESOURCES

Journals

Archives of American Art Journal. Produced by the Archives of American Art. Quarterly publication.
Art and Architecture Information Guides. Produced by Gale Research Company.
Metropolitan Museum Journal. Produced by the Metropolitan Museum of Art. Annual publication.

Portal Sites, Directories, and Pathfinders

Archives USA
Archives USA is a current directory of over 5,400 repositories and over 124,000 collections in the United States. Access is provided through institutional subscription.
http://archives.chadwyck.com/infopage/ausa_abt.htm

French Ministry of Culture
Pathfinder of Libraries and Research Centers Documenting the Art of France.
http://web.culture.fr/culture/sedocum/histart.htm

"This Directory is provided as a means to access nearly 3,000 libraries and library departments with specialized holdings in art, architecture, and archaeology throughout the world. Data recorded for each institution includes address, telephone and tele-facsimile numbers, hours of operation, annual closings, and listings of professional personnel. It also includes electronic mail addresses of individual librarians and direct links to institutional home pages." *(Quoted from Web site.)*
http://iberia.vassar.edu/ifla-idal/

Portal to locate primary source material and copyright holders of art and literature.
http://www.columbia.edu/cu/libraries/indiv/rare/guides/Resources.html

Portal site for worldwide museum home pages.
http://www.museumlink.com/

UNESCO Archives Portal
http://portal.unesco.org/ci/ev.php?URL_ID =
    5761&URL_DO = DO_TOPIC&URL_SECTION
    = 201&reload = 1049451919

University of California Los Angeles Arts Library
http://www.library.ucla.edu/libraries/arts/websites/
    wwwart.htm

A portal site of over 4,900 Web sites describing hold-
    ings of manuscripts, archives, rare books, historical
    photographs, and other primary sources for schol-
    arly research. The lists only include actual reposito-
    ries. The resources are divided geographically.
http://www.uidaho.edu/special-collections/Other.
    Repositories.html

A portal site created by the University of Waterloo li-
    brary to organize and provide access to Web sites
    of scholarly fine arts societies across the world. In-
    cludes a URL stability ranking.
http://www.scholarly-societies.org/finearts_soc.html

Major Microforms Collections in Art

The University of Maryland Library has compiled
a descriptive list of major art-related collections on
microfiche and microfilm. Included are archival
holdings, exhibit catalogs, periodicals, photographs,
ephemera, and indexes from international sources.
Provides increased access to rare sources. *(Adapted
from the University of Maryland Libraries Web site,
2002.)*

Libraries at the University of Maryland
College Park, MD 20742-7011
(301) 405-9064
Access: No appointment required. Monday through Thursday 8:30 A.M. to 10:00 P.M. Friday 8:30 A.M. to 5:00 P.M.
Saturday 10:00 A.M. to 5:00 P.M. and Sunday 1:00 P.M. to
10:00 P.M. Microforms and microfiche located on-site.
lg72@umail.umd.edu
http://www.lib.umd.edu/ART/guides/microform.html

Catalogs

SCIPIO, updated daily, contains more than 715,000
    records (as of August 2000) for auction sale cata-
    logs from all major North American and European
    auction houses as well as important private sales.
    An expanding group of contributors includes lead-
    ing art libraries in North America and the United
    Kingdom.
http://web.culture.fr/

Printed Resources for Locating Fine Arts Manuscript Collections

Artzen, Etta, and Robert Rainwater. *Guide to the Lit-
    erature of Art History.* (1980) Chicago; American
    Library Association. 616 p.
A critical bibliography containing over 4,160 entries
    designed for research into the history of art. Fully
    annotated entries; some contain content analysis.
    Contents include "Bibliography; Directories; Sales
    Records; Visual Resources; Dictionaries and Ency-
    clopedias (includes general biographical dictionar-
    ies); Iconography; Historiography and Methodology;
    Sources and Documents; Histories and Handbooks;
    Architecture; Sculpture; Drawings; Painting; Prints;
    Photography; Decorative and Applied Arts; Periodi-
    cals; Series. Includes author and title index and a
    classified subject index, which complements the de-
    tailed table of contents by bringing together the liter-
    ature according to country, region, culture, historical
    period, and major art movements" (Etta Artzen).

Besterman, Theodore. *Art and Architecture: a bibli-
    ography of bibliographies.* (1981) Totowa, N.J.;
    Scarecrow Press. 216 p.
Comprehensive collection of bibliographies from
    around the world. Subjects include art, archeology,
    architecture, ceramics, painting, cinematography,
    and special subjects.

Bronner, Simon J. *American Folk Art: A Guide to
    Sources.* (1984) New York, N.Y.; Garland Publish-
    ing. 313 p.
"Bibliography of American folk art, with 950 cita-
    tions grouped in 13 topical sections. Includes a
    brief introductory essay to each section, and author
    and subject indices."[1]

Duplessis, Georges. *Catalogue de la Collection de
    pieces sur les beaux-arts, imprimees et manu-
    scrites.* (1881) Paris; Picard. 224 p.
An annotated catalog of the Academy's manuscript
    collections, including The Royal Academy of Paint-
    ing, The Royal Academy of Music, and The Royal
    Academy of Architecture. Established in 1648 by
    King Louis the 14th, the royal academies are affili-
    ated with a long history of European masters.

Fenwick, Simon, and Greg Smith. *The Business of
    Watercolour: a guide to the Archives of the Royal
    Watercolour Society.* (1997) Great Britain; U.P.
    Cambridge. 326 p.
The Royal Watercolour Society was founded in 1804
    to provide a network for watercolor artisans. The
    archives of the Royal Watercolour Society secures
    the history of the artists and the intellectual devel-
    opments of the medium, emphasizing British

artists. Sales of major pieces and surveys on the purpose and techniques of watercolor from 1750 to modern times are included.

Federal Works Agency Work Projects Administration. *Subject Index to Literature on Negro Art.* (1941) Chicago, Ill.; Chicago Public Library Omnibus Project.

An older index compiled from the Union Catalog of Printed Materials on the Negro in the Chicago Libraries. Subjects include art and artists, awards, federal art projects, galleries and museums, patronage, painters, and private collections. This is a valuable research guide for those interested in African American art.

Gale Research Co. *Who's Who In Art.* (1998) Great Britain; Art Trade Press Ltd.

The first edition of *Who's Who In Art* was published in 1927. This publication is a comprehensive collection providing biographical details of living artists within Britain and Ireland. International artists are represented in limited numbers. All forms of painting, drawing, graphic art, and sculpture are included. Inclusion in the publication is at the discretion of the artist. Important resources within the book are aims and activities of academies, groups, and societies, as well as monograms, signatures, and obituaries. Details about estates and primary source material can be found throughout the publication.

Hoffberg, Judith W., and Stanley W. Hess. *Directory of Art Libraries and Visual Resource Collections in North America.* (1978) Published for the Art Library Society of North America. New York, N.Y.; Neal-Schuman.

Contains index subjects and special collection summaries for 632 libraries and 703 visual resource collections, arranged alphabetically within state or province.

Igoe, Lynn Moody. *250 Years of Afro-American Art.* (1981) New York & London; R.R. Bowker Company.

An annotated bibliography intended for scholarly research into Afro-American artists, art works, and art history. Sources include books, periodicals, newspapers, exhibition catalogs, announcements, fliers, dissertations, theses, and primary source materials. The artists include anyone who was born in the United States with African ancestry or who functioned as an artist within the United States. Photographers, commercial artists, and architects have been excluded. In all, this book contains 25,000 citations that document the life and work of 3,900 artists.

Keaveney, Sydney Starr. *American Painting: A Guide to Information Sources.* (1974) Detroit, Michigan; Gale Research Company. 235 p.

This work is part of the Gale Research Company's Art and Architecture series. The author attempts to be inclusive when defining "American" by including artists trained in other countries who worked in the United States. Evaluative comments are added to help the researcher choose appropriate materials. American painting and American painters are the focus of the book. Illustrators, cartoonists, and artists who specialize in a medium other than painting have been omitted.

Kleinbauer, W. Eugene and Thomas P. Slavens. *Research Guide to the History of Western Art.* (1982) Chicago; American Library Association. 228 p.

Research Guide to the History of Western Arts is an information guide to the range of resources in the humanities. The series consists of six titles covering arts, linguistics, music, literature, religion, and philosophy. Each volume has two parts; the first part is compiled by professionals within each discipline, and the second is an annotated list of major reference works relating subject scholarship with bibliography.

Marquis Who's Who. *Who's Who in American Art.* (2001) New Providence, N.J.; Reed Elsevier Inc.

A biennial directory profiling 11,000 contributors to the visual arts in the United States, Canada, and Mexico. The biography portion is arranged alphabetically and includes "vital statistics, professional education and training, works in public collections, commissions, exhibitions, publications, positions held in schools, museums and organizations, memberships in art societies, honors and awards, research statements, media, dealer and mailing address." People other than artists are included based on position and experience in the art world. People such as administrators and curators of major museums, scholars and librarians of prominent institutions, and widely published art writers and critics are represented. The geographic index breaks down biographical entries by state and city, allowing research by region.

Pacey, Philip, ed. (Primary sources by: Irene Whaley) *Art Library Manual: a guide to resources and practice.* (1977) London and New York; Art Libraries Society. 423 p.

This publication is a guide to developing art library collections. A wide variety of materials are addressed, including bibliographies, art library catalogs, periodicals, published and unpublished sources, organization, museum and gallery publications, exhibition catalogs, sales catalogs, patents, trade literature, abstracts and indexes, theses, primary sources, out-of-print materials, reprints, microforms, slides and filmstrips, loan collections of original works, sources of special materials, art organizations and associations. This book provides a road map to finding and exploiting all types of materials used for fine arts research.

Pacht, Otto and J. J. G. Alexander. *Illuminated Manuscripts in the Bodleian Library, Oxford.* (1969–1973) London; Oxford U.P.
Comprehensive index of the illuminated manuscripts housed in the Bodleian Library at Oxford.

Pollard, Elizabeth B. *Visual Arts Research: a handbook.* (1986) New York; Westport. 165 p.
Visual Arts Research: a handbook presents the process involved in fine arts research. Topics that are discussed are the common organization of art research material in libraries, computerized databases, reference tools available for art-related research, an annotated list of art periodicals and extensive bibliography with over 450 items. This book approaches methods in research by accounting for information needs and the sources available to fulfill them.

Pro Quest Information and Learning. *Dissertation Abstracts Online.* (1861–2003) Ann Arbor, Michigan; Xerox University Microfilms.
"Dissertations on all academic topics accepted at accredited institutions since 1861." *(Quoted from Web site.)* http://www.oclc.org/firstsearch/databases/details/dbinformation_Dissertations.html

R. R. Bowker. *American Art Directory.* (1997) New Providence, N.J.; Reed Elsevier Inc. 906 p.
The *American Art Directory* is an annual publication first printed in 1898. The directory contains four major sections. Section one contains The Museums, Libraries, and Associations indexes. The listing is comprised of over 2,013 main museums, 289 main libraries, 614 associations, and 110 corporations with art holdings. Section two contains details on art schools, art history, and architecture. The third section has listings of art museums, international art schools, art education, periodicals, and topical information about the arts. The last section investigates specific collections, providing access through a subject index that provides the name and location of the holding organization.

Sokol, David M. *American Architecture and Art: a guide to information sources.* (1976) Detroit, Michigan; Gale Research Company. 341 p.
Contains general histories, publications, and biographies about specific architectural forms, individual architects, urban architecture and city planning, painting collections, colonial painting, nineteenth- and twentieth-century painting and painters, as well as individual sculptors, craftsmen, and exhibition catalogs.

NOTE

1. "A Bibliography of the History of Art," Research Libraries Group Eureka database, Record no. XRIL102349-G. http://eureka.rlg.org/.

CHAPTER 8
Performing Arts Archives
Willem Rodenhuis

INTRODUCTION

Performing arts should be seen as a form of art that requires action and performance in order to obtain its intended effect or meaning. Performing a play, an opera, a symphony, a sonata, or choreography requires by necessity an audience for the appreciation of that particular piece of art. Moreover, such a performance can be characterized by its *here and now* manifestation. Only by bringing together time, space, artist(s), and audience can the process of mutual immanent communication get achieved, which forms the essentials of the performing arts.

This condition differs basically for the form of art that belongs in the field of the plastic arts (for example, sculpture and painting). Once complete, the painting or the sculpture *is* the art, as meant for by the artist. After finishing the product, the artist's physical presence is no longer needed for the process of appreciation between, for example, the painting (or sculpture) and the viewer.

Sculptures, photographs, and cinematography are products that exist on their own. A sculpture, a photo, or a film can be seen and appreciated *independently* from an interpreter or an artist—at any time and at any place.

Discussing the performing arts gives implication to how wide the range of artistic production is. In the first place, one could focus on the field of drama, such as theater, whether on the basis of a written script or nonverbal drama such as mime performances. Puppetry and other forms of folkish entertainment, such as the circus, add considerable richness to drama. This is also true for worldwide existing forms of dramatic play. Drama is an artistic form of expression that has been practiced by many civilizations in the world,

both past and present. World history can be told through the richness of drama, which has been used through the ages, and in many cases, these genres still find their audiences. This is certainly true for the European-based *commedia dell'arte,* the Japanese *kabuki, noh,* and *butoh,* and India's *kathakali.* One could refer to as many forms of drama as there are civilizations in the world. This phenomenon is unlikely to come to an end during our times.

Likewise, the world of music comes in a rich palette of different forms and varieties, such as instrumental music, pop music, symphonies, sonatas, operas, operettas, and musicals. And they all contribute to the sensation of *omnipresence* in our consciousness. Music, like drama, whether secular or religious, is appreciated in both elite and popular forms, finding both its particular audiences. Contemporary distribution of music through radio, television, records, CDs, and the Internet have caused an immense influence on the public effects of music production.

Dance is yet another large part of the performing arts. It is the oldest and the most basic form of the performing arts. One can easily determine a wide scale of different forms and audiences. By character, dancing implies music. Dance is, in essence, an interdisciplinary form of art. This principle has found its way through expression in all forms: from ballet to break dancing and from folk dance to the sophisticated temple dances of Bali.

In this chapter, ample attention is given to the emergence of archives that are dedicated to the performing arts. When discussing the objectives and functions of archives and library collections in this field, the first step is to find a solution to the above-mentioned contradiction, which implies that archives, libraries, and museums should be able to preserve the *live character,* or better, the *performative character* of these very holdings—which they cannot do. Performing arts collections offer as many sources as possible, but can never provide the piece of art itself: the sensation of the audience member that what is performed fits miraculously into one's framework of personal history, emotions, and desires.

Among the sources available are textbooks, playbills, diaries, scrapbooks, designs, theater models and stage sets, costumes, props, musical instruments, printed music, and all kinds of objects such as performers' personal belongings, drawings and paintings depicting scenes from plays and performances, and so on. And from individual artists when performing or in private circumstances, statues, caricatures, photos, films, microfilms, recordings of performances, diapositives, videotapes, microfilms, CD-ROMs, and so on. The development of academic interest in the performing arts as its own discipline has resulted in important research collections. International organizations such as the International Association of Music Libraries, Archives, and Documentation Centers (IAML), International Association of Music Information Centers (IAMIC), and International Association of Libraries and Museums for the Performing Arts (SIBMAS) have given shape to the academic interest in the performing arts. Moreover, they are in the front row when implementation of new technologies for research is at stake. After a short introduction on the academic development in the field and its effect on the growth of performing arts collections and archives, an outline will be given on present-day collections, the role of the Internet, and the growing demands for contact among colleagues all over the world.

Theater Studies: A Developing Discipline

Despite several important exceptions through the centuries, drama as a form of art was largely influenced by scholars who advocated it as a form of literature. This vision implied that a drama could be appreciated by just *reading* it and not necessarily by *seeing* it performed on stage.

Plato was among those who have underlined the interaction between the performance of a play and its audience. In his *Politeia,* his readers are warned about the strong emotions that arise from poetics, which could form into drama. Plato had the inclination to see emotional outbursts as negative; he favored that man

be in full control his mind. In Plato's view, an audience should be educated in order to consume and evaluate the feelings evoked from a play. In response to Plato's cautious attitude, Aristotle's *Poetica* reads as a brilliant analysis and an effective guideline for the appreciation of the fifth-century Athenean drama. Unfortunately, Aristotle has been misread from the seventeenth century up until the early twentieth century, where emphasis was put on his famous rules instead of his descriptions of the shared emotional impact of a play on the audience.

Other authors should be mentioned here as well: eighteenth-century French philosopher Denis Diderot (1713–84) stressed in his famous essay *Paradox sur le Comédien* (published posthumously in 1830) the psychological attitude to be practiced by an actor when performing: the emotions evoked should not be really felt by the actor. If so, the illusion would be over. His German colleague Johann Wolfgang von Goethe left several accounts of his experiences as an audience member in theater performances, and also renowned is his description of his experiences during performance of Carlo Goldoni's *La Locandiera* in Rome in 1789. Wolfgang also (re)introduced the oeuvre of William Shakespeare in Germany (*Götz von Berlichingen,* 1773) by translating and sometimes adapting these famous plays. In doing so, he offered his readers a brilliant overview about the possible effects of a theater performance on an audience.

A totally non-European tradition has been acquainted with the fourteenth-century Japanese actor and theater leader Zeami, whose writings offer a rich account of the practice of the acting profession, set against the background of the Noh theater.

As stated earlier, in the tradition of studying the theater, these opinions have proven to be marginal, as the main focus was on theater as an aspect of literature. This was extremely true for the academic world, where almost by tradition paradigms tend to be conservative. However, in the second half of the nineteenth century a gradual shift in focus was achieved. In Germany it was Theodor Wund, who in 1846 began lecturing at the University of Berlin, stressing the importance of the performance of a play instead of the literary text. Others were soon to follow, such as Wilhelm Creizenach at the University of Cracow in Poland and George Pierce Baker of Harvard University. These activities led to a provisional climax in 1892 when in Vienna the exhibition *die Internationale Ausstellung für Musik und Theaterwesen* (the International Exhibition on Music and Theater) was held on theatrical sources, which were given considerably more importance than literary texts. This exhibition was well received and called attention to the academic community the importance of archival holdings that were dedicated to the conservation of the performing arts. This inspiriation was clearly felt, resulting with the steady emergence of theater collections in Europe and in the United States. Although theater collections often began modestly as smaller departments within larger bodies (such as the Theater Museum in Vienna being installed as a department of the National Museum for the Arts), an important shift was made from the private sphere to the public realm. Putting it differently, during the eighteenth and nineteenth centuries theater items had been acquired by fans, lovers of theater, who devoted their collection to a particular actor or actress. By the end of the nineteenth century these collections won the interest of academics, who could use these holdings for systematic, professional research of the phenomenon of theater. Together with the deployed activities by scholars and performing artists, several societies for the study of theater were founded in the early twentieth century. In Germany the work of Arthur Kutscher and Carl Niessen have become famous; in Russia Vsevolod Vsevolodsky-Gerngross published his *History of the Russian Theater* in 1929. Josef Gregor and René Fülöp-Miller in 1927 published a similar work of general scope, *Das Russische Theater.* In England Edward Gordon Craig published a book about his own work as a theater director and about his cooperation with Adolphe Appia, the Swiss theatrical designer. And he did it in a style that inspired many scholars in the field. In Italy Sylvio d'Amico wrote his first study on the theater, *Storia del Teatro Drammatico,* in the late 1930s. All these publications could be made as there were relevant sources at the disposal of the researchers. Collectors such as Auguste Rondel in Paris, actress Clara Ziegler in Munich, Robert Neiiendam in Copenhagen, and Josef Gregor in cooperation with Franz Hadamowsky in Vienna contributed considerably by making vast donations toward the development of the theater studies. Apart from the collections that were built around a branch society, a national museum, or a university, another important input was secured by the libraries and archives that were associated with European national theater companies and opera houses, such as the Paris-based Comédie Française, the famous opera house La Scala in Milan, the royal theaters in Brussels, Copenhagen, and Stockholm, Covent Garden in London, and the Moscow Art Theater. (Many of these institutions are still active today and in full swing when adapting their role as an information center to the requirements of the digital era.)

This process of founding theater societies, in combination with archives, museums, or libraries, took place within a few decades at the beginning of the twentieth century. Alongside this development, academic interest grew and widened, which resulted in two clusters of scientific activity. On one side, historical research emerged, while on the other, a theoretic approach got ample attention as well. For the study of the history of theater, scholars could rely on the many resources available in collections, such as diaries, biographies, descriptions of plays and performances by members of the audience, drawings and paintings depicting scenes or theater interiors, designs, and props, and the like. The theoretical approach enabled scholars to link the theater world to existing notions proven to be valid in the study of literature, such as text interpretation and analysis and philosophy. Here the heritage of the great dramatists of the past offered a fruitful guideline for research.

Initially the separation from the study of literature by those who dedicated themselves to the study of the theater led to a strong opposition between the two. However, the interdisciplinary character of theater studies as such resulted in the end to a constructive cooperation and new findings. This is certainly true for the integrated study of non-Western forms of performing arts, when taking into account some of the results of an anthropological methodology. The ritual as a touchstone for theatrical production was a concrete result of this approach, as the interest in nonliterary forms of theater, such as the *commedia dell'arte* and other vital forms of folk theater.

In the course of the twentieth century, a debate arose about the incorporation of mass media, such as radio, film, and television, in the field of theater studies. For these forms of communication people relied heavily on the principle of acting *as if*—the very basis of the theatrical fiction. This debate resulted in two views on theater studies as an academic discipline: an enlarged one, including film and television production, and a limited one, concentrating more strictly on the theater, as presented on some sort of stage. In his *Dynamics of Drama: Theory and Method of Analysis,* Bernard Beckerman formulated in his famous definition of the theater the essential process between actor and audience, when stating that "Theater occurs when one or more human beings, isolated in time and space, present themselves in imagined acts to another or others" (Beckerman, p. 20). He added to this definition a schedule: A (actor) impersonates B (person) while C (audience) watches.

Martin Esslin stressed in his study *The Field of Drama* the importance of the use of the notion *drama,* indicating all forms of role-play, be it on stage, a film, or television (Esslin, p. 34).

In the course of the second half of the twentieth century, theater researchers developed a vivid interest for the findings in psychology and sociology. Role-playing and identity, both individual and collective, were notions that got their attention. A growing exchange of views with regard to these fields of interest paved the way to a deeper understanding of theatrical processes and of the universal forms these processes resulted in. The dominance of Western views when discussing the theater and its reach could be seen in another light, enabling non-Western forms of performing arts to win appreciation from a worldwide audience. The French scholar Patrice Pavis wrote an excellent study, *Theater at the Crossroads of Culture,* summarizing the challenges, needs, and objectives of present-day inter-cultural theater production.

In an earlier work of reference *Dictionnaire du Théâtre,* Pavis has made an effort to coin terms in use among theater researchers and those active in other disciplines. This lexicographical attention has proven to be rewarding, when wishing to explain to colleagues in related fields of academic interest what the trade of theater studies is about.

Having come to this point in this short outline it may be obvious that the performing arts have seen an increasing popularity among academics, apart from the support of all kinds of audiences through the ages. The professional attention paid to the performing arts has in the past one and one-half centuries led to specific demands to the collections that house all kinds of material. Theater collections in general have the task to meet the needs of two large groups of users, or visitors, of certain collections. On the one hand the lovers of the theater, the fans that will never cease to express their enthusiasm for the theater as such, and the professional researchers, enthusiasts without a doubt as well, who are also studying theater whether in its historical or in its theoretical context. Apart from these two categories, a performing arts collection may expect visits by critics and journalists preparing for their (research) articles. Another vital function is the delivery of pictorial material for all kinds of reproduction, be it in printed form in books and articles or be it for the production of film documentaries and television productions. The main task is therefore increasing the access to a collection and the grade of detailed information per item that one may expect. Here the last decade has shown a stormy development, which was enabled by the application of computer technology.

Performing Arts Collections

Before going into some specific performing arts collections in today's world, attention should be given to the organizational framework that dome these collections. By describing several variations in character, mission, and proportion of holdings, an overview on these collections will emerge, adding to the understanding of the specific position performing arts collections have in the world of archives, museum collections, and libraries.

First, there are libraries, or sections of libraries, that foster special collections dedicated to the performing arts. These libraries sometimes have national status, such as the Bibliothèque de l'Arsenal in Paris, which houses all the literature and archives related to the performing arts in France and is also a branch library of the prestigious Bibliothèque Nationale de France. Then there are research libraries that belong to a university library, such as the Harvard Theater Collection of Harvard University, or the performing arts library of the University of Amsterdam. Special collections on dance, circus, or other possible fields of interest are easily to be expected in these collections. Libraries also play a vital role when related to a theater school, or acting school. In Rome the Biblioteca e Raccolta Teatrale di Burcardo is part of the Italian organization for the collection of copyrights, the Società Italiana degli Autori ed Editori. Moreover, this library houses a fine museum collection as well, serving as a basis for thematic temporary exhibitions. This exception to a kind of a general rule illustrates the many possible forms that a particular collection can have.

Museums form another nucleus, where one may expect holdings with regard to the performing arts. Apart from exhibitions, these institutions organize based on props, models, and recordings in all forms. One may easily rely on a research library as well. Museums show a tendency to focus on the particular forms of theater by a certain country or by the same language.

Archives can be found in both a library and a museum. This is depending on how a collection is connected with other larger bodies in a given country.

Performing arts collections have benefited through the years of their international bonds that were shaped into several Non-Governmental Organizations (NGO) operating within the framework of the United Nations Educational, Scientific, and Cultural Organization (UNESCO). Active worldwide is the International Association of Music Libraries (IAML), a large body uniting hundreds of libraries and archives in the field of music of all kinds. This is also true for the International Association of Museums and Libraries of the Performing Arts (SIBMAS). SIBMAS in its turn is affiliated with the International Council of Museums (ICOM), and with the International Federation of Library Associations and Institutions (IFLA). The International Federation for Theater Research (FIRT-IFTR) unites theater researchers from all over the globe and is a sister organization of SIBMAS. Congresses have proven to be an effective instrument to mobilize skills and working experience from colleagues active in the same professional circumstances. Though practical matters and available equipment may differ considerably, the uniting factor between staff members and others who work as professionals for the preservation of collections is the sharing of each other's objectives and love for the performing arts.

Through the years several important initiatives have been taken, focusing to find ways to give expression to the notion of worldwide cooperation. This is for instance true for IAML, being one of the founding organizations in 1967 of the Répertoire International de la Littérature Musicale (RILM), which has grown to be an indispensable bibliographic source for musicologists. Répertoire International des Sources Musicales (RISM) is another source of information that helps researchers in their daily work. Both reference works are nowadays available in a digital form, easing considerably the access to the information provided.

Although considered a small body when comparing with the above-mentioned organizations, SIBMAS has been active since its foundation in 1954 motivating its members. An important tool to upkeep professional links between each other was the publication in 1967 of *Performing Arts Libraries and Museums of the World,* edited by André Veinstein and Rosamond Gilder (Paris: Editions du Centre National de la Recherche Scientifique, 1967). In New York Benito Ortolani took in the 1980s the initiative for another work of reference, the *International Bibliography of Theater* [IBT] (Brooklyn, N.Y.: Theater Research Data Center, Brooklyn College, published annually). Several SIBMAS members cooperated with Canadian Don Rubin's project the *World Encyclopedia of Contemporary Theater* (1990–96) [WECT] (London and New York: Routledge, 1994), apart from the many bilateral forms of assistance that members render to their colleagues. This is especially true for all kinds of references, the delivery of photos, film reels, and videotapes, editorial support for publication, and the assistance with the development of exhibitions.

Several Kinds of Institutions Active in the Field of the Performing Arts

A closer look at the body of performing arts collections learns that a total of four sections can be determined. This is true for both the music collections and the theater collections.

In the first place, one finds museums presenting their collection of *realia* and *artefacts* to a public of lovers of the art and professional researchers. This often occurs in combination with the maintenance of a library, a collection of handwritten manuscripts, diaries, letters, musical scores, and the like. Fine examples of these museums can be found in Vienna (Österreichisches Theatermuseum), Munich (Deutsches Theatermuseum), London (Theater Museum), Stockholm (Drottningholms Slottsteater), Copenhagen (Teatermuseet), Helsinki (Teaterimuseet), Česky Krumlov Castle Theater, Athens (Greek Theater Museum), and Lisbon (Museu Nacional do Teatro). Many more museum collections exist that are dedicated to the performing arts, but the collections here referred to are only listed as an example.

A second category consists of libraries and archives that are part of a larger body. Occasionally one can find in these collections museum-like holdings as well, but this is not a necessity. The larger body may be a national library or a university, such as the Bibliothèque Nationale in Paris, the New York Public Library in New York City, the Società Italiana degli Autori ed Editori in Rome, the Moscow State Art Library in Moscow, and the Universiteit van Amsterdam in Amsterdam. A third kind of collections consists of those institutions that primarily function as information centers for the performing arts, however, mostly in combination with a museum. A few examples are the Divadlo Ustav in Prague, the Institut de Teatro in Barcelona, the Theater Instituut Nederland in Amsterdam, the Archief en Museum voor het Vlaamse Cultuurleven in Antwerpen, and the Vlaams Theater Instituut in Brussels, as well as other numerous documentation keeping up tasks in the field of music, dance, and theater in the United States, Canada, South America, Asia, and Australia.

The fourth and last category are those collections that are part of a theater or opera house, like the Paris-based collections of the Opéra de Paris and the Comédie Française, in Brussels the Opéra de Monnaie, the Scala di Milano in Milan, Covent Garden Opera House in London, and the Opera Narodowi in Warsaw.

Finding the addresses of these institutions has been made possible in the past decade by updating the above-mentioned guide *Performing Arts Libraries and Museums* by Paul Ulrich. Initially he published an extended printed version in 1996, to be followed by a digital version freely accessible since early 2002, the *SIBMAS International Directory of Performing Arts Museums and Institutions*. In the following entry, due attention will be paid to the challenge and possibilities the digital world has to offer to the field of the performing arts collections.

Performing Arts Collections and the Digital World

Getting in contact with institutions for the performing arts has never been easier than through today's facilities offered by the World Wide Web. Moreover, big efforts are made to make catalogs readable and accessible by archives, museums, and libraries. Clustering of data is the new goal, leading to the presentation of integrated information through portals. New technology and protocols such as the 2001 agreed *Dublin Core* and the earlier Z 39.50 protocol facilitate this sophisticated application of datasets that has been made available and still finds growing users in larger organizations. Experimental use of this function is about to be evaluated and to be presented to larger unities in the field of research collections. Academics are the first to benefit a lot from this technological innovation. The same is true for critics and journalists. In the past it was the researcher that had to go in person to a specific collection, causing a lot of energy to be spent on traveling fees, hoping for a positive result and discovery of the information wished for. Today, the Internet makes it possible to research catalogs from one's desk, and in doing so research on the spot, while at home or in the office. A shift has been realized from static information, preserved in card catalogs to a dynamic form of information that can be made available on demand.

A small *tour d'horizon* will convincingly illustrate what has been achieved in the field of the performing arts. First of all, the dome organizations should be mentioned here. Without exception these organizations have developed Web sites over the past decade. Then there have emerged specific research sites, concentrating on disciplines such as dance, theater, circus, and all genres of music and the like. Thirdly, catalogs of libraries and museums offer their abundance of information and data to anyone in the world who wishes to use it. Overall, any Web site allows visitors to get in contact with staff members, ready for consultation and capable to solve detailed questions that may have come forward during the process of research.

Searching the Internet will easily prove the wide spread of all kinds of information concerning aspects of the performing arts. The Berlin-based librarian Paul Ulrich did a tremendous job adding to the framework of the printed reference work in *Performing Arts Libraries and Museums* (1967), listing over 8,000 entries of institutions housing relevant collections in the field of music, theater, and dance. During the production process, he could rely on the support of a small task group of colleagues, both active in SIBMAS and in related organizations. This magnificent digital directory is accessible free of charge and can be used by one click when on the homepage of SIBMAS at http://www.theaterlibrary.org/sibmas/sibmas.html. A special service has been built in, enabling the editor to add corrections to the data on the spot. Should a user of the directory wish to correct elements of the information provided, like a telephone number or a new zip code, then one click is enough to reach the editor and tell him the correct information. This procedure adds to the dynamic character of the directory, something that would be impossible in a printed copy of the same directory. Another benefit of this kind of dissemination of data is that it is no longer necessary to send questionnaires to all the institutions involved, a troublesome and risky procedure, seen from the point of view of the production of a reliable work of reference. This saves a lot of money as well and prevents errors and missing deadlines for the presentation of data.

Search engines like Google, OCLC's initiative NetFirst, AltaVista, and Yahoo! support this process of retrieval. Using Internet search engines and its effectiveness can be hampered by the absence of a professional editor to the information provided. Access, reliability, and actuality of the information presented are the conditions that should be met without discussion when active on the Web. NetFirst has tackled this problem by screening the content of the Web sites, before adding them to the domain. The same is true for a similar European initiative called DutchESS

(Dutch Electronic Subject Service) and Renardus. Here making use of subject specialists for selection, description, and reviews of Internet sources guarantees a relevant input in the database for the benefit of a circle of academic users.

Yet, it is helpful when one has a certain overview on the framework that initiates the many performing arts collections in the world. Apart from Paul Ulrich's digital directory this contribution ends by listing several organizations and institutions, thus providing a stronghold when searching the Web for performing arts collections. Each of the sites provides many related links, offering new horizons for detailed research. Access to all kinds of information with respect to the performing arts has never been easier since the past decade. Efforts by dozens of professionals worldwide offer a secure basis on which the growth of reliable data can flourish.

Organizations

European Network of Information Centres for the Performing Arts (ENICPA)
http://www.enicpa.org/

This site covers a network of information centers focusing on the performing arts in Europe. Special attention is given to special events, such as festivals, that are held throughout the year.

Performing Arts Data Service (PADS)
http://www.pads.ahds.ac.uk/

This initiative in Great Britain groups several libraries and archives in the U.K., allowing researchers to peep in the holdings before deciding to travel.

Performing Arts Special Interest Group of Museums Australia (PASIG)
http://amol.org.au/pasig/

Australian performing arts collections present themselves through this tool. Theater, music, and dance have been put together in an effective way.

Institute for Cultural Memory Bucharest (CIMEC)
http://www.cimec.ro/arte/perf.htm

Although CIMEC stands for a large cultural institution, the drama section in this site is for those who are interested in the present situation of drama in Romania. An agenda is presented to people planning to visit the country or to get an overview on the repertoire performed.

Stage of Central Europe and Newly Independent States (SCENIS)
http://www.scenis.org/

This Web site concentrates on the former states belonging to the Warsaw Pact, or to the Soviet Union. Theater life and production is presented in a context of broader cultural and social development, and this site provides an interesting overview for those who are active as playwrights, directors, actors, and musicians and their oeuvres.

International Association of Museums and Libraries of the Performing Arts (SIBMAS)
http://www.theaterlibrary.org/sibmas/sibmas.html

This NGO has been discussed above. The site offers, among current affairs and congress proceedings of the past, a direct and free access to the SIBMAS International Directory of Performing Arts Museums and Institutions.

International Federation for Theater Research (FIRT-IFTR)
http://www.firt-iftr.org/firt/home.jsp

FIRT-IFTR is a partner organization to SIBMAS, uniting theater researchers and is an indispensable research tool for academics and students in the field of the performing arts.

Theater Library Association (TLA)
http://www.brown.edu/Facilities/University_Library/beyond/TLA/TLA.html

This organization is the North American branch for the performing arts collections and their staff. The Web site allows direct contact with colleagues in the field.

American Society for Theater Research (ASTR)
http://www.inform.umd.edu/ASTR/index.html

This is the North American organization of theater researchers and students and is directly related with FIRT, and is very prominent in the field.

International Association of Music Libraries (IAML)
http://www.IAML.org/

The NGO for those who are active in music libraries and archives, musicologists and library staff alike. It fosters and stimulates special skills for those who are working with scores, music instruments, and special collections with music holdings.

International Association of Music Information Centres (IAMIC)
http://www.iamic.net/

The Web site offers a possibility for contact with this worldwide operating organization, uniting information centers for contemporary music, inclusive pop, and jazz in 38 countries.

Résource International des Sources Musicales (RISM)
http://www.rism.harvard.edu/rism/Welcome.html

This well-known international initiative has been working for decades to present a bibliographic overview on musical sources. A digital form is available as well as the printed version.

Nordic Center for Theater Documentation (NCTD)
http://www.nb.no/nctd/

In this Web site, one finds the results of cooperation with regard to the presentation of the performing arts in Denmark, Norway, Iceland, Sweden and Finland. The site allows an overview on contemporary repertoire and activities like festivals in the region.

The New York Public Library for the Performing Arts
http://www.nypl.org/research/lpa/lpa.html

This unique institution, located next to the Lincoln Center, houses a large collection of American theater production and its history. Through this Web site an easier access is secured, facilitating catalog research at a distance. It contains special collections in theater, musical, dance, and personal archives of celebrities in the field.

International Bibliography of Theater (IBT), Theater Research Data Center at Brooklyn College
http://www.cuny.edu/

This bibliography was discussed above. This Web site allows contact with the editorial team.

The WWW Virtual Library: Theater and Drama
http://www.brookes.ac.uk/VL/theater/

This site was built up as a virtual library, enabling lovers of the theater and professionals to get acquainted with theater productions and manuscripts from all over the world. Nowadays a fine tool for researching new repertoire, and possible translations of repertoire in many languages are offered.

Circustuff: the Circus Portal
http://www.circustuff.com/

This site offers information about the circus in its many forms and the history behind it. Moreover, courses are offered, as well as tips for literature, props, and tricks.

The Circus Collection of the Library of the University of Amsterdam
http://www.uba.uva.nl/

Together with the circus collections in the British Museum, the Library of Congress, and the Bibliothèque Nationale de France, the University Library of Amsterdam houses one of the world's four largest collections in this discipline. Access for research is secured by the online catalog.

International Theater Institute (ITI)
http://iti-worldwide.org/

This NGO unites theater makers from all over the world. The Web site has a vivid function in keeping the contacts among colleagues going.

Le Département des Arts du Spectacle de la Bibliothèque Nationale de France
http://mistral.culture.fr/culture/sedocum/bnf-das.htm

The site offers a complete overview on the holdings of this important archive of the theater in the past and of today in France and other French-speaking countries.

Museums and Information Centers for the Performing Arts

The Theater Museum (London)
http://www.theatermuseum.org/

This museum near Covent Garden houses the heritage of United Kingdom's drama and theater production. The Web site offers an effective entrance to the holdings.

Institut del Teatre (Barcelone)
http://diba.es/iteatre/frames.html

This collection focuses primarily on the theater in Catalonia, an independent cultural entity in the Kingdom of Spain. A rich collection is presented on the Web site. The institute is merged with a museum, a theater school and the performing arts section of the University of Barcelone.

Czech Theater Institute (Prague)
http://www.divadlo.cz/

Through this Web site, the Czech theater presents itself to the world. The Czech Theater Institute secures a reliable overview on contemporary Czech theater production and its adherent activities.

Vlaams Theater Instituut (Brussels)
http://www.vti.be/

Flanders, the Dutch-speaking part of the Kingdom of Belgium, is renowned for its rich theater production and history. The Web site offers an effective entrance to this, in combination with an overview on contemporary activities such as festivals and playwrights.

Theater Instituut Nederland (Amsterdam)
http://www.tin.nl/

The Web site allows an online catalog research. Moreover, a detailed overview is offered on the museum collection, special collections in the archive, and all kinds of promotional activities throughout the year.

The National Resource Centre for Dance
http://www.surrey.ac.uk/NRCD/

This British Web site unites the many dance collections in the country and their holdings.

Eurofestival Infocenter
http://www.euro-festival.net/

The many European festivals programming the performing arts, being theater, dance, and music, are grouped in this Web site.

Theater Communications Group
http://www.tcg.org/

Many of the European theater productions and their troupes are put together on this site. Information on the several national policies toward cultural production has been added for the convenience of the visitor.

Greek Theater Museum (Athens)
http://www.theater-museum.gr/index.htm

This fine collection presents itself on the Web through this elegant Web site.

Biblioteca e Raccolta Teatrale del Burcardo (Rome)
http://www.theaterlibrary.org/

Discussed earlier, this collection is presented in combination with the other elements of the institute: archives, museum, and library concentrating on the history of Italian performing arts. As an extra service a vast field has been mounted with links to all kinds of disciplines in the field of the performing arts.

Museo Teatrale alla Scala (Milan)
http://www.museoteatrale.com/

This collection dedicates itself to the presentation of the rich history of this famous opera house in Milan. Apart from the museum collection, a large library is available and searchable as well.

Česky Krumlov Castle Theater
http://www.ckrumlov.cz/uk/i_index.htm

Through the Web site a detailed overview is given on the several elements of this famous castle complex in the Czech Republic. The Baroque theater in the castle is well preserved over the centuries and one of the jewels in the crown of European theater history.

Drottningholms Slottsteater (Stockholm)
http://www.drottningsholmsteatern.dtm.se/index.htm

With Česky Krumlov this theater is one of the few remaining eighteenth-century theaters in Europe, still in its original state of being. The Web site offers an effective insight in the theater, its annex theater collection, and the programming throughout the season.

Österreichisches Theatermuseum (Vienna)
http://www.theatermuseum.at/

Located in a wonderful eighteenth-century city palace the museum houses a rich collection, covering the history of Austrian performing arts. Thematic exhibitions complete the functioning of this museum in present Vienna.

Comédie Française (Paris: Museum and Library)
http://www.comedie-francaise.fr/

Through this Web site access is secured to the oldest still-existing (since 1680) theater company in the world. Programming, repertoire, and educational activities are presented along with the history of this renowned cultural institution.

STS: Schweizerischen Theatersammlung (Bern)
http://www.theatersammlung.ch/

This collection covers the history and present production in the field of the performing arts in Switzerland. The collection is maintained in close cooperation with the universities of Bern and Basel.

Research Sites

The Theatron Project
http://www.theatron.org/ec.html

Theatron focuses on the digital representation of theater buildings that belong to the heritage of European cultural history. Donated with European funds for the development of digital application in scientific research, this Web site shows the first results of the cooperation between several universities in Europe.

Shakespeare Globe USA
http://www.shakespeare.uiuc.edu/

A virtual visit to the rebuilt Globe theater in London is facilitated through this Web site. Moreover, additional information on historical background and repertoire is freely offered.

Skenotheke, Images of the Ancient Stage
http://www.usask.ca/antharch/cnea/skenotheke.html

The University of Saskatoon hosts this digital initiative, covering vast areas of the classical studies. Actual findings are promptly added, as of related Web sites in the field. The main focus, however, remains on the classical theater.

Classical Drama Sites
http://www.webcom/shownet/medea/cldrama.html

This site provides a digital overview on Web sites dealing with issues of the classical drama.

BIBLIOGRAPHY

Arnott, James. "An Introduction to Theatrical Scholarship." *Theater Quarterly* 10, no. 39 (1981): 29–42.

Beckerman, Bernard. *Dynamics of Drama: Theory and Method of Analysis.* New York: Drama Book Specialists, 1970.

Esslin, Martin. *The Field of Drama.* London: Methuen, 1987.

Pavis, Patrice. *Dictionnaire du Théâtre.* Paris: Dunod, 1997.

———. *Theater at the Crossroads of Culture.* London: Routledge, 1992.

Rubin, Don, ed. *The World Encyclopedia of Contemporary Theater.* 6 vols. London: Routledge, 1994–2000.

Schoenmakers, Henri. "Between Reasonless Passion and Passionless Reason: Theater in the Nineties." In *The Humanities in the Nineties, a View from the Netherlands,* edited by E. Zürcher and T. Langendorff, 175–205. Amsterdam and Rockland, Mass.: Swets & Zeitlinger, 1990.

CHAPTER 9
Sports Archives
Jackie R. Esposito

INTRODUCTION

Sports archives are ubiquitous in nature—a combination of primary source materials created by and about a specific sport, media guide and publicity publications, and memorabilia reflecting the sports enthusiast or the fan. Since sports in the United States fall into three basic categories, professional, collegiate, and recreational, it is important to understand that archival collections for sports are as diverse as the sports themselves. It is also critical to conduct searches with as broad a set of parameters as possible. In 1969, Philip Brooks argued in his book *Research in Archives: The Use of Unpublished Primary Sources* (New Providence, N.J.: R. R. Bowker, 1969) that "the riches that lie in countless repositories can be mined productively only if the seeker knows what he is looking for, where he may expect to find it, and how to recognize it...." The latter is particularly relevant for sports research.

Sports collections are inclusive of a wide gamut of archival collections. Every record type such as individual athlete and coach papers, sport foundation and development, conditioning and training, legal issues, and medicine to financial records, tournaments and championships, broadcasting, history, and gender equity is a distinct search possibility. Therefore, the depth and breadth of a collection is the critical piece of knowledge for a successful archival search.

At a minimum, any given sport will be represented by a hall of fame museum, which depicts the career of specific athletes and chronicles the history of their sport. Halls of fame offer biographies, press clippings, photographs, memorabilia, and reminiscences of athletes chosen by that sport to represent its best. While these collections may indeed document a specific ath-

lete well, they do not often embody a comprehensive history of the sport developed for scholarly research. Rather the target audience is the fan, who is interested in glitz more than substance. There are several exemplary research collections housed within halls of fame but these are the exception, not the norm.

Major sport organizations collect institutional records that document the management and operations of sports. For example, the National Collegiate Athletics Association, as the regulatory organization for collegiate sport, collects records concerning rules, procedures, compliance, individual programs, specific athletes, tournaments, and educational benefits. This archival collection contains records for all participatory schools but does not comprehensively document each one of them. This phenomenon is repeated with the U.S. Olympic Commission collection, the International Association for Sport Information, and other organizational collectors. Their goal is to document sports as it applies to their specific mission, therefore, a good program may receive little or no notice while a violating program will receive extensive documentation.

Detailed archival collections of primary source materials representing sports, sports organizations, athletes, and sport research are often held within university archives. In addition to documenting the rich sporting history of a particular institution, university archives often supplement their collection with professional research organization records that document the academic side of the sport. For example, Penn State University Archives house over 600 cubic feet of Penn State athletic history alongside the records of the International Society of Biomechanics, the North American Society for Sport History, and the American Academy of Kinesiology and Physical Education, to name but a few. This combination of resources allows the scholarly researcher the opportunity to place sports research in context of its related academic disciplines: kinesiology, sport medicine, sport psychology, and so on.

Sports researchers need to be aware of the variety of sports resources available and prepare their searches in advance with as much detail as possible. The importance of communication of research need and access to repository information is critical for archival researchers. David Kepley argues in his article on "Reference Services and Access" in *Managing Archives and Archival Institutions* edited by James G. Brashers (Chicago: University of Chicago Press, 1989) that "the heart of the reference process lies in understanding the researcher's questions and suggesting the kinds of records that the institution and other related repositories have that may be of use." For sports research, this process is the basis for a search success or failure.

There is one additional caveat for the sports researcher to consider—identifying resources on the earlier history of women's sports is often problematic. Do not assume that women's sports follow the same pattern of development as the men—they did not. Therefore, women's archival resources do not follow the same search patterns. Often, information about women's participation in sports is hidden within papers of male coaches, administrators, trainers, and managers. Utilizing the expertise of a given archive, finding aids and the knowledge of the archivist is essential.

PRINT RESOURCES

There are few print resources to help researchers in locating information for sports archival collections. The International Association for Sports Information (IASI) at http://www.iasi.org/ is a unique international association "that brings together a worldwide network of information experts, librarians, sport scientists and managers of sport libraries" to document sport. IASI compiles a *World Directory of Sport Libraries, Information and Documentation Centres* (Gloucester, Ont.: IASI, 1996), maintains an active listserv, and publishes a newsletter for its members. The most recent print version of the directory dates from 1996 and "aims to promote access to sport information resources and services throughout the world." It con-

tains information on more than 100 organizations and is organized alphabetically by country. Each entry contains a postal address, phone and fax numbers, languages in which staff can communicate, collection descriptions, hours of operation, and other research access information. Because of its international focus, this slim volume (62 pages) is extraordinarily useful to the scholar interested in completing a comparative, international sport study.

Donald L. Deardorff II has compiled an excellent resource guide for the sports researcher, entitled *Sports: A Reference Guide and Critical Commentary, 1980–1999* (Westport, Conn.: Greenwood Press, 2000). Deardorff has reviewed sports monographs, serials, and various other publications by subject. He annotated each item with his own analysis of the value of the publication and placed them in the context of the usefulness for that particular subject, for example, sports marketing, women in sports, and so on. Appendix 2 of his book evaluates halls of fame, libraries, museums, periodicals, and Web Sites.

Several other print compilations are worth noting: Doug Gilbert's *Sports Halls of Fame: A Directory of over 100 Sports Museums in the United States* (Jefferson, N.C.: McFarland & Co., 1992), Matthew Rosenberger's *Sports Resource Directory* (Chicago, Ill.: M. G. R. Enterprises, 1993), and Victor Danilov's *Hall of Fame Museums: A Reference Guide* (Westport, Conn.: Greenwood Press, 1997). For the serious sports library or researcher, Human Kinetics is, arguably, the best sport publisher in the business today. The range of subjects covered by Human Kinetics is inclusive of all physical disciplines and a wide coverage of specific sports. The Web site listing both monographs and serials is available at http://www.humankinetics.com/.

There is a wide range of academic and popular sports periodicals. Academic journals are particularly useful due to the inclusion of footnotes and bibliographies for citations of archival collections. The following is a short list of those titles particularly relevant for the sports researcher: *American Journal of Sports Medicine; Athletic Administration; Baseball Research Journal; Exercise and Sport Sciences Review; International Journal of the History of Sport; International Journal of Sport Nutrition; Journal of Physical Education, Recreation, and Dance; Journal of Sport and Exercise Psychology; Journal of Sport and Social Issues; Journal of Sport History; Journal of Strength and Conditioning Training; NCAA News; NCAA Sports Sciences Education Newsletter; Physical Educator; Research Quarterly for Exercise and Sport;*

SABR Bulletin; Sport Science Review; Women in Sport and Physical Activity Journal; Women's Sport and Fitness; Inside Sports; The Sporting News; and *Sports Illustrated.*

The standard archival search tools are somewhat helpful, especially if a wide range of search terms is applied. The Library of Congress National Union Catalog of Manuscript Collections (NUCMC) provides a comprehensive research tool for collections cataloged between 1959 and 1993. NUCMC was superceded in electronic form by the Research Libraries Information Network (RLIN). NUCMC contains copies of catalog cards and descriptions of collections in various repositories. It utilizes Library of Congress subject headings and can be unwieldy due to its multiple-volume structure.

Two other paper resources worth consulting are (1) *Directory of Archives and Manuscripts* (Phoenix, Ariz.: Oryx Press, 1988), published by the National Historical Publications and Records Commission in 1978 and 1988. The directory contains repository name, address, policy and procedures, and a summary of collection holdings. (2) *Subject Collections: A Guide to Special Book Collections and Subject Emphases as Reported by University, College, Public, and Special Libraries and Museums in the United States and Canada* by Lee Ash (New Providence, N.J.: R. R. Bowker Co., 1993) is a handy two-volume compilation that contains information arranged by subjects both broad and specific. It includes more than 65,000 entries from more than 5,000 institutions, both libraries and archives. Due to publication strictures, print resources have their limitations. Technological developments and standardization of reporting provide solutions to search problems found in paper.

DIGITAL RESOURCES

Electronic search engines and library online catalogs have replaced print resources for many researchers. As mentioned previously, RLIN contains NUCMC records created since 1993 that are not contributed to a national computer database. This limitation must be considered serious by researchers since it excludes such prominent academic institutions as Harvard University, Notre Dame University, and Big 10 colleges, to name just a few.

Archives USA is, arguably, the best single electronic database devoted to primary source collections. Created in 1997, this electronic subscription, or CD-ROM product, has holdings from more than 4,000

archival institutions and more than 100,000 records. The database includes a directory of repository names, locations, contact information, hours of service, and collection descriptions. It also includes collection records from NUCMC pre-1993, *Index to Personal Names,* and *Index to Subject Names.* In addition, Archives USA includes collections microfilmed by the *National Inventory of Documentary Sources* (NIDS). Archives USA has a feature that allows E-mails directly to holding repositories. NIDS has its own stand-alone CD-ROM product with search capabilities throughout the entire finding aid. Both Archives USA and NIDS products are fairly expensive and usually owned by research libraries with large archival depositories. The most direct way to access them is to locate a research library that has a subscription and request user status.

SportDiscus, on the other hand, is the best (bar none) electronic resource for sports researchers. Discus is a full-text electronic subscription, or CD-ROM product, that covers practical and research literature on physical education, sport, physical fitness, exercise psychology, sports medicine, biomechanics, coaching, training, and kinesiology. It also provides comprehensive indexing of the Microfilm Publications of the International Institute for Sport and Human Performance. Discus is a product of the Sport Information Resource Centre and contains more than 500,000 records from 1975 through the present. An additional 22,000-plus records are added annually and the database is updated monthly. The Sport Information Resource Centre (SIRC) at http://www.sirc.ca/ is the "world's leading bibliographic database producer of sport, fitness, and sports medicine." SportDiscus is SIRC's best selling product.

Gretchen Ghent from the University of Calgary oversees the North American Sport Libraries and Information Network (NASLIN) Scholarly Sports Web site at http://www.sportquest.com/nasline. This phenomenal resource was created in 1989 to "facilitate communication and resource sharing among sports librarians." In addition to its online presence, NASLIN publishes a semiannual newsletter that includes an extensive bibliography. NASLIN hosts a biennial conference and offers educational programs. It is affiliated with the International Association for Sports Information, Canadian Association for Sports Heritage, and the International Association of Sports Museums and Halls of Fame.

The INSEP Media Library Catalogue, at http://www.insep.fr/Sid/catalog.htm, is a full-text database including 15,000 monographs, 2,000 theses and dissertations, 700 congressional proceedings, and 790 specialized periodicals. This resource is a good complement to both SportDiscus and NASLIN capabilities.

Great Outdoors Research Page (GORP) Web site at http://www.GORP.com/ is one of the best commercial recreational sport Web sites. Although a commercial site, it provides excellent information on destinations, activities, gear, trip planning, and print resources. The other useful Web site for recreational sport enthusiasts and researchers is the National Park Service ParkNet at http://www.nps.gov/. The site provides detailed information for all national parks and includes extensive visitor information. But its true value as a Web site resides in the links it provides for researchers to the historical past of the sites and the "learn NPS" links for educators. Both provide incredibly useful information about the history, culture, and learning that can take place at any of the U.S. national parks.

There are several additional Web sites worth exploring. The American Association for Health, Physical Education, Recreation and Dance site at http://www.aahperd.org/ is devoted to "promoting health lifestyles through high quality programs in health, physical education, recreation, dance and sports." The Amateur Athletic Union site at http://www.aausports.org/ details the activities and role of the "largest, volunteer, non-profit sports organization in the United States". The American College of Sports Medicine Web site at http://www.acsm.org/ includes information on "scientific research, education, and practical application of sports medicine and exercise science" for physical performance. A similar Web site is located at http://www.sportsmedicine.com/.

The premier commercial sports broadcasting network, ESPN, also maintains an active and useful Web site at http://www.espn.com/. Its print counterpart is the Sporting News at http://www.sportingnews.com/. The Exploratorium at http://www.exploratorium.edu/sports/ is one of the nation's major hands-on science centers. Located in San Francisco, a large component of the virtual and physical exhibits is dedicated to the science of sport. A good example of one of the many commercial sports Web sites is http://www.hickoksports.com/. It focuses on sports history for North American sports including biographies and glossaries. The sports product industry is represented at http://www.sportlink.com/ and the sports awards network can be located at http://www.worldsport.com/.

The sports researcher *must* use discretion when surfing the World Wide Web. Many fans and supporters of individual sports have created Web sites for their team. The majority of these sites have limited usefulness for the serious researcher. Evaluate each Web site for authority, objectivity, accuracy, and currency. Alternatively, utilize only the national resources that have proven their value before trusting an individual Web site.

SAMPLE ARCHIVAL COLLECTIONS

International Association for Sport Information
1600 James Naismith Drive
Gloucester, Ontario, Canada, K1B 5N4
http://www.sirc.ca/iasi.html

International Association for Sports Museums and Halls of Fame (IASMHF)
180 No. LaSalle Street, Suite 1822
Chicago, IL 60601
(312) 551-0810
http://www.sportshalls.com/

College and University Archives

Haverford College
70 Lancaster Avenue
Haverford, PA 19041-1392
(610) 896-1000
http://www.haverford.edu/
C.C. Morris Cricket Library and Collection

Indiana University
107 So. Indiana Avenue
HPER Building 031
Bloomington, IN 47405
(812) 855-4420
http://www.indiana.edu/~libhper/index.html
Health, Physical Education, and Recreation Library

University Archives
Notre Dame University
Hesburgh Library
Notre Dame, IN 46556
(574) 631-6448
http://www.sports.nd.edu/
Joyce Sports Research Collection

University Archives
Penn State University
104 Paterno Library
University Park, PA 16802

(814) 865-7931
http://www.libraries.psu.edu/crsweb/speccol/univarch.html

All-Sport Museum
American Association for Physical Education and
Kinesiology records
Hugo Bezdek papers
Department of Intercollegiate Athletics records
Charles "Rip" Engle papers
Exercise and Sport Science Department records
Maxwell Garret papers
Dorothy Harris Sports Psychology papers
Mary Jo Haverbeck papers
Health, Physical Education, and Recreation, College of
Records
International Society of Biomechanics records
North American Society for Sport History records
Joseph V. Paterno papers
Pennsylvania State Association for Health, Physical Edu-
cation, and Recreation records
H. Ridge Riley papers
Sports Archives
G. Thomas Tait papers
Budd Thalman papers
Eugene Wettstone papers
Women's Intercollegiate Athletics Association records
Women's Recreation Association records

Springfield College
Reference Archives
Springfield, MA 01109
http://AAHPERD.spfldcol.edu/
American Association for Health, Physical Education,
Recreation, and Dance records

University Archives
University of California at Los Angeles
330 Powell Library
Box 951575
Los Angeles, CA 90095-1575
http://univ-archives@library.ucla.edu/
(310) 825-4068

William Coit Ackerman Awards
Associated Students of UCLA
Department of Intercollegiate Athletics
"Bunker Bill's Bruins" Football Scrapbook
"Card Stunts" Scrapbook
John Jackson Biographical File
Dorothy Mason Peel Memorabilia
Margaret Sitko Memorabilia

Archives and Special Collections
University of Connecticut
Thomas J. Dodd Research Center
405 Babbidge Road, Unit 1205
Storrs, CT 06269-1205

(860) 486-2524
http://www.lib.uconn.edu/DoddCenter/ASC/
Division of Athletics

Special Collections
University of Delaware Library
Newark, DE 19717-5267
(302) 831-2229
http://www.lib.udel.edu/ud/spec/findaids/
David M. Nelson papers

University of Illinois
University Archives
Room 19 Library
1508 W. Gregory Drive
Urbana-Champaign, IL 61801
(217) 333-0708
http://www.uiuc.edu/

Avery Brundage papers
Campus Recreation Division records
Division of Intercollegiate Athletics records
Thomas K. Cureton, Jr. papers
David O. Matthew papers
Stuart C. Staley papers
Student Affairs records
Robert Zuppke papers

University of Michigan
1150 Beal Avenue
Ann Arbor, MI 48109-2113
(734) 764-3482
http://www.umich.edu/~bhl/
Division of Intercollegiate Athletics records

University Archives
University of New Hampshire
18 Library Way
Durham, NH 03824-3592
(603) 862-2714
http://www.unh.edu/library/
Charles E. Holt Archives of American Hockey

Special Collections
University of Scranton
Scranton, PA
(570) 941-6341
http://academic.uofs.edu/department/spcoll/ath_dep_col.html
Department of Intercollegiate Athletics records

University of Texas at Austin
217 Gregory Gymnasium
Austin, TX 78712
(512) 471-4890
http://www.utexas.edu/
Todd-McLean Physical Culture Collection

Special Collections
J. Willard Marriott Library
University of Utah
295 South 1500 East
Salt Lake City, UT 84112
(801) 581-8864
http://www.skiarchives.org/
Utah Ski Archives

Yale University
University Archives
P.O. Box 208240
New Haven, CT 06520-8246
(203) 432-9657
http://www.yale.edu/
Walter C. Camp papers

Halls of Fame

Alabama Sports Hall of Fame and Museum
2150 Civic Center Boulevard
Birmingham, AL 35203
(205) 323-6665
http://www.alasports.org/

The hall honors Paul "Bear" Bryant, Hank Aaron, Joe Louis, Joe Namath, Jesse Owens, Satchel Paige, Willie Mays, Bobby Allison to name but a few.

American Football Association Hall of Fame
P.O. Box 43885
Las Vegas, NV 89116-1885
(702) 431-2100
http://www.afafootball.com/

Site features rules, events, and sponsors for adult eight-on-eight flag football.

ASA National Softball Hall of Fame
2801 NE 50th Street
Oklahoma City, OK 73111-7203
(405) 424-5266
http://www.softball.org/

Established in 1957, the hall includes exhibits dedicated to players, teams, tournaments, and the Olympics.

Babe Ruth Museum
216 Emory Street
Baltimore. MD 21230
(410) 727-1539 Ext.3011
http://www.baberuthmuseum.com/

The museum holds archives of Babe Ruth and Cal Ripken records, the archives of the Baltimore Colts, Baltimore Orioles and Baltimore Ravens, as well as Baltimore's Negro Baseball Leagues.

College Football Hall of Fame
111 South Street
South Bend, IN 46601
(574) 235-9999
http://collegefootball.org/

The hall honors more than 800 college football players from the earliest years of the sport to the present.

International Bowling Museum and Hall of Fame
111 Stadium Plaza
St. Louis, Mo 63102
(800) 966-BOWL
http://www.bowlingmuseum.com/

Opened in 1984, the museum documents the history of the sport and chronicles its playing legends.

International Boxing Hall of Fame
1 Hall of Fame Drive
Canastata, NY 13032
(315) 697-7095
http://www.ibhof.com/

Its mission is to "honor and preserve boxing's rich heritage, chronicle the achievements of those who excelled and provide an educational experience...."

International Gymnastics Hall of Fame
120 No. Robinson E. Concourse
Oklahoma City, OK 73102
(405) 235-5600
http://www.ighof.com/

Representing gymnastics stars from around the world, the hall recognizes both competitive achievement and continuing participation in the sport.

International Motorsports Hall of Fame
P.O. Box 1018
Talladega, AL 35161
(256) 362-5002
http://www.motorsportshalloffame.com/

Opened in 1990, the hall features tributes to famed drivers and features more than 100 exhibits. The facility also includes the Automobile Racing Club of America Hall of Fame, the Western Auto Mechanics Hall of Fame, the Quarter Midgets of America Hall of Fame, the World Karting Hall of Fame, and the Alabama Sportswriters Hall of Fame.

International Museum of the Horse
4089 Iron Works Parkway
Lexington, KY 40511
(859) 233-4303
http://www.imh.org/

The museum is "the largest and most comprehensive equestrian museum in the world. It is dedicated to telling the intriguing story of the horse and his relationship with man."

International Swimming Hall of Fame
1 Hall of Fame Drive
Fort Lauderdale, FL 33316
(954) 462-6536
http://www.ishof.org/

The hall immortalizes "the achievements and contributions of those who have excelled in the sport" in addition to providing a "world-wide focal point for swimming and its many disciplines."

International Tennis Hall of Fame
194 Bellevue Avenue
Newport, RI 02840
(401) 849-3990
http://www.tennisfame.com/

Created in1954 to preserve the historic legacy of the game, the hall enshrines its greatest players and provides a facility for junior competitors.

Lacrosse Museum and Hall of Fame
113 West University Parkway
Baltimore, MD 21210-3300
(410) 366-6735
http://www.lacrosse.org/halloffame/

The hall was founded in 1957 to honor "men and women, past and present" who personify the goals and achievements of lacrosse.

Little League Baseball Museum
P.O. Box 3485
Williamsport, PA 17701
(717) 326-3607
http://www.littleleague.org/museum/

The museum documents the history of the program from its earliest beginnings in 1939 as a three-team league.

Naismith Memorial Basketball Hall of Fame
1150 W. Columbus Avenue
Springfield, MA 01101-0179
(413) 781-6500
http://www.hoophall.com/

Dedicated in 1968, the hall documents the achievements of the sport's elite as well as its history.

National Baseball Hall of Fame Library
25 Main Street
Cooperstown, NY 13326
(607) 547-0350
http://www.baseballhalloffame.org/

Dedicated in 1939 to recognize the 100th anniversary of the birth of the sport, the hall documents the history of the sport, honors its players, and examines its cultural impact worldwide.

National Ski Hall of Fame
P.O. Box 191
Ishpeming, MI 49849
(906) 485-6323
http://www.skihall.com/

The hall is dedicated to the preservation of U.S. ski history.

National Track & Field Hall of Fame
One RCA Dome, Suite 140
Indianapolis, IN 46225
(317) 261-0500
http://www.usatf.org/

The hall recognizes the achievements of "the sport's volunteers and athletes."

National Wrestling Hall of Fame
405 W. Hall of Fame Drive
Stillwater, OK 74075
(405) 377-5243
http://www.wrestlinghalloffame.org/

The hall "preserves the heritage of the sport, celebrates new achievements, and encourages the youth of the land to aspire to lofty goals."

Negro Leagues Baseball Museum
1616 E. 18th Street
Kansas City, MO 64108-1610
(816) 221-1920
http://www.nlbm.com/

Opened in 1991, the museum is arranged on a "timeline of African American and baseball history from 1860s–1950s."

Pro Football Hall of Fame
2121 George Halas Drive NW
Canton, OH 44708
(216) 456-8175
http://www.profootballhof.com/

Opened in 1963, the hall "serves as a hallowed honoring spot for the greats of the pro football world."

Soccer Hall of Fame
18 Stadium Circle
Oneonta, NY 13820
(607) 432-3351
http://www.soccerhall.org/

Established in 1979, the hall is dedicated to "preserving the history and sport of soccer in the United States."

U.S. Field Hockey Hall of Fame
One Olympic Plaza
Colorado Springs, CO 80909
(719) 866-4567
http://www.usfieldhockey.com/

The hall documents the achievements of athletes and coaches for contributions to the sport.

United States Golf Association Museum and Library
P.O. Box 708
Far Hills, NJ 07931
(908) 234-2300
http://www.usga.org/

Established in 1934, the museum documents the developments of the game and chronicles the accomplishments of its greatest participants.

U.S. Hockey Hall of Fame
801 Hat Trick Avenue
Eleveth, MN 55734
(218) 744-5167
http://www.ushockeyhall.com/

More than 100 "great American hockey people" from all competitive levels of the sport are enshrined in the hall.

United States Olympic Commission
Olympic Hall of Fame
1750 E. Boulder
Colorado Springs, CO 80909
(719) 578-4622
http://www.usoc.org/

Established in 1979, the Olympic Hall of Fame "celebrates the achievements of America's premier athletes in the modern Olympic games."

Volleyball Hall of Fame
444 Dwight Street
Holyoke, MA 01040
(413) 536-0926
http://www.volleyhall.org/

Opened in 1987, the hall features profiles of over 50 inductees as well as the Court of Honor, the Morgan Award winners, and Mintonette Medal of Merit winners.

Women's Basketball Hall of Fame
700 Hall of Fame Drive
Knoxville, TN 37915
(865) 633-9000
http://www.wbhof.com/

The hall opened in 1999 and "honors the past, celebrates the present and promotes the future of women's basketball."

World Figure Skating Museum & Hall of Fame
20 First Street
Colorado Springs, CO 80906
(719) 228-3450
http://www.worldskatingmuseum.org/

This museum is dedicated to documenting the history and achievements of international ice-skating.

Miscellaneous

Amateur Athletic Foundation (AAF) of Los Angeles
The Paul Ziffren Sports Resource Center
2141 W. Adams Blvd.
Los Angeles, CA 90018
(323) 730-4640
http://www.aafla.org/

The AAF operates "the largest sports research library in North America."

Berman-Bogdan Productions, Inc.
65 Beacon Street
Haworth, NJ 07641
(201) 384-7715
http://www.footagefinders.com
jbb@footagefinders.com
Pathe Newsreel Footage

Hospitality Industry Archives
Conrad N. Hilton Collection
229 C.N. Hilton Hotel & College Street, UH
Houston, TX 77204-3028
(713) 743-2470
http://www.mhmonline.uh.edu/
American Football League founding

International Motor Racing Research Center
610 S. Decatur Street
Watkins Glen, NY 14891-1613
(607) 535-9044
http://www.racingarchives.org/

The center documents the history and heritage of amateur and professional motor racing.

National Archives and Records Administration
700 Pennsylvania Avenue NW
Washington, D.C. 20408
(866) 272-6272
http://www.archives.gov/

U.S. President's Commission on Olympic Sports

National College Athletics Association
6201 College Boulevard
Overland Park, KS 66211-2422
(913) 339-0035
http://www.ncaa.org/

In addition to maintaining an extensive archive of NCAA policies, procedures, regulations, and activities, the NCAA also offers a Hall of Champions. The hall "celebrates the journey of the NCAA student-athlete."

National Sporting Library
102 The Plains Road
P.O. Box 1335
Middleburg, VA 20118-1335
(540) 687-6542
http://www.nsl.org/

The library "fosters interest and stimulates research in field and turf sports."

Mahoning Valley Historical Society
648 Wick Avenue
Youngstown, OH 44502
(330) 743-2589
http://www.mahoninghistory.org/

Old Timers Association, Baseball Players
John Elosh Papers

The Sporting News Research Center
10176 Corporate Square Drive
Suite 200
St. Louis, MO 63132
(314) 993-7787
http://www.sportingnews.com/archives/research
archives@sportingsnews.com

The center features a complete run of back issues of *The Sporting News,* media guides, books, guides, periodicals, and an extensive clippings file.

Women's Sports Foundation
342 Madison Avenue
Suite 728
New York, NY 10173
(212) 972-9170
http://www.womenssportfoundation.org/

The foundation is the "#1 information resource on women's sports."

BIBLIOGRAPHY
Sources

Ash, Lee. *Subject Collections: A Guide to Special Book Collections and Subject Emphases....* New Providence, N.J.: R. R. Bowker, 1993.

Brooks, Philip C. *Research in Archives: The Use of Unpublished Primary Sources.* Chicago, Ill.: University of Chicago Press, 1969.

Danilov, Victor J. *Hall of Fame Museums: A Reference Guide.* Westport, Conn.: Greenwood Press, 1997.

Deardorff, Donald L., II. *Sports: A Reference Guide and Critical Commentary, 1980–1999.* Westport, Conn.: Greenwood Press, 2000.

Gilbert, Doug. *Sports Hall of Fame: A Directory of over 100 Sports Museums in the United States.* Jefferson, N.C.: McFarland & Co., 1992.

International Association for Sports Information. *World Directory of Sports Libraries, Information and Documentation Centers.* Gloucester, Ont.: IASI, 1996.

Kepley, David. "Reference Services and Access." In *Managing Archives and Archival Institutions,* ed. James G. Brashers. Chicago, Ill.: University of Chicago Press, 1989.

National Historical Publications and Records Commission. *Directory of Archives and Manuscripts.* Phoenix, Ariz.: Oryx Press, 1988.

Rosenberger, Matthew G. *Sports Resource Directory.* Chicago, Ill.: M. G. R. Enterprises, 1993.

Su, Mila Chin Ying. "Collegiate Women's Sports and a Guide to Collecting and Identifying Archival Materials." Master's Thesis, Pennsylvania State University, 2002.

Journals for Sports Researchers

American Journal of Sports Medicine. Thousand Oaks, Calif.: Sage Publications, Inc.

Athletic Administration. Cleveland, Ohio: Bashian Pub. Co.

Baseball Research Journal. Washington, D.C.: Society for American Baseball Research.

Exercise and Sport Sciences Review. Hagerstown, Md.: Lippincott, Williams & Wilkins.

International Journal of the History of Sport. London: F. Cass.

International Journal of Sport Nutrition. Champaign, Ill.: Human Kinetics Publishers, Inc.

Journal of Physical Education, Recreation, and Dance. New York: National Physical Education Society.

Journal of Sport and Exercise Psychology. Champaign, Ill.: Human Kinetics Publishers, Inc.

Journal of Sport and Social Issues. Thousand Oaks, Calif.: Sage Periodicals Press.

Journal of Sport History. Radford, Va.: North American Society for Sport History.

Journal of Strength and Conditioning Training.

NCAA News. Shawnee Mission, Kans.: National College Athletic Association.

NCAA Sports Sciences Education Newsletter.

Physical Educator. Indianapolis, Ind.: Phi Epsilon Kappa Fraternity.

Research Quarterly for Exercise and Sport. Washington, D.C.: American Alliance for Health, Physical Education, Recreation, and Dance.

SABR Bulletin: Newsletter of the Society for American Baseball Research.

Sport Science Review. Champaign, Ill.: Human Kinetics Publishers, Inc.

Women in Sport and Physical Activity Journal. Fort Worth, Tex.: Women of Diversity Productions.

Women's Sport and Fitness. New York: Conde Naste.

Inside Sports. Evanston, Ill.: Inside Sports, Inc.

The Sporting News. St. Louis, Mo.: Sporting News Pub. Co.

Sports Illustrated. Chicago, Ill.: Time, Inc.

CHAPTER 10
Business Archives
Gregory S. Hunter

Business archives are important sources of historical information. Accessing that information, however, is different than using other archival collections *because* business archives exist to serve the parent institution rather than scholarship. To understand the similarities and differences between business archives and other archives, this article will discuss the following:

- History and development of business archives
- Challenges and opportunities in contemporary business archives

This chapter will conclude with a listing that covers the broad range of business archives found in North America.

HISTORY AND DEVELOPMENT OF BUSINESS ARCHIVES

Some archives are established to fulfill a legal mandate. Government archives, in particular, are usually established after the passage of legislation. The federal, state, or local law provides the purpose of the archives and details the responsibilities that it must discharge. The authorizing legislation, however, cuts both ways: while it permits some activities, the government archives cannot go beyond its legal mandate. This became an issue in several U.S. states in the 1980s, where the archives realized that they lacked oversight authority for digital imaging systems or electronic records programs.

Other archives are established to promote research and scholarship. The first historical society in the United States was the Massachusetts Historical Society, which was founded in 1791. From this beginning,

the historical society movement swept the United States, preserving and making available for research a great deal of valuable historical documentation.[1]

The earliest college and university archives were also established to promote scholarship. As universities adopted the German seminar model for graduate education at the end of the nineteenth century, it became important to have primary sources available for both faculty and students. From these efforts grew some of the finest scholarly collections in the nation.[2]

Business archives, however, differ from other types of archives in one major respect: business archives exist to serve the parent corporation rather than the world of scholarship. While many business archives are open to outside researchers, usually under specified conditions, this is not their primary purpose. Especially in difficult economic times, a corporation maintains an archive because it makes business sense.

The first professionally managed corporate archive was established at the Firestone Tire & Rubber Company in 1943. As early as 1937, the Firestone family had hired former Ohio state archivist William D. Overman to process the papers of the founder of the company Harvey Firestone and his sons. Realizing the importance of the company's activities to the war effort, the company hired Overman on a permanent basis in 1943.[3]

Business archives grew in the 1940s and 1950s. Archival programs were established at Alcoa, Armstrong Cork, Bank of America, Coca-Cola, Eastman Kodak, Eli Lilly, Ford Motor Company, Lever Brothers, New York Life Insurance, Procter & Gamble, Sears Roebuck, and Time, Inc. This growth slowed in the 1960s when only four new business archives were established: the Chicago Board of Trade, the Educational Testing Service, Gulf Oil, and the International Business Machines Corporation (IBM).[4]

The 1970s was a decade of unprecedented growth in business archives fueled by three factors: (1) interest in history sparked by the U.S. bicentennial, (2) an expanding economy for much of the decade, and (3) a change in corporate culture that emphasized the importance of collective memory. During the 1970s archival programs were established at Anheuser-Busch, Atlantic Richfield, Chase Manhattan Bank, Corning Glass Works, Deere & Co., Ford Foundation, Georgia-Pacific Co., Gerber Products, International Harvester (now Navistar), J. Walter Thompson Company, Los Angeles Times, Nabisco, Nationwide Insurance, the New York Stock Exchange, United Technologies, Walt Disney Productions, Wells Fargo Bank, and Weyerhaeuser Company.[5]

The growth of business archives slowed in the 1980s and 1990s. Nevertheless, archival programs were established at such major corporations as American Express, American International Group, General Mills, Kraft Foods, Microsoft, Motorola, Phillips Petroleum, and Texas Instruments.[6]

Many of these business archives no longer exist; unfortunately, archives have not been immune from business cycles and management trends. Economic downturns, right sizing, and outsourcing all have had an effect. Business archives that have survived these shifts have demonstrated their continuing contribution to the corporation.[7]

Two of the most famous examples of business archives demonstrating their value to their parent corporation are:

- Wells Fargo & Co. was once faced with a $480 million suit alleging that it had misappropriated an idea to start a credit card operation. Using materials from the bank's archives dating back to the 1960s, lawyers were able to prove that Wells Fargo had developed the idea itself.[8]
- When Mount St. Helens erupted in Washington in 1980, Weyerhaeuser was faced with the enormous task of salvaging downed timber. The extent of the damage reminded old-timers at Weyerhaeuser of Typhoon Frieda in 1962 where even more timber was downed. Documents relating to the earlier disaster's salvage operations were readily available in the company's archive. Weyerhaeuser based its Mount St. Helens operations on this information and employed 650 loggers and 600 trucks over three years to complete the job.[9]

There are numerous other examples that show the value of a business archive to its parent corporation: documentation for trademark and copyright disputes, valuation of assets at the time of mergers or divestitures, increasing sales through marketing programs using historical advertising and packaging, and promoting a positive public image of the corporation. Because of the proprietary nature of business, most of these examples never reach the press.[10]

CHALLENGES AND OPPORTUNITIES IN CONTEMPORARY BUSINESS ARCHIVES

Contemporary business archives face a number of challenges. Some flow from the unique nature of the business environment; others are a factor of the changing nature of records and affect archives of all types. Depending upon whether one is an optimist or a pessimist, these challenges can offer opportunities for a business archive to demonstrate its value to the corporation.

Among the issues business archivists face today are: selection and appraisal, digital records, litigation and investigations, and an interface with records management.

Selection and Appraisal

Organizations of all kinds are awash in records, a surprising amount that continues to be on paper. Despite all the hype surrounding the paperless office, trees still have much to fear in the contemporary business.[11]

One major challenge facing business archivists is determining how much of this increasing volume of records has archival value. Appraisal has been called the archivist's "first responsibility"[12]—if we do not select the proper materials, all of our subsequent activities (the arrangement, description, preservation, and so on) are a waste of scarce institutional resources.

Since the 1980s, archivists have devoted a great deal of effort to understanding and refining appraisal theory and practice.[13] Business archivists also have been part of the discussions, with the most important contribution being a volume edited by James M. O'Toole.[14] As with other aspects of business archives, the challenge is to shape a body of historical documentation that meets the needs of the business as well as scholarship.

Digital Records

Although contemporary businesses continue to produce and retain paper, much of the mission-critical information now is in digital form. These digital records present new challenges for the business archivist.

Jeff Rothenberg of the Rand Corporation has identified a "unique collection of core digital attributes." According to Rothenberg, if we are to preserve digital records, we must preserve their ability to be copied perfectly, accessed without geographic constraint, disseminated at virtually no incremental cost, and machine-readable in all phases of their creation and distribution. In addition, documents that are "born digital" tend to be dynamic, hyperlinked, and interactive—additional attributes that may need to be preserved.[15]

The ultimate goal is to preserve the *integrity* of the digital record. In 1996, the Commission on Preservation and Access and the Research Libraries Group formed the Task Force on Archiving of Digital Information. This task force identified five aspects of information integrity:

- *Content.* The intellectual substance found in the information objects.
- *Fixity.* The content must be fixed as a discrete object in order to be a record. If a digital object is subject to change without notice, then its integrity may be compromised.
- *Reference.* For a digital object to maintain its integrity, one must be able to locate it definitively and reliably among other objects over time.
- *Provenance.* The integrity of an information object is partly embedded in tracing its source.
- *Context.* Digital objects interact with other elements in the wider digital environment.[16]

Analog records exhibit the five characteristics noted above; we are so accustomed to the analog records, however, that we tend to take these characteristics for granted. With digital records, we can take almost nothing for granted if we are to have a reliable record over time.

Business archivists are beginning to acquire and preserve a vast array of digital records: E-mail messages, Web site pages, Computer Aided Design (CAD) drawings, digital photographs and videos, records from Electronic Document Management Systems (EDMS), content management systems, and data warehouses. How future researchers will access these records is still unclear; preservation rather than access is the immediate focus of the business archivist.

Litigation and Investigations

The business environment has always been a litigious one. The last few years, however, have seen a number of high-visibility cases that often involve business records:

- The Enron case was one of the largest forensic records case in history. Investigators pored through 10 thousand computer backup tapes, 20 million sheets of paper, and more than 400 computers and handheld devices. The electronic data alone was up to 10 times the size of the Library of Congress.[17]
- Microsoft's protracted antitrust investigation by the federal government often hinged on internal Microsoft documents. The government was able to review an estimated 3.3 million Microsoft documents, including megabytes of E-mail messages dating from the early 1990s. These internal documents often contradicted Microsoft's public statements about its approaches and actions.[18]

Into this environment walks the business archivist, arguing for the preservation of historical records at a time when others within the organization would prefer to slash and burn the entire corporate memory. The business archivist must constantly communicate the importance of an archival *program* and how it differs from the wholesale retention of records in cubbyholes quickly forgotten. As noted above, the core archival responsibility is determining the value of records and retaining only a small, historically valuable subset of the entire records universe.

Interface with Records Management

Archival programs are not the only ones experiencing change. A related profession, records management, is also facing new challenges. Unlike archivists who deal only with records of enduring value, records managers are responsible for the entire life cycle of records.[19]

Researchers need to understand the different access to records in the physical custody of archivists and records managers. When records are transferred to archives, the records are administered according to the archives' policies and procedures, including references by nonemployees. In contrast, records managers do not set policies for access by outside researchers; each department that creates the records makes this determination. Researchers should be forewarned that it would be highly unusual for a business to grant access to records in the physical custody of records managers.[20]

One of the major responsibilities of records management is the efficient storage of inactive records in facilities called records centers. These facilities have been a target for outsourcing to private companies specializing in records storage. Outsourcing storage, unfortunately, has lowered the presence of records management and weakened many records programs.

This can have implications for archives. One of the ways that archives identify records of potential historical value is by working with records managers. Archivists provide input for establishing retention periods and review records eligible for destruction. Any diminution in the role of records management would make it more difficult for archivists to identify records of potential interest to internal and external researchers.

DIRECTORY OF BUSINESS ARCHIVES

The following information is taken from the 5th edition of the *Directory of Corporate Archives in the United States and Canada,* published by the Society of American Archivists. This edition includes companies that maintain their historical records themselves, as well as companies that contract out with historical consulting firms to maintain their archives collections for them. The latter are marked by an asterisk.

The 5th edition of the *Directory* was edited in 1997 by Amy Fischer of Procter & Gamble and Liz Holum Johnson of H.B. Fuller Company. Since 1999 an online version has been edited and maintained by Gregory S. Hunter and is available at http://www.hunterinformation.com/corporat.htm.

Since 1997 there has been no systematic effort to update directory listings, though many archives have sent updates for the online edition. Therefore, some in the following listing may contain inaccuracies. Researchers are advised to contact a corporation directly before embarking on a research project.

Campbell Soup Company
Building 81
Camden, NJ 08103
Contact: Jan Dickeler, librarian, archivist
609-342-4800, ext. 2425
Fax: 609-342-5241
Type of business: Food industry
Hours of service: Varies; contact archivist directly
Conditions of access: Each request considered separately
Holdings: 1869–present; bulk dates, 1900–196(?)

Holdings include memorabilia of the Campbell Soup Company, such as print advertisements, labels, in-house publications, photographs, company history, Campbell Kid dolls, toys, premiums, and licensed products.

Caterpillar, Inc.
100 N.E. Adams
Peoria, IL 61629
Contact: Nicole Thaxton, corporate archivist
309-675-5869
Fax: 309-675-5948
Thaxton_Nicole_L@cat.com
Type of business: Manufacturing, capital goods
Conditions of access: By appointment only
Holdings: 1850–present; bulk dates, 1883–present

Archive contains records, correspondence, photos, and memorabilia pertaining to the history of Caterpillar and its predecessor and acquired companies.

CBS News
524 West 57th Street
New York, NY 10019
Contact: Neil Waldman, director of sales and licensing
212-975-4321
Fax: 212-975-5442
Type of business: Stock footage, television, and radio broadcasting
Hours of service: 9:00 A.M.–5:00 P.M.
Conditions of access: Stock footage sales available through CBS news archives
Holdings: 1954–present

Film and videotape material that were produced in connection with CBS news broadcasts. Collection includes complete news broadcasts as well as outtakes. Retrieval tools include catalog cards and in-house database.

Chas. Schwab & Company Inc.

Corporate Records and Archives
280 Valley Drive
Brisbane, CA 94005
Contact: Russ Stephens
415-636-6161
Hours of service: M–F, 8:00 A.M.–5:00 P.M.

Chase Manhattan Corporation
2 Chase Plaza, 27th Floor
New York, NY 10081
Contact: Jean Hrichus, archivist
212-552-8330
Fax: 212-552-8293
Type of business: Banking and financial services
Hours of service: M–F, 9:00 A.M.–5:00 P.M.

Conditions of access: By appointment only
Holdings: 1799–present; bulk dates, 1930–present
Total volume: 5,000 cubic feet

This archive collection includes noncurrent records of the Chase Manhattan Bank, N.A. and their predecessors that have lasting administrative, legal, or historical value. Heavily used materials include the photograph collection, early water company records of the Bank of Manhattan Company and Chase publications. The merger between Chemical Bank and Chase Manhattan Corporation in August 1995 produced an additional 1,000 cubic feet of records documenting the predecessors of Chemical Bank and Manufacturers Hanover Trust. These records are included in the total volume listed.

Chicago Mercantile Exchange
30 S. Wacker Dr.
Chicago, IL 60606
312-648-5413
Fax: 312-466-7436
Type of business: Futures and options exchange
Hours of service: 7:00 A.M.–4:00 P.M.
Conditions of access: Restricted; contact archivist for admittance
Holdings: 1890–present; bulk dates, 1950s–present
Total volume: 800 cubic feet

CIGNA Corporation
1601 Chestnut Street, TL05D
Philadelphia, PA 19192-2057
Contact: Leslie Simon, archives manager; Aimee Felker, associate archivist
Simon: 215-761-4903; fax: 215-761-5588
Felker: 860-726-3844; fax: 860-726-2915
history@cigna.com
Type of business: Insurance and financial services
Hours of service: M–F, 9:00 A.M.–4:00 P.M.
Conditions of access: All outside access is by individual review
Holdings: 1865–present; bulk dates, 1950–present
Total volume: Approximately 3,200 cubic feet

Collections include administrative, financial, marketing and public affairs publications and photographic and artifactual records of CIGNA and its predecessor and subsidiary companies.

Coca-Cola Company
P.O. Drawer 1734
Atlanta, GA 30301
Contact: Philip F. Mooney, manager of archives department
404-676-3491
Fax: 404-676-7701
Type of business: Food industry

Hours of service: M–F, 9:00 A.M.–5:00 P.M.
Conditions of access: All outside access is by individual review
Holdings: 1880–present; bulk dates, 1920–present
Total volume: 2,000 linear feet

Collections include administrative, financial, legal, and marketing and public relations files. Extensive holdings of photography and audiovisual materials are available. Collections heavily weighted toward advertising, marketing, and promotional activities in the United States; some files on overseas operations.

Colgate-Palmolive Company
300 Park Avenue
New York, NY 10022
Contact: Carla Mikell, coordinator of corporate communications
212-310-2191
Type of business: Manufacturer of consumer goods
Hours of service: By appointment only
Conditions of access: By appointment only
Holdings: Late nineteenth century to present; bulk dates, 1920s, 1950s, 1960s

Holdings are product samples, print ads, and a few books and periodicals.

Colonial Life and Accident Insurance Company
1200 Colonial Life Boulevard
Columbia, SC 29202
Contact: Jeanette Bergeron, archivist
803-798-1000
Type of business: Insurance and insurance-related services
Hours of service: M–F, 9:00 A.M.–5:00 P.M.
Conditions of access: Restricted; access requires written approval
Holdings: 1937–present
Total volume: 2,000-plus cubic feet

Holdings include historical, legal, and administrative records of the company, its subsidiaries, founders, and chief executive officers. Bedsides paper documents, the collection includes photographs, slides, microfiche, blueprints, videotapes, and artifacts.

Compaq Computer Corporation
Global Records Management
9440 Louetta, MSC 500103
Spring, TX 77379
Contact: Leslie Williams Brunet, corporate archivist
lesley.brunet@compaq.com

Corning, Inc.
Department of Archives and Records Management
HP-AB-02-2
Corning, NY 14831

Contact: Michelle L. Cotton, archives and records management supervisor
607-974-8457
Fax: 607-974-8612
Type of business: Manufacturing and health services
Hours of service: 8:00 A.M.–5:00 P.M., by appointment only
Conditions of access: Corporate personnel; limited outside access for scholarly research
Holdings: 1851–present; bulk dates, 1900–present
Total volume: 500 cubic feet

Archive contains corporate records, photographs, illustrations, and audiovisual materials. The bulk of the collection consists of documents dealing with the business affairs, research and development, manufacturing, and marketing of products. Approximately 300,000 photographs and 2,000 artifacts support the written documentation.

CTB/McGraw Hill
20 Ryan Ranch Road
Monterey, CA 93940-5703
Contact: Chase Weaver
408-393-7920
Type of business: Educational test publishing company
Conditions of access: By appointment only
Holdings: 1926–present
Total volume: 770 linear feet

Archives contain test products of the California Test Bureau and CTB/McGraw-Hill.

DaimlerChrysler Corporate Historical Collection
CIMS 410-11-21
12501 Chrysler Freeway
Detroit, MI 48288
313-252-2902
Type of business: Manufacturing, capital goods
Hours of service: M–F, 8:30 A.M.–4:30 P.M.
Conditions of access: Not open to the public; inquiries to be sent via U.S. mail
Holdings: 1914–1999

Holdings include product information, photographs, manuals, technical information, and general corporate history.

Deere & Company
John Deere Road
Moline, IL 61265
Contact: Leslie J. Stegh, archivist
309-765-2763
Fax: 309-765-2751
ls61856@deere.com
Type of business: Manufacturing capital goods and consumer goods; insurance and insurance-related services
Hours of service: M–F, 8:00 A.M.–4:30 P.M.

Conditions of access: By permission of the archivist
Holdings: Twentieth century; 1837–present

Archive materials relate to the history of Deere & Company and its products.

Delta Air Lines, Inc.
Delta Air Transport Heritage Museum
P.O. Box 20585, Dept. 914
Atlanta, GA 30320-2585
Contact: Marie Force, archivist
404-714-2371
Fax: 404-715-2037
marie.force@delta.com
Type of business: Transportation
Hours of service: M–F, 9 A.M.–5 P.M.
Conditions of access: Outside requests for information subject to approval by the Delta Air Transport Heritage Museum and Delta Air Lines Corporate Communications
Holdings: 1924–present; bulk dates, 1941–1990
Total volume: 11,000 cubic feet

Corporate collections include Delta Air Lines administrative, financial, legal marketing, technical operations, and public relations files related to crop-dusting activity from 1924–1966 and passenger service from 1929–present. Also contains records from airlines affiliated with Delta through mergers and route acquisitions: Chicago & Southern (C&S) Airlines, Western Airlines, Northeast Airlines, and limited Pan Am records and artifacts. Extensive holdings include photographic materials, flight schedules, uniforms, and passenger-service equipment.

Digital Equipment Corporation
153 Taylor St., TAY-2/E 12
Littleton, MA 01460
Contact: Craig St. Clair, corporate archives
508-952-3559
Fax: 508-952-3560
stclair@rdvax.enet.dec.com
Type of business: Computer manufacturer
Hours of service: M–F, 9:00 A.M.–5:00 P.M.
Conditions of access: By permission of the archivist
Holdings: 1975–present
Total volume: 3,000 cubic feet

The archive holds the permanent records of the company including executive papers, speeches, correspondence, memoranda and project files, engineering drawings and business plans, digital publications, product and technical manuals, employee periodicals, public-relations materials, shareholder materials, marketing brochures, videotapes, press releases, and oral histories plus artifacts ranging from computer modules to vintage full-size computers.

Dow Chemical Company
205 Post Street
Midland, MI 48640
Contact: E. N. Brandt, company historian; Kathy Thomas, librarian
517-832-0870
Fax: 517-832-0871
Type of business: Chemical manufacturing
Hours of service: M–F, 8:00 A.M.–12:00 P.M.
Conditions of access: Open to public with some restricted collections; photographs may be borrowed; staff may make copies of requested print materials
Holdings: 1872–present; bulk dates, 1887–present

Archive contains historical records of the Dow Chemical Company, with a special collection of papers of founder Herbert H. Dow. A-V materials include photographs, films, videos, audiocassettes, and advertisements. Printed matter consists of biographies, product and location histories, annual reports, Dow publications, collected papers of key personnel, and miscellaneous other topics relating to company history.

Dow Corning Corporation
2200 West Salzburg Road
Auburn, MI 48611
Contact: Gayann Nash, HES archivist
517-496-8429
Fax: 517-496-6609
Type of business: General manufacturing
Conditions of access: Restricted
Holdings: 1960–present
Total volume: 5,000 cubic feet

Eastman Kodak Company
343 State Street
Rochester, NY 14650-1206
716-724-3041
Fax: 716-724-1985
Type of business: General manufacturing
Hours of service: M–F, 8:00 A.M.–5:00 P.M.
Conditions of access: Letter describing research needs required; requests will be evaluated as to whether there is enough material to warrant a visit to the company.
Holdings: 1880s–present

The collection is varied, consisting of early business correspondence, photographs, advertisements, and biographies of corporate officers through the years. The collection is an adjunct to the business library and no one person is specifically assigned to administer it.

Ernest and Julio Gallo Winery
600 Yosemite Boulevard
Modesto, CA 95354

Contact: Pat Hall, legal department
209-579-3169
Fax: 209-579-4969
Type of business: Food and beverage industry

Fireman's Fund Insurance Company Archives*
777 San Marin Drive
Novato, CA 94998

Holdings consist of administrative records, biographical material, correspondences and speeches of founders and executives, property files, logbooks and code books, anniversary material, written and pictorial documentation of the 1906 earthquake and fire in San Francisco, a large photograph collection of natural disasters and fires, and photographs providing insights to the developments of the shipping industry in the second half of the nineteenth century. Records of subsidiaries and acquired institutions, particularly the American Insurance Company and Home Mutual are well represented.

Forbes
P.O. Box 95
1400 Route 206 North
Bedminster, NJ 07921
Contact: Whoy Yurn Shang
908-781-2360
Fax: 908-719-7964
whoys@aol.com
Type of business: Publishing
Hours of service: M–F, 9:00 A.M.–5:00 P.M.
Conditions of access: Restricted; outside requests must be submitted in writing on letterhead, and requests are subject to approval by senior administrators.
Holdings: 1917–present
Total volume: Approximately 2,000 cubic feet

Holdings consist of company records, company publications, print and broadcast advertising, photographs, clippings, and company artifacts.

Ford Motor Company
Ford Industrial Archives
Schaefer Court, Suite 180
14441 Rotunda Drive
Dearborn, MI 48120
Contact: Elizabeth Adkins, manager of archives services; Darleen Flaherty, assistant corporate archivist
313-845-0556
Fax: 313-248-4921
Type of business: Automotive manufacturing
Hours of service: M–F, 8:00 A.M.–4:30 P.M.
Conditions of access: Access policy currently under review
Holdings: 1903–present; bulk dates, 1950–1980
Total volume: 7,000 cubic feet

Majority of the collection falls into the category of executive correspondence and international operations; large collection of executive speeches and corporate newspapers and periodicals; hundreds of smaller collections on a wide assortment of Ford Motor Company activities/programs/buildings. In December 1964, a major donation of Ford archival materials, along with 460,000 photos and negatives, was made to the Henry Ford Museum Archives, Research Center, P.O. Box 1970, Dearborn, Michigan, 48121, Phone: 313-271-1620, ext. 650, fax: 313-271-9621. The museum holds the bulk of early Ford historical records, 1903–1950.

Frito Lay Corporation
P.O. Box 650423
Dallas, TX 75265-0423
Contact: Suzanne Ogden
214-334-4732
Fax: 214-334-2019
Type of business: Food industry

Gap, Inc.
1 Harrison St.
San Francisco, CA 94105
Contact: Laurie Banducci
415-952-4400
Type of business: Apparel retailing

General Mills, Inc.
One General Mills Blvd.
Minneapolis, MN 55440-1113
Contact: Katie Dishman
763-764-2679
Fax: 763-764-4921
katie.dishman@genmills.com
Type of business: Food industry
Hours of service: M–F, 8:30 A.M.–4:30 P.M.
Conditions of access: Open to all employees and by phone only to outside researchers
Holdings: 1890–1994; bulk dates, 1930–1950
Total volume: 1,000 cubic feet

Holdings are mostly promotional and advertising materials including print ads, audio-visual reports, packaging, price lists as well as detailed annual reports and other information related to the history of the corporation.

Georgia-Pacific Corporation
P.O. Box 105605
133 Peachtree Street, 2nd Floor
Atlanta, GA 30348
Contact: Linda E. Long, records manager; Shirley Ming
404-852-6674

Fax: 404-527-0887
Type of business: General manufacturing
Hours of service: M–F, 8:00 A.M.–5:00 P.M.
Conditions of access: Restricted access
Holdings: 1927–present; bulk dates, 1960–present

Gerber Products Company
445 State Street
Fremont, MI 49412
Contact: Sherrie Anderson, corporate librarian
616-928-2631
Type of business: Food industry
Hours of service: M–F, 8:00 A.M.–5:00 P.M.
Conditions of access: Not open to the public
Holdings: 1900–present

Archive collection includes clippings, photos, promotional pieces, products, bulletins, employee announcements, and company publications.

Goodyear Tire & Rubber Company*
The University of Akron
Polsky Building
Akron, OH 44325-1701
Contact: John Miller, archival services
330-972-7670
Fax: 330-972-6170
Type of business: General manufacturing
Hours of service: 8:30 A.M.–5:00 P.M.
Conditions of access: Limited; requests for archival information will be answered by writing or faxing Mr. John Miller. For general information on the company founders and it namesake, Charles Goodyear, the inventor, please write to the corporation at 1144 E. Market St., Akron, OH 44316-0001.
Holdings: 1898–present; bulk dates 1920s, 1940s
Collection includes photos, letters, and other materials relating to the beginning and development of the company: its historic achievements, its products, its contributions to aviation and transportation and its involvement in world affairs.

Guardian Life Insurance Company of America
201 Park Avenue South
New York, NY 10003
Contact: Karen L. Dickinson, assistant corporate secretary
212-598-7499
Fax: 212-420-9516
Type of business: Insurance and insurance-related services
Hours of service: By appointment only
Conditions of access: External use is limited; requests must be submitted in writing. Researchers are advised to consult Anita Rapone, *The Guardian Life Insurance Company, 1860–1920: A History of a German-American Enterprise,* (New York: New York University Press, 1987).
Holdings: 1860–present

Total volume: 110 cubic feet

The collection documents business activities primarily of the company's home office, with some materials relating to its field offices, industrial branch, and European business. The records consist of minutes, annual reports, legal documents, financial ledgers, stock certificates, insurance policies and registers, correspondence, publications, photographs, and artifacts.

Hallmark Cards, Inc.
2501 McGee, #453
Kansas City, MO 64141
Contact: Sharman Robertson, corporate archivist
816-545-6992 or 816-274-3534
Fax: 816-274-2947
Type of business: Manufacturing consumer goods
Hours of service: M–F, 8:00 A.M.–5:00 P.M.
Conditions of access: Restricted to in-house; all other requests must be in writing
Holdings: Corporate collection: 1910–present; design collection: late eighteenth and early twentieth centuries
Total volume: 2,000 cubic feet

The corporate archives houses any material related to the history and development of the company. This includes publications, correspondence, photographs, product samples, and oral histories. The design collection contains more than 40,000 greeting cards dating to the late eighteenth century published in the United States and Europe. Also housed in the archive are the collections of Louis Prang and Andrew Szoeke.

Harley-Davidson Motor Company
3700 W. Juneau Avenue
Milwaukee, WI 53208
Contact: Susan Fariss, archivist; Martin J. Rosenblum, historian
Fariss: 414-935-8973
Rosenblum: 414-935-4974
Fax: 414-935-8786
sfariss@omnifest.uwm.edu
Type of business: Motor vehicle manufacturing
Conditions of access: Physical access restricted; outside requests for information filled on a case-by-case basis
Holdings: 1903–present

Holdings consist of company publications, print and broadcast advertising, motorcycling memorabilia, motorcycles, and technical manuals and more than 40,000 photographs of motorcycles, parts and accessories, facilities, employees, and the founders. Holdings also include a wide variety of other documentation for company brands and acquired companies.

Harper Collins Publishers
10 East 53rd Street
New York, NY 10022
Contact: Donna Slawsky, library and records manager
212-207-7132
Fax: 212-207-7946
slawsky@harpercollins.com
Type of business: Publishing
Hours of service: M–F, 9:00 A.M.–5:00 P.M.
Conditions of access: Appointment with manager
Holdings: Published books, early 1900s–present; corporate memos, 1960s–present; catalogs, 1847–present
Total volume: 1,800 square feet

Archive contains books published by Harper Collins, Harper & Row, Harper & Brothers, T. Y. Crowell, J. B. Lippincott and other acquired imprints from early 1900s to present; corporate memos from the 1960s to the present; catalogs from 1847 to present.

The Hartford Family Foundation (Atlantic & Pacific Co.) Archives
8 Lone Oak Road
Basking Ridge, NJ 07920
Contact: Avis Anderson, HFF; Debbie Waller, director of archival services, The History Factory, 14140 Parke Long Court, Chantilly, VA 20151-1649
703-631-0500
Fax: 703-631-1124
http://www.historyfactory.com/
Type of business: Family foundation
Hours of service: M–F, 9:00 A.M.–5:30 P.M.
Conditions of access: Restricted; outside requests for information subject to approval by the executive director and The History Factory.
Holdings: 1865–1990
Total volume: 108 linear feet

Holdings are comprised of A&P business records including advertisements, annual reports, sales brochures, anniversary publications and memorabilia, and product packaging. Storefront signs and machinery are retained. Papers of the Hartford family include oral histories, photographs, correspondences, marriage certificates and genealogy, movies, and memorabilia.

Jim Henson Productions
117 East 69th Street
New York, NY 10021
Contact: Karen Falk, archivist; Lauren Bien, associate archivist
212-794-2400
Fax: 212-570-1147
Type of business: Entertainment

Conditions of access: Restricted to company personnel; outside requests at the discretion of the archivist

Herman Miller, Inc.
855 East Main Avenue
P.O. Box 302, MS 0220
Zeeland, MI 49464
Contact: Robert W. Viol, corporate archivist
616-654-5680
Fax: 616-654-3597
Type of business: Furniture and consumer goods manufacturer
Hours of service: M–F, 8:00 A.M.–5:00 P.M., by appointment only
Conditions of access: Some collections open to the public; call for an appointment
Holdings: 1905–present; bulk dates, 1930–present
Total volume: 1,500 linear feet

The Herman Miller Archives manages the following collections: administrative records, including the papers of the company's founder; Herman Miller specific publications; photography dating from 1905 to present; drawings and blueprints depicting furniture designed by Charles Eames, George Nelson, Gilbert Rohde, and others; oral histories; audiovisuals; corporate art; Herman Miller furniture collection; and reference library. Also included are 1,000 furniture artifacts and 500 art objects.

Hershey Community Archives*
P.O. Box 64
Hershey, PA 17033
Contact: Pamela C. Whitenack, archivist
717-566-8116
Fax: 717-566-8004
pwhitenack@hersheyarchives.com
http://www.hersheyarchives.org/
Type of business: Food industry, amusement parks, financial company, resorts, town models
Hours of service: M–F, 8:00 A.M.–4:30 P.M.; appointments recommended
Conditions of access: Open to internal clients; outside access to collections vary; contact archivist
Holdings: 1857–present; Bulk dates, 1903–present
Total volume: 1,800 cubic feet

The records of Hershey Foods Corporation, Hershey Entertainment and Resorts, Hershey Trust Company, The M.S. Hershey Foundation as well as the records of many local organizations and individuals. The holdings include oral histories, business records, product packaging and advertising, maps, architectural plans, and more than 12,000 photographs.

Hewlett-Packard Company
3000 Hanover Street, 20BR
Palo Alto, CA 94304
Contact: Anna Mancini
415-857-6276
Type of business: Computer and information systems
Hours of service: M–F, 8:30 A.M.–5:00 P.M.
Conditions of access: Limited use
Holdings: 1938–present
Total volume: 1,500 cubic feet

Resources include records of chief executives, central administration, and corporate labs that are of continuing administrative and historical value. Materials also include oral histories, photographs, internal publications, ephemera, and a historical product collection.

Hormel Foods Corporation
P.O. Box 800
Austin, MN 55912
Contact: V. Allan Krejci
507-437-5355
Fax: 507-437-9803
Type of business: Food industry
Hours of service: M–F, 7:00 A.M.–4:00 P.M.
Conditions of access: Restricted; outside requests for information subject to approval from the archivist and the public-relations director
Holdings: 1860–present

Holdings consist of artifacts and documents dating back to 1860; family photos, business correspondences, and advertising dating from late 1800s; product packaging from 1920s and tins from the 1900s.

Hudson's Bay Company
Records Management & Heritage Services
401 Bay Street, Suite 2407
Toronto, Ontario, Canada
M5H 2Y4
Contact: Brenda Hobbs, manager of records and historical information; Yanick Dubé, records analyst for artifacts and archives; for donated archives, contact Judith Beattie at 204-945-2626
Hobbs: 416-861-4148
Dubé: 416-861-4704
Fax: 416-861-6248
brenda.hobbs@hbc.com; yanick.dube@hbc.com
Type of business: Retailing
Hours of service: M–F, 8:00 A.M.–5:00 P.M.
Conditions of access: Donated records open to all; corporate records open to research by appointment only
Holdings: Provincial Archives of Manitoba (donated records): 1671–1970; corporate collection: museum pieces, 1660–present; archival material: 1850–present

Total volume: Museum pieces: 800 artworks, 400 artifacts; archival material: 1,500 cubic feet (corporate collection only)

Hughes Aircraft Company
Building C4/Mail Station 4
4881 West 145th Street
Hawthorne, CA 90250
Contact: Patricia D. Sinclair
310-973-0093
Fax: 310-973-3530
pdsinclair@ccgate.hac.com
Type of business: Electronics, aerospace
Conditions of access: Restricted; outside requests subject to approval
Holdings: 1940s–present
Total volume: 1,500 cubic feet

IBM Corporation
Archives
LS 120, CSB
Route 100
Somers, NY 10589
Contact: Paul C. Lasewicz, corporate archivist
914-766-0611
Reference requests: 914-766-0612
Fax: 914-766-0616
lasewicp@us.ibm.com
Type of business: Information technology
Hours of service: M–F, 8:30 A.M.–4:30 P.M.
Conditions of access: Limited public access
Holdings: 1890–present; bulk dates, 1940–1985
Total volume: 10,000 cubic feet of print documentation; 2,500-plus films/videotapes; 1,500 business machines

The IBM archive documents the growth and development of one of the world's leading technology companies. Strengths of the collection include: The Thomas J. Watson Sr. papers, corporate communications (press releases, publications, and advertisements), annual reports, product documentation, photographs, and A/V materials. Also of note is an extensive collection of precision business equipment ranging from eighteenth-century adding machines to nineteenth-century clocks to twentieth-century mainframe computers.

JC Penney Company
6501 Legacy Drive, MS 4118
Plano, TX 75024
Contact: Jeff Pirtle, company archivist and museum manager
972-431-5128
Fax: 972-431-5300
jpirt2@jcpenny.com
Type of business: Retail
Hours of service: M–F, 8:00 A.M.-5:00 P.M.

Conditions of access: Most collection closed to the public; access granted by special request
Holdings: 1876–present; bulk dates, 1902–1932, 1950–present
Total volume: 1,500 linear feet

The JC Penney Archives and Historical Museum contains both the corporate records of the JC Penney Company and the personal papers of Mr. James C. Penney, founder, as well as store photographs, advertisements, catalogs, and other audiovisual records. The museum collection focuses on JC Penney merchandise, period fashions from 1900 to the 1950s and toys and other artifacts.

Kellogg Company
One Kellogg Square
P.O. Box 5399
Battle Creek, MI 49016-3599
Contact: Alinda Arnett
616-961-2981
Fax: 616-961-3075
alinda.arnett@kellogg.com
Type of business: Food industry
Hours of service: M–F, 8:00 A.M.–4:45 P.M.
Conditions of access: Open to authorized Kellogg personnel; outside users only with the approval of the public affairs department
Holdings: 1907–present
Total volume: 5,000 linear feet

Company documents, ad reprints, marketing materials, photographs, premiums, training films, commercials, slide presentations, purchasing documents, public-affairs records, and trademark and patent information are just a portion of the collections housed in Kellogg's Archives.

Kraft Foods, Inc.
6350 Kirk St.
Morton Grove, IL 60053
Contact: Becky Haglund Tousey, Michael R. Bullington
Tousey: 847-646-2981
Bullington: 847-646-0187
Fax: 847-646-7699
btousey@kraft.com; mbullington@kraft.com
Type of business: Food industry
Hours of service: M–F, 8:00 A.M.–4:00 P.M.
Conditions of access: Not open to researchers; contact through mail or telephone for unclassified information
Holdings: 1880–present; bulk dates, 1920–present
Total volume: 6,000 cubic feet

Lennox International, Inc. Archives*
2100 Lake Park Boulevard
Richardson, TX 75080

Contact: Karen O'Shea, vice president, public relations; Debbie Waller, director, archival services, The History Factory; 14140 Parke Long Court, Chantilly, VA 20151-1649
703-631-0500
Fax: 703-631-1124
http://www.historyfactory.com/
Type of business: Air conditioning and heating manufacturer
Hours of service: 9:00 A.M.–5:30 P.M.
Conditions of access: Restricted; outside requests for information subject to approval by public relations and The History Factory
Holdings: 1890s–present
Total volume: 261 linear feet

Holdings are comprised of records of Lennox International Inc. and its subsidiary companies, Lennox Industries Inc., Heatcraft Inc., Lennox Global Ltd., and Armstrong Air Conditioning Inc. Employee and dealer publications; technical and installation manuals; catalogs and brochures; bulletins; cost and pricing lists; sales and marketing materials; product samples; demonstration kits; correspondence and news clippings; advertisements; memorabilia; audiovisual material; and over 1,200 negatives arc retained. The collection also contains biographical and correspondence files and scrapbooks of executives, as well as material relating to the heating and air conditioning industry.

Levi Strauss & Co.
1155 Battery St.
San Francisco, CA 94111
Contact: Lynn Downey, historian
415-501-6577
Fax: 415-501-6443
ldowney@levi.com
Type of business: Apparel manufacturing
Conditions of access: Restricted; phone reference only for nonemployees; access to the collections subject to approval of historian and global communications department
Holdings: 1906–present (All corporate records prior to 1906 were lost in earthquake and fire. Some nineteenth-century invoices and advertising materials have been purchased in this century.)

Holdings (in order of volume, greatest to least) consist of: clothing, marketing materials, photographs, documents (correspondence, speeches, newsletters, financial records, legal records), audio and video tapes, phonograph records, artifacts, oral history tapes and transcripts, and books.

Eli Lilly and Company
Lilly Corporate Center
Indianapolis, IN 46285
Contact: Lisa E. Bayne, archivist

317-276-2173
Fax: 317-276-7000
Type of business: Pharmaceutical
Hours of service: M–F, 8:00 A.M.–4:00 P.M.
Conditions of access: In-house use only
Holdings: 1876–present

The archive contains important records and artifacts used by Eli Lilly and Company in more than a century of operations. These records document corporate structure, programs, policies, decisions, product lines, and communications. The archive also preserves papers, photographs, and memorabilia of the Lilly family.

Thomas J. Lipton Company
800 Sylvan Avenue
Englewood Cliffs, NJ 07626
Contact: Edythe Masten, archivist; Mary F. Pfeil
201-894-7645
Type of business: Food industry
Hours of service: M–F, 9:00 A.M.–4:45 P.M.
Conditions of access: Open to company and to inquiries from outside
Holdings: 1890–present

Archive contains photographs, advertising, memorabilia, and files.

Little Caesar Enterprises, Inc.
2211 Woodward Avenue
Detroit, MI 48201-3400
Contact: Sharon Arend, company historian
313-983-6176
Fax: 313-983-6197
Type of business: Fast food (pizza), sports, and entertainment
Hours of service: M–F, 9:00 A.M.–5:00 P.M.
Conditions of access: Restricted; internal only

Documents and photos for all of the companies owned by Mike and Marian Ilitch (founders of Little Caesars), which includes the Detroit Red Wings hockey team, the Detroit Tigers baseball team, the historic Fox Theatre, and Olympia Arenas Inc., as well as Little Caesars. Records include publications, printed material, advertisements, packaging, ephemera, photos, videos, and films.

Longaberger Company
95 Chestnut Street
P.O. Box 73
Dresden, OH 43821-0073
Contact: Marge Shipley, director of historical archives; Holly L. Noland, historian
Shipley: 614-754-6311
Noland: 614-754-2887

Fax: 614-754-6439
Type of business: General manufacturing

Lucent Technologies
Archives
101 Crawfords Corner Road
Room 11G-104
Holmdel, NJ 07733
Contact: Edward Eckert, corporate archivist
732-332-5597
Fax: 732-332-5920
Type of business: Telecommunications
Hours of service: M–F, 8:00 A.M.–5:00 P.M.
Conditions of access: Limited public access
Holdings: 1869–present
Total volume: 2,000 cubic feet of print documentation;
12,000 images, 4,000 films, and 4,000 artifacts

The Lucent Technologies Archives was established in 1996 to document the history and ongoing business activities of Lucent Technologies and the R&D activities of Bell Laboratories. The collections contain material from Lucent's predecessor companies, Western Electric and AT&T, which were formed in the 1800s. The archive also manages two company museums that are open to the public and an international traveling exhibit program.

McDonald's Corporation
2010 East Higgins Road
Elk Grove, IL 60007
Contact: Lois Dougherty, archivist
708-952-2348
Fax: 708-952-2342
Type of business: Fast-food restaurants

The McGraw-Hill Companies
Archives and Business Information Center
1221 Avenue of the Americas, 48th Floor
New York, NY 10020
212-512-4005
Fax: 212-512-4646
Type of business: Publishing and information services
Hours of service: M–F, 9:30 A.M.–5:30 P.M.
Conditions of access: Internal access
Holdings: 1884–present
Total volume: 300 linear feet

Contains materials related to McGraw-Hill Companies and its predecessors including the McGraw and Hill Publishing Companies. The collection includes photographs, board minutes, significant issues of McGraw-Hill Publications, advertisements, and other information on both the corporate and the business unit levels of the corporation.

MCI Corporation Archives*
1133 19th Street
Washington, D.C. 20036
Contact: Adam Gruen, corporate historian
202-736-6290, ext. 6115
Fax: 202-736-6289
agruen@mcimail.com
Type of business: Telecommunications and internet working
Hours of service: 9:30 A.M.–5:00 P.M.
Conditions of access: Restricted; outside requests for information subject to approval by corporate historian
Holdings: 1963–present
Total volume: 650 cubic feet, and growing

Holdings consist of employee publications, videos, slides, and limited photographs, artifacts, executive papers and speeches, financial and administrative records, oral histories, press releases and daily news clippings, legal documentation, and extensive online historical reference material.

Merck & Company, Inc.
Merck Archives
P.O. Box 100
WSCUP-50
Whitehouse Station, NJ 08889-0100
Contact: Joseph M. Ciccone, J.D., corporate archivist
908-423-3765
Fax: 908-735-1197
ws_archives@merck.com
Type of business: Pharmaceutical
Hours of service: M–F, 8:30 A.M.–4:00 P.M.
Conditions of access: The archive can be contacted in writing, by telephone, by E-mail, or in person. Interested scholars may conduct research at the archive through prior arrangement with the corporate archivist. Access is subject to approval of the corporate archivist.
Holdings: 1880s–present

Collection consists of: documents such as publications and sales materials, photographs of Merck people, products, and facilities, oral histories of key figures in Merck history, artifacts, and other items related to Merck and the companies with which Merck has merged and acquired, including Sharp & Dohme, Mulford, and Powers-Weightman-Rosengarten.

Merrill Lynch & Co., Inc.*
World Financial Center
South Tower
New York, NY 10080
Contact: Jean Tepsic, project archivist, The Winthrop Group
Type of business: Banking, financial service
Conditions of access: Internal use only

Holdings: 1885–present; bulk dates, 1914–present
Total volume: 150 cubic feet

The collections consist of papers of partners, past presidents, and CEOs including William A. Schreyer, Roger E. Birk, Donald Regan, and Charles E. Merrill. Also includes files concerning partners and management meetings, photographs, promotional materials, publications, and other corporate records as well as documentation of various antecedent companies, including underwritings.

Metropolitan Life Insurance Company
1 Madison Ave.
1M-F
New York, NY 10010
Contact: Daniel B. May, company archivist
212-578-8818
Fax: 212-689-0926
Type of business: Insurance and insurance-related services
Hours of service: M–F, 8:45 A.M.–4:30 P.M.
Conditions of access: Open to all researchers with legitimate questions about MetLife
Holdings: 1868–present; bulk dates, 1890–present
Total volume: 1,000 linear feet

Materials document the development of Metropolitan Life Insurance Company. Areas of special interest: photographs of buildings, activities and personnel, company sponsored public-health education publications, advertising and promotional material, internal publications, papers of selected executives, and general subject files.

Microsoft Corporation
One Microsoft Way
Redmond, WA 98052
Contact: Nicole Pelsinsky, knowledge asset and archives collections manager; Peggy Crowley, museum research analyst
Pelsinsky: 425-705-4803
Crowley: 425-705-2964
Fax: 425-706-7329
nicolepe@microsoft.com; peggyc@microsoft.com
Type of business: Computer software
Conditions of access: Restricted; outside requests for information subject to approval

The Microsoft archive collects all versions of Microsoft domestic and international products, including documentation and original packaging. Scope also includes computer hardware, business records, artifacts and awards, market research, marketing materials, photographs and digital images, and audio and video.

Miles Laboratories, Inc.
P.O. Box 40

Elkhart, IN 46515
Contact: Donald N. Yates, supervisor, employee communications
219-262-7966
Type of business: Pharmaceuticals
Hours of service: M–F, 8:00 A.M.–5:00 P.M.
Holdings: 1882–present; bulk dates, 1938–1979
Total volume: 750 linear feet

Holdings include advertising and other records (boxed vertical files, photographs, film and artifactual) documenting business development of Miles Laboratories, Inc., founded in 1884. Public card catalog and tapes are also available.

Mitre Corporation
202 Burlington Road
Bedford, MA 07130-1420
Contact: David W. Baldwin, corporate archivist
617-271-7854
Fax: 617-271-3877
dbaldwin@iegate.mitre.org
Type of business: Education related
Hours of service: M–F, 8:00 A.M.–4:00 P.M.
Conditions of access: Restricted to corporation personnel and qualified researchers only
Holdings: 1943–present; bulk dates, 1959–present
Total volume: 1,100 cubic feet

Holdings contain materials relating to the history of command, control, communications and information systems. They include photographs, slides, motion picture film, audio and video tape recordings, microforms, annual reports, house organs, press clippings, training brochures, memorabilia, work-tasks documentation, minutes, and correspondence.

MONY Financial Services Archives*
1740 Broadway
New York, NY 10019
Contact: Eileen Ast, vice president of corporate communications; Debbie Waller, director of archival services, The History Factory
703-631-0500
Fax: 703-631-1124
http://www.historyfactory.com/
Type of business: Mutual life insurer; life, disability income and annuities, mutual funds, and securities
Hours of service: 9:00 A.M.–5:30 P.M.
Conditions of access: Restricted; outside requests for information subject to approval by creative services and The History Factory
Holdings: 1840s–present
Total volume: 400 linear feet

The MONY archive is comprised of records from the executive office, corporate affairs, and all product management and support management operations. Policy contracts, advertisements, photographs, annual reports, sales material and memorabilia are retained. More than 50 titles of home office and agency publications, numerous agency/agent biographical files and a special collection of famous policyholders' files are examples of material within the collection.

Monsanto Company
800 North Lindbergh Boulevard
St. Louis, MO 63167
Contact: Charlotte J. Kuhn, (contractor) archives coordinator; Steven Poth (contractor) associate archives coordinator
314-694-8752 or 314-694-4873
Fax: 314-694-8748
Charlotte.J.Kuhn@monsanto.com; Steven.D.Poth@monsanto.com
Type of business: Pharmaceutical, agriculture, nutrition, biotech, and formerly chemicals
Hours of service: M–F, 8:00 A.M.–5:00 P.M.
Conditions of access: Restricted; apply to contact person who must clear with Monsanto Management
Holdings: 1886–present

Archive contains company records starting from 1901 with material from several chemical companies bought by Monsanto: Swann, Chemstrand, Lion Oil, Cochrane, Schwanigan, among others; includes three company histories and one published history of the company. Also included are photographs, press releases, movies, and videos.

Motorola, Inc.
Motorola Museum of Electronics
1297 East Algonquin Road
Schaumburg, IL 60196
847-538-2967
Fax: 847-576-6401
Type of business: Electronics
Hours of service: M–F, 9:00 A.M.–5:00 P.M., by appointment only
Holdings: 1928–present; bulk dates, 1940–present
Total volume: 1,000 cubic feet

Museum houses catalogs, photographs, sound recordings, film and video recordings, correspondences, service manuals, advertising and promotional material, speeches and publications. Biographical materials include those of Paul Galvin, Robert Galvin, Daniel E. Noble, Elmer Wavering; and oral interviews with key employees.

Navistar International Transportation Corp.
29642 School House Road

Mokena, IL 60448-1700
Contact: Greg Lennes, secretary and records manager
312-836-2149
Fax: 312-836-2192
Type of business: Manufacturing capital goods
Hours of service: M–F, 8:30 A.M.–4:15 P.M.
Holdings: 1831–1950s; bulk dates, 1902–1950s
Total volume: 2,000 linear feet

The archive contains the business records of Navistar and its predecessor company, International Harvester Company, founded in 1902.

NBC News Archives
30 Rockefeller Plaza
New York, NY 10112
Contact: Michael Sosler, director
212-664-3797
Fax: 212-703-8558
http://www.nbcnewsarchives.com/
Type of business: Newspaper and magazine publishing and broadcasting
Hours of service: M–F, 9:00 A.M.–6:00 P.M.; other hours by appointment.
Conditions of access: Research, screening, and duplication; royalty fees charged
Holdings: Mid-1930s–present; bulk dates, late 1950s–present

Archive contains stock shots and background material on every conceivable subject including historical and news events throughout the world and documentary and magazine show footage.

New England Life Insurance Company (New England Financial)
501 Boylston Street
Boston, MA 02117
Contact: Phyllis E. Steele, archivist
617-578-4312
Fax: 617-578-5523
psteele@NEFN.com
Type of business: Insurance and investment services
Hours of service: M–Th 9:15 A.M.–5:15 P.M.
Conditions of access: Company associates: Open in accordance with corporate policy on the confidentiality of information. General public: Written application to archivist stating nature of research project; access conditional upon approval by the archivist and the vice president of public relations.
Holdings: 1843–present; bulk dates, 1843–1999
Total volume: 1,800 linear feet

Archive contains records of the New England Life Insurance Company, and its predecessor company, New England Mutual Life Insurance Company. Records include: annual reports and annual statements; board of directors' minutes and files; correspondence and administrative files of company officers; marketing and advertising files; product information files; personnel directories; company publications (books, pamphlets, magazines, newsletters, manuals); research and planning reports; nineteenth-century insurance applications, policies, policy registers, and policy ledgers from 1843–1890; nineteenth- and early twentieth-century policy dividend, loan and valuation records; nineteenth- and early twentieth-century financial records, including ledgers of accounts, cash books, and stock and bond registers; files about company agencies; departmental and subsidiary information files; scrapbooks; photographs and other audiovisual media; and company artifacts.

New York Stock Exchange, Inc.
11 Wall Street
New York, NY 10005
Contact: Steven Wheeler, archivist
212-656-2252
Fax: 212-656-5629
Type of business: Securities exchange
Hours of service: M–F, 9:00 A.M.–5:00 P.M., by appointment only
Conditions of access: Reference requests must be submitted by letter.
Holdings: 1792–present; bulk dates, 1817–present
Total volume: 2,000 cubic feet

Administrative records of the New York Stock Exchange and its affiliates, information on listed companies, members and member firms, records of stock sale prices, house organs, books on the history of the stock market, photographs, films, videotapes and artifacts.

New York Times Company
New York Times Archives
122 E. 42nd St., 14th Fl.
New York, NY 10168-0002
Contact: Charles St. Vil
212-499-3581
Fax: 212-499-3382
Type of business: Newspaper and magazine publishing, broadcasting
Hours of service: M–F, 9:00 A.M.–5:00 P.M., by appointment only
Conditions of access: Authorization may be required; some files restricted
Holdings: 1851–present; bulk dates, 1920s–1970s
Total volume: 500 cubic feet

Archive holdings include financial, legal, and historical records of the New York Times Company and

newspaper; personal and business papers of the publishers and other major executives, editors, writers; correspondences with business associates, persons in the news and readers; maps; and blueprints, diagrams, photos, awards, memorabilia; a few films, video and audio tapes.

Norfolk Southern Corporation
185 Spring Street, SW
Atlanta, GA 30303
Contact: Roger D. Powers
404-529-2326

Northwest Airlines*
2700 Lone Oak Parkway A4285
Eagan, MN 55121
Contact: Kyle F. Hjelmstad, administrator-corp. records
612-727-7348
Fax: 612-726-4721
Type of business: Airline

Northwestern Mutual Life
720 East Wisconsin Avenue
Milwaukee, WI 53202
Contact: David V. Hingtgen
414-299-1961
Type of business: Insurance and insurance-related services

Ocean Spray Cranberries, Inc.
One Ocean Spray Drive
Lakeville-Middleboro, MA 02349
Contact: Christine Hormell, corporate records and archives manager
508-946-1000
Fax: 508-946-7704
Type of business: Agriculture
Hours of service: M–F, 9:00 A.M.–5:00 P.M.
Conditions of access: For business use and restricted internally by collection
Holdings: 1900–present; bulk dates, 1930–present
Total volume: 700 linear feet

Ocean Spray Cranberries, Inc. is an agricultural marketing cooperative responsible for developing and marketing products derived from the crops grown by our grower-owners. Collections include print advertisements, packaging samples, film and commercial reels, publications, minutes of board meetings, financial statements and annual reports, legal, marketing and consumer correspondence, research and development documents, organizational charts, and photographs.

Pacific Bell
140 New Montgomery St.
San Francisco, CA 94105-3799

Contact: Don T. Thrall, director and archivist
415-441-3918
Type of business: Communications
Hours of service: M–F, 9:00 A.M.–3:30 P.M.
Holdings: 1896–present; bulk dates, 1906–present
Total volume: 449 linear feet, plus 34 file cabinets

The collection includes papers from past company presidents, Bell system companies' annual reports, trade journals, house organs, reference books, maps, floor plans, equipment blue prints, circuit description sheets, motion picture film, videotapes, and photographs.

Paine Webber*
1285 Avenue of the Americas
New York, NY 10020
Contact: Linda Edgerly, consulting archivist, The Winthrop Group
212-865-6181
Type of business: Securities industry
Conditions of access: Requests must be made in advance and in writing; recent correspondences and subject files closed to outside research
Holdings: 1870s–1986; bulk dates, 1950–1985
Total volume: 45 cubic feet

Holdings include annual reports, press coverage and news releases, biographical files on major figures in the company's history, reference files on antecedent and subsidiary companies, correspondences and office files of the chairman of the board and executive assistant to the chairman, and samples of printed material and advertising of the company and its antecedents.

Parke-Davis Research Institute
2270 Speakman Drive
Mississauga, Ontario L5K 1B4, Canada
Contact: Jody Wagner
905-822-3520
Fax: 905-822-1049
Type of business: Pharmaceuticals

Pendleton Woolen Mills*
220 NW Broadway, Box 3030
Portland, OR 97208-3030
Contact: The Winthrop Group
503-226-4801
Type of business: Textiles and garments
Conditions of access: Restricted; outside requests subject to approval by management
Holdings: 1870s–present; bulk dates 1910–present
Total volume: 700 cubic feet

Pendleton is a closely held corporation, founded in 1909. Holdings include personal papers, business records, photographs, and products.

Phillips Petroleum Company
Corporate Archives
C-20, Phillips Building
Bartlesville, OK 74004
Contact: Kathy Triebel, corporate archivist
918-661-7326
Fax: 918-662-2600
kbtrieb@ppco.com
Type of business: Energy
Hours of service: M–F, 8:00 A.M.–5:00 P.M.
Conditions of access: Limited; by permission of the corporate archivist
Holdings: 1874–present
Total volume: 700 cubic feet

The Phillips corporate archives contains the corporate records of Phillips Petroleum Company and its subsidiaries as well as its founders, Frank and L. E. Phillips; biographical data files; financial reports; organization charts; advertisements and publicity campaign materials; company publications and employee newsletter; executive speeches; more than 800,000 photographs and negatives; audio and video taped oral histories; and maps and many other artifacts.

Piper Jaffray, Inc.
222 South Ninth Street
P.O. Box 28
Minneapolis, MN 55440
Contact: Jane Johnson, records manager
612-342-6707
Fax: 612-342-6088
Type of business: Securities industry
Hours of service: M–F, 8:15 A.M.–4:45 P.M.
Conditions of access: Prior approval necessary
Holdings: 1895–present; bulk dates, 1930–present
Total volume: Approximately 90 cubic feet

Holdings include files of founding partners, materials relating to the internal structure of the company, and other documents that reflect the business of the company. The archive includes documents, photos and other miscellaneous materials.

Polaroid Corporation
119 Windsor Street, 1st Floor
Cambridge, MA 02139
Contact: Nasrin Rohani
617-577-3309
Hours of service: M–F, 9:00 A.M.–5:00 P.M.

Conditions of access: The archive functions as an internal resource, but will provide materials for publishers and outside researchers.
Holdings: 1936–present
Total volume: 2 million items

The Polaroid corporate archive was founded in 1984 in anticipation of the company's 50th anniversary in 1987. Since its founding, the archive has produced 72 reference volumes, including catalogs of individual collections and topics pertaining to the company's history. Major collections include: examples of early products, cameras and test photographs, vectograph collection, photographs representing many Polaroid film types, fine prints, and advertising and packaging collections.

Polo Ralph Lauren Corporation
Photography
650 Madison Avenue
New York, NY 10022
Contact: Pamela Robin Anderson, Cybil Genevieve Walsh Powers
212-765-7950
Fax: 212-765-7240
Type of business: Clothing, fashion

Procter & Gamble Company
One Procter & Gamble Plaza
Cincinnati, OH 45202
Contact: Edward Rider, corporate archivist
513-983-5443
Fax: 513-983-1193
rider.em@pg.com
Type of business: Consumer products
Hours of service: M–F, 8:30 A.M.–5:30 P.M.
Conditions of access: Restricted; outside requests for information subject to approval of corporate archivist and public relations department
Holdings: 1837–present; bulk dates, 1880s–present
Total volume: 4,000 cubic feet

Archival material includes papers of the founding partners, financial records, brand records, company publications, print and broadcast advertising, 19,000-plus products, 250,000-plus photographs of packaging, facilities and employees, and a wide variety of other documentation for P&G brands and acquired companies.

Prudential Insurance Company of America
Prudential Plaza
Newark, NJ 07101
Contact: Jon W. Goldberg, assistant public relations consultant

201-877-8533
Type of business: Insurance and insurance-related services
Conditions of access: While the archive is no longer open to the public, specific research inquiries may be addressed to the above address
Holdings: 1875–present

Collection contains archival records dating from Prudential's founding in 1875 to the present day.

Red Wing Shoe Company
314 Main Street
Red Wing, MN 55066-2300
Contact: Jayne Ann Valley
612-388-8211
Type of business: Clothing manufacturing

R. J. Reynolds Tobacco Company
401 North Main Street
P.O. Box 2959
Winston-Salem, NC 27102
Contact: Barry Miller, business information center
910-741-7545
Fax: 910-741-7546
fn_miller@co.forsyth.nc.us
Type of business: Tobacco industry
Hours of service: M–F, 8:00 A.M.–4:30 P.M.
Conditions of access: For internal use only
Holdings: 1875–present; bulk dates, 1913–present

Safeway Inc.
5918 Stoneridge Mall Road
Pleasanton, CA 94588-3229
http://www.safeway.com/
925-467-3000
Type of business: Food industry

Holdings include company memorabilia and publications.

Sara Lee Corporation Archives*
3 First National Plaza
Chicago, IL 60602
Contact: Theresa Herlevsen, executive director of communications and public relations; Debbie Waller, director of archival services, The History Factory, 14140 Parke Long Court, Chantilly, VA 20151-1649
703-631-0500
Fax: 703-631-1124
Type of business: Manufacturer, marketer, and distributor of consumer products
Hours of service: 9:00 A.M.–5:30 P.M.
Conditions of access: Restricted; outside requests for information subject to approval by Sara Lee Corporate Affairs and The History Factory.

Holdings: 1890s–1996
Total volume: 432 linear feet

The Sara Lee Corporation archive documents the evolution of the corporation from Nathan Cummings's acquisition of the C.D. Kenny Company in 1939 to its current position as a leading international manufacturer and marketer of consumer products. The corporate collection consists of executive papers, including speeches, biographical material, and photographs, as well as acquisition files and correspondence. The archive retains historical product packaging, photographs, histories, and biographical material of more than 70 subsidiary companies and the Sara Lee Foundation.

Joseph E. Seagram & Sons, Inc.
375 Park Avenue, Suite 3509
New York, NY 10152-0192
Contact: Carla Caccamise Ash, curator of collections; Barry M. Winiker, assistant to the curator
Ash: 212-572-7379
Winiker: 212-572-7364
Fax: 212-572-7510
carla_caccamise_ash@seagram.com; barry_winiker@seagram.com
Type of business: Beverages and entertainment
Conditions of access: Closed to outside research
Holdings: Yet to be fully determined; varies with company
Total volume: Yet to be fully determined; varies with company

Collections include Seagram papers, photographs, and publicity relating to the Seagram Building (by architect Mies van der Rohe); papers, letters, invoices, and photographs about commission, including the Seagram County Court House Archives; and past art projects, such as exhibitions on the Seagram Plaza and in the Seagram Gallery; correspondences and contracts with lenders, engineers, and so on. Tropicana Dole Beverages has recently begun to organize historic photographs, promotion, material, and papers relating the development of the company. Universal Studios, Inc. has begun a major project to create an archive of historic material from all divisions of the company—movies, theme parks, television, and music.

Sears, Roebuck & Co. Archives
Sears, Roebuck & Co.
CLL-116B
3333 Beverly Road
Hoffman Estates, IL 60179
Contact: Kathy Bryan, on-site archivist, The History Factory
847-286-7458 or 8321
Fax: 847-286-1914
Type of business: Retail merchandising

Hours of service: 8:00 A.M.–4:00 P.M.
Conditions of access: Lengthy research by appointment only; internal requests given priority
Holdings: 1888–present (1905–1960 majority of material)
Total volume: 5,000 linear feet

The largest portion of the collection includes Sears general and specialty catalogs. The collection also includes news releases, employee publications, annual reports, executive speeches, biographical data, administrative and financial documents as well as merchandising material, artifacts and historical memorabilia, and products. Photographs and records documenting Sears catalog merchandising distribution centers and retail stores are also retained.

Shell Oil Company Archives*
One Shell Plaza
Houston, TX 77001
Contact: H.R. Hutchins, manager of corporate communications; Debbie Waller, director of archival services, The History Factory, 14140 Parke Long Court, Chantilly, VA 20151-1649
703-631-0500
Fax: 703-631-1124
Type of business: Oil, gas, and petrochemical
Hours of service: 9:00 A.M.–5:30 P.M.
Conditions of access: Restricted; outside requests for information subject to approval by corporate communications and The History Factory
Holdings: 1920s–present
Total volume: 275 linear feet

Holdings are comprised of corporate records as well as records of subsidiary companies. The archive is rich in marketing and advertising material including original posters, direct mailers, promotional items, and products and service station accessories. Annual reports, executive speeches, numerous employee and industry publications, as well as board of directors meeting files are retained. Photographs of production and refinery facilities as well as educational films and videos are retained.

The Sherwin-Williams Company
101 Prospect Street, NW
Cleveland, OH 44115-1075
Contact: Kathleen Carnall, archivist
216-566-3082
Fax: 216-566-3312
Type of business: General manufacturing
Hours of service: By appointment only
Conditions of access: Limited to telephone requests only (or mail)
Holdings: 1866–present; bulk dates, 1880–1930
Total volume: 3,000-plus items

Materials include general papers detailing the history of the company and its officers, advertisements, decorating guides and color selectors, photographs, cans and bottles of paints and sundries, formulas, signs, books and periodicals published by the company, and other papers and artifacts of the company and its subsidiaries.

State Farm Insurance Company
One State Farm Plaza
Bloomington, IL 61701
Contact: Dan Barringer, company history unit
309-766-6007
Fax: 309-766-6169
Type of business: Insurance and insurance-related services
Hours of service: M–F, 8:00 A.M.–4:15 P.M.
Conditions of access: Outside requests are subject to approval
Holdings: 1922–present

Company history unit is responsible for keeping historical records, photographs, artifacts, and advertising material.

Texaco, Inc.
Archives
2000 Westchester Avenue
White Plains, NY 10650
Contact: Craig St. Clair, corporate historian
914-253-4058
Fax: 914-253-6115
stclacg@texaco.com
Type of business: Energy
Hours of service: M–F, 8:30 A.M.–5:00 P.M.
Conditions of access: Limited public access
Holdings: 1902–present
Total volume: 1,500 linear feet

The Texaco archive provides a record of Texaco's growth and development from the company's beginnings in Southeast Texas to today's multinational enterprise. Included in the collection are corporate and executive records, product specifications and research documentation, an extensive advertising collection in print, film and video, an artifact collection that ranges from early drilling machinery to vintage gasoline pumps, plus approximately 250,000 photographs.

Tiffany & Company
15 Sylvan Way
Parsippany, NJ 07054
Contact: Annamarie V. Sandecki, archivist
212-755-8000
Type of business: Jeweler, silver manufacturer, luxury goods retailer
Hours of service: By appointment only

Conditions of access: Free upon application by letter to scholars, authors, and museum professionals; for all others an access fee of $250 is charged
Holdings: 1837–present; bulk dates, 1860s–present
Total volume: 2,000 cubic feet

Archive contains material pertaining to the history of Tiffany & Co. (founded in 1837) including its retail operations and silver and jewelry manufacturing facilities. Extensive documentation on the design, manufacture, and sale of silver including blueprints, design resources, and work records (1840–present). Collection of jewelry sketches and gemstone records (1840–present), information on commemorative medals; press-clipping books; World's Fair records (1853–1940); catalogs and publications (1845–present); and some retail records including store photographs, employee records, and limited correspondence files. Archives also contain the Permanent Collection of Jewelry and Silver.

Time Inc.
Room 26-52D
Rockefeller Center
New York, NY 10020
Contact: Bill Hooper
212-522-1063
Fax: 212-522-2403
Type of business: Publishing and communications
Conditions of access: Restricted; written applications will be considered on their merit
Holdings: 1922–present

Holdings include photographs, slides, motion picture films, oral history, volumes of publications, annual reports, house organs, press clippings, books, promotion materials, minutes, correspondence, volumes of Time Inc. history, and other memorabilia.

Toyota Motor Sales, USA, Inc.
Toyota USA Archives and Research Center
19001 South Western Avenue, Mail Drop A404
Torrance, CA 90509-2991
Contact: Cindy Knight, lead archivist
310-618-4053
cindy_knight@notes.toyota.com
Type of business: Motor vehicle sales
Hours of service: M–F, 8:00 A.M.–5:30 P.M.
Conditions of access: Limited external access

Toyota Motor Sales USA, established in 1957, is the U.S. marketing arm of Toyota Motor Corporation. The archive, a new unit of TMS, is currently under development. The archive will document the 40-year history of Toyota in the United States, and the research center will house a collection of relevant published information sources. Toyota company records include photographs, publications, product literature, advertising, executive papers, films, videotapes, and memorabilia.

Union Pacific Railroad
1416 Dodge Street
Room 114
Omaha, NE 68179
Contact: Donald D. Snoddy, director
402-271-3305
Fax: 402-271-6460
Type of business: Transportation
Hours of service: M–F, 9:00 A.M.–3:00 P.M.
Holdings: 1862–present; bulk dates, 1910–present
Total volume: 2,500 cubic feet

Holdings include correspondences, architectural and mechanical drawings, engineering files, and more than 500,000 images relating to Union Pacific, Missouri Pacific, and subsidiary roads and their role in the development of transportation in the West.

United Parcel Service
55 Glenlake Parkway, NE
Atlanta, GA 30328
Contact: Jill Swiecichowski, archivist
404-828-4371
Fax: 404-828-6971
jswiecichowski@ups.com
Type of business: Transportation
Hours of service: M–F, 9:00 A.M.–5:00 P.M.
Conditions of access: By appointment
Holdings: 1907–present
Total volume: 200 cubic feet

The archive contains office files and records of UPS founders and managers, correspondences, speeches, printed materials, audiovisual materials and publications.

Walt Disney Company
500 S. Buena Vista Street
Burbank, CA 91521-1200
Contact: David R. Smith, archivist
818-560-5424
Fax: 818-842-3957
Type of business: Entertainment, leisure
Hours of service: M–F, 8:00 A.M.–5:30 P.M.; by appointment only
Conditions of access: Open to students, writers, and others working on serious research projects
Holdings: 1920–present

Archival material includes photographs, business records, tape recordings, books, press clippings, annual reports, awards, house organs, memorabilia, merchandise samples, posters, correspondence, original art, phonograph records, and other material documenting the history of all the Disney enterprises.

Wells Fargo & Company
Historical Services, MAC A0101-026
420 Montgomery Street, 2nd Floor
San Francisco, CA 94163
Contact: Keri Koljian
415-396-3669
Fax: 415-391-8644
koljian@wellsfargo.com
Type of business: Banking and financial services
Hours of service: M–F, 9:00 A.M.–5:00 P.M.
Conditions of access: Permission of the archivist
Holdings: 1852–present
Total volume: 8,000 linear feet

Holdings consist of information sources that document the origins, development, operations, and impact of Wells Fargo & Company and all of it subsidiaries, affiliates, and merger partners from 1852 to the present.

Westinghouse Savannah River Company
P.O. Box 3151
Aiken, SC 29801
803-725-4037
Fax: 803-725-4360
Type of business: Utilities

Weyerhaeuser Company
Archives NP-190
P.O. Box 9777
Federal Way, WA 98063-9777
Contact: Megan Moholt, research archivist; Kenneth House, technical archivist
Moholt: 253-924-5051
House: 253-924-6208
Fax: 253-924-7150
megan.moholt@weyerhaeuser.com; kennethhouse@weyerhaeuser.com
Type of business: Forest products
Hours of service: M–F, 8:00 A.M.–4:30 P.M.
Conditions of access: External researchers must submit a request describing the scope and content of their project. Some parts of the collection are closed to all outside research.
Holdings: 1880–present; bulk dates, 1900–present
Total volume: 2,500 cubic feet

A collection of business records relating to the history of Weyerhaeuser Company, its antecedent, merged, and subsidiary companies, and materials relating to the people associated with them. The major part of the collection consists of correspondence and office files, financial records, advertising campaigns, oral histories, and audiovisual and printed materials.

Wm. Wrigley Jr. Company
410 North Michigan Avenue
Chicago, IL 60611
Contact: Linda Hanrath, corporate librarian and archivist
312-645-3921
Fax: 312-644-0081
76376.2113@compuserve.com
Type of business: Food industry
Hours of service: M–F, 9:00 A.M.–4:30 P.M.
Conditions of access: Restricted; requests are handled on an individual basis
Holdings: 1889–present; bulk dates, 1930–present
Total volume: 600 linear feet

Holdings consist of photographs, slides, tape recordings, annual reports, financial reports, house organs, press clippings, memorabilia, minutes, articles of incorporation, and correspondence.

The World Bank Group
1818 H St., NW
Washington D.C. 20433
Contact: Elisa Liberatori Prati, Bank Group archivist; Jim Huttlinger, reference officer
Prati: 202-458-1552; fax: 202-614-1024
Reference Desk: 202-473-2841; fax: 202-477-1499
eliberatoriprati@worldbank.org; archives@worldbank.org
Type of business: Economic and social development
Hours of service: M–F, by appointment only
Conditions of access: Open for IBRD and IDA items that are 20 years old or older (see access policy at http://archives.worldbank.org/, catalog subsite)
Holdings: 1946–present
Total volume: 135,000 cubic feet

Holdings comprise the records of the International Bank for Reconstruction and Development (IBRD), the International Development Association (IDA), the International Finance Corporation (IFC), and the Multilateral Investment Guarantee Agency (MIGA). The records comprise correspondence and reports on lending and investment projects, aid coordination, economic conditions, and so on, supplemented by audiovisual records.

NOTES

1. For more information on the development of archives, see Gregory S. Hunter, *Developing and Maintaining Practical Archives* (New York: Neal Schuman, 1997), chap. 1.

2. There are historical societies and university archives that specialize in business collections.

Among the best collections are the Minnesota Historical Society, Baker Library of Harvard University, Duke University, and the Hagley Museum and Library. See Laura Linard and Brent M. Sverdloff, "Not Just Business as Usual: Evolving Trends in Historical Research at Baker Library," *American Archivist* 60, no. 1 (winter 1997): 88–98.

3. Elizabeth W. Adkins, "The Development of Business Archives in the United States: An Overview and a Personal Perspective," *American Archivist* 60, no. 1 (winter 1997): 10–11. Unfortunately, Firestone no longer maintains an in-house archives.

4. Adkins, "Development of Business Archives," 12–13.

5. Adkins, "Development of Business Archives," 12–13.

6. Adkins, "Development of Business Archives," 15.

7. For more on this point, see Gord Rabchuk, "Life after the 'Big Bang': Business Archives in an Era of Disorder," *American Archivist* 60, no. 1 (winter 1997): 34–43; James E. Fogerty, "Archival Brinkmanship: Downsizing, Outsourcing, and the Records of Corporate America," *American Archivist* 60, no. 1 (winter 1997): 44–55.

8. Frederick Rose, "In the Wake of Cost Cuts, Many Firms Sweep Their History out the Door," *Wall Street Journal*, 21 December 1987, p. 23.

9. Ellen Lawson, "Manager's Journal: Companies Plumb the Past to Protect the Present," *Wall Street Journal*, 16 January 1989, p. A8.

10. For one of the best discussions of the value of business archives, see George David Smith and Laurence E. Steadman, "Present Value of Corporate History," *Harvard Business Review* 59 (November/December 1981): 164–173.

11. For an excellent discussion of why paper will continue to remain important for organizations, see Abigail J. Sellen and Richard H. R. Harper, *The Myth of the Paperless Office* (Cambridge: MIT Press, 2002).

12. Richard J. Cox and Helen W. Samuels, "The Archivist's First Responsibility: A Research Agenda to Improve the Identification and Retention of Records of Enduring Value," *American Archivist* 51 (winter/spring 1988): 28–51.

13. The literature on appraisal is quite extensive for the last 20 years. A comprehensive listing can be found in the bibliography at the end of Hunter, *Practical Archives*. Among the most important sources are the following: Frank Boles, *Archival Appraisal* (New York: Neal-Schuman, 1991); Hans Booms, "Society

and the Formation of a Documentary Heritage: Issues in the Appraisal of Archival Sources," *Archivaria* 24 (summer 1987): 69–107; Richard J. Cox, *Documenting Localities: A Practical Model for American Archivists and Manuscript Curators* (Lanham, Md.: Scarecrow Press and the Society of American Archivists, 2001); Luciana Duranti, "The Concept of Appraisal and Archival Theory," *American Archivist* 57 (spring 1994): 328–44; F. Gerald Ham, *Selecting and Appraising Archives and Manuscripts,* (Chicago: Society of American Archivists, 1993); Leonard Rapport, "No Grandfather Clause: Reappraising Accessioned Records," *American Archivist* 44 (spring 1981): 143–50; Helen Willa Samuels, *Varsity Letters: Documenting Modern Colleges and Universities* (Chicago: Society of American Archivists and Scarecrow Press, 1992).

14. James M. O'Toole, ed., *The Records of American Business* (Chicago: Society of American Archivists, 1997). For more on the appraisal of business records, see Francis X. Blouin, Jr., "A New Perspective on the Appraisal of Business Records: A Review," *American Archivist* 42 (July 1979): 312–20; Mark Greene, "Store Wars: Some Thoughts on the Strategy and Tactics of Documenting Small Business," *Midwestern Archivist* 16 (1991): 95–104; Stuart Strachan, "The Acquisition of Business Records: A New Zealand Approach," *Archives and Manuscripts* 6, no. 5 (November 1975): 177–84; JoAnne Yates, "Internal Communication Systems in American Business Structures: A Framework to Aid Appraisal," *American Archivist* 48 (spring 1985): 141–158.

15. Jeff Rothenberg, *Avoiding Technological Quicksand: Finding a Viable Technical Foundation for Digital Preservation* (Washington, D.C.: Council on Library and Information Resources, 1999), 3.

16. John Garrett and Donald Waters, *Preserving Digital Information: Report of the Task Force on Archiving Digital Information* (Washington, D.C.: Commission on Preservation and Access and the Research Libraries Group, 1996), 11–19. See also Hunter, *Preserving Digital Information,* 5–10.

17. Edward Iwata, "Enron Case could be Largest Corporate Investigation," *USA Today,* 19 February 2002, p. B6.

18. Jerry Adler, et al., "When E-Mail Bites Back," *Newsweek,* 23 November 1998, pp. 45–47.

19. The life cycle concept, as developed at the National Archives and Records Administration at the end of the Second World War, stated that all records go through stages: from creation or receipt, through active use and semi-active use, to ultimate disposition (destruction or preservation in an archives).

20. Records in the custody of records managers, as well as all other corporate records, must be produced in response to a subpoena. As Enron learned, destruction of records when required for an investigation can result in criminal penalties.

CHAPTER 11
Military Archives
Carrie Bohman

INTRODUCTION

Military records are very rich resources documenting the armed conflicts of a particular country. They also document the individuals who serve their country in the various armed forces. Interest in military records runs the gamut from genealogists researching those family members who served their country to scholars analyzing international foreign policy through the primary source documents of specific individuals, governmental agencies, or veteran organizations.

This chapter highlights the various military archives or resources at the international, national, state, and local levels. Some institutions or archival repositories hold a combination of paper records. The Department of Veterans Affairs, a governmental agency charged with maintaining specific military records, or an institution holding the individual papers of a military figure, such as General Ulysses S. Grant, are examples of institutions with extensive paper records. Repositories may also hold photographs, film, and oral histories. I have also included online resources that will facilitate research for an individual who may not be able to visit the particular repository. In such a situation, an online finding aid or an index may be locally available. As online resources are very broad and cover a lot of material, I will begin by examining online resources at the international level.

ONLINE INTERNATIONAL MILITARY RESOURCES

Armed Forces of the World compiled by the Information Center of the Canadian Forces
http://wps.cfc.dnd.ca/links/milorg/index.html

Allows a researcher to consult individual countries and locate their armed forces' collections and indexes. Completeness varies depending on the country.

The Parallel History Project on NATO and the Warsaw Pact
http://www.isn.ethz.ch/php/

Established in 1999, the Parallel History Project has undertaken the large-scale declassification of communist era military materials in Central and East European archives. This collection contains thousands of documents on the security aspects of the Cold War. A researcher will find a selection of annotated documents, most of them in facsimile and in English translation. Archival collections range from the Berlin Crisis of 1961 to the United States air raid of Libya in 1986.

The Commonwealth War Graves Commission
2 Marlow Road
Maidenhead
Berkshire SL6 7DX, United Kingdom
(01628) 634221
Fax: (01628) 771208
http://www.cwgc.org/ (includes online searchable database)

Maintains records related to graves, cemeteries, and memorials commemorating Commonwealth servicemen and women who died during both world wars. Links to other related resources for other countries.

Australian War Memorial
http://www.awm.gov.au/index_noflash.asp/

Site contains several searchable databases. The Collections database includes art, photographs, film, sound and private records, the database for official records of the National Archives of Australia, and library resources. Information on researching family and military history through biographical database and research guides.

Canadian Virtual War Memorial maintained by the Canadian Veteran Affairs Department
http://www.virtualmemorial.gc.ca/

This site contains a registry of information about the graves and memorials of more than 116,000 Canadians and Newfoundlanders who gave their lives for their country. Also contains additional information and resources regarding Canadian military history and observances.

Canadian Letters and Images Project
http://www.mala.bc.ca/history/letters/

The Canadian Letters and Images Project is an online archive of the Canadian war experience, from any war, as told through the letters and images of Canadians themselves. The online collections highlight individual collections from both the front lines and home front experiences. The history department at Malaspina University College is responsible for the project. The objective is to create a searchable online archive of the personal side of Canada's war experience.

King's College London Liddell Hart Centre for Military Archives
http://www.kcl.ac.uk/lhcma/home.htm

Collections include papers of individual military officers as they relate to World War I, the Allied forces during World War II and D-Day, proliferation of nuclear warfare, and the Palestinian and Israeli conflict. Content notes and access information provided.

The Second World War Experience Centre
5 Feast Field, Horsforth,
Leeds, West Yorkshire LS18 4TJ, UK
+44 (0) 113 258 4993
+44 (0) 113 258 2557
enquiries@war-experience.org
http://www.war-experience.org/index.html

Archival collection dedicated to World War II experiences of individuals serving in the armed forces. Also documents how civilian populations experienced the war.

Polish Military Archives
http://www.loc.gov/rr/european/archiwum.html

This project is sponsored by the U.S. Department of Defense and the Library of Congress as they make available the microfilm of declassified records from the Central Military Archives (Centralne Archiwum Wojskowe, CAW) in Warsaw covering the early years of the Cold War, primarily 1945–50. Documents include letters, memoranda, and policy papers of the Polish Cabinet of Ministers, the Minister of Defense, the General Staff, and other military bodies.

Irish Defence Forces
http://www.military.ie/military_archives/index.html

Documentation from 1913 to the present, including overseas service with the United Nations.

New Zealand and Commonwealth War Graves Commission
http://www.cultureandheritage.govt.nz/History/HPU/CWGC.htm

The commission is responsible for commemorating members of the Armed Forces of the Commonwealth who died during the world wars of 1914–18 and 1939–45 and for the care of their graves throughout the world. New Zealand is one of six Commonwealth or former Commonwealth countries that participate in the work of the Commission, the others being the United Kingdom, Canada, Australia, South Africa, and India.

MILITARY RECORDS IN THE UNITED STATES

U.S. Military Records at the National Archives and Records Center

Military service records, either the Personnel File or Pension File, contain pertinent information for the genealogist or researcher. The National Archives and Records Administration (NARA) maintains and makes available for research the military service files for individuals no longer in active service. The individual military branches do not maintain these files any longer.

An initial step in researching military service records is to consult NARA's General Index to Pensions Files, 1861–1934, Microfilm Publication T288. This index is on microfilm rolls that are available at the National Archives regional branches. The pension application to which this index applies relates chiefly to army, navy, and Marine Corps service performed between 1861 and 1916. Most of the records relate to Civil War service; some relate to earlier service by Civil War veterans; others relate to service in the Spanish-American War, the Philippine Insurrection, the Boxer Rebellion, and the Regular Establishment. There are no federal pension records for service in Confederate forces. Links or contact information for Confederate pension records are located in the discussion of Civil War records.

Each card in the general index gives a veteran's name, rank, unit, and term of service; names of dependent(s); the filing date; the application number; the certificate number; and the state from which the claim was filed. The darker cards relate to naval service. The index is arranged alphabetically. The National Archives has a list of the microfilm roll numbers online at http://www.nara.gov/genealogy/t288.html. Researchers can contact the regional office closest to their location to conduct this research. Using the information from the index card, a researcher can now order copies of the veteran's military and pension records directly from the National Archives in Washington, D.C. The pension records contain more useful genealogical information than the military records. The military records generally contain copies of the muster roll cards for the military unit, enlistment papers, and a physical description of the soldier. In some cases, they also contain discharge papers. If the researcher locates the veteran's surname in the General Pension index, the researcher can then order the pension from the National Archives.

Paper copies of military service and pension records can be ordered by mail from the facility that holds the records—either the National Archives Building in Washington, D.C., or the National Personnel Records Center in St. Louis, Missouri. To order military service records from 1775–circa 1916, use NATF Form 86. For military records from circa 1917–present, use Standard Form 180. For military pension records, use NATF Form 85. For more information about these records and instructions for ordering them, see the information about military records on NARA's genealogy page at http://www.nara.gov/genealogy/.

To order NATF Forms 85 and 86, contact the National Archives and Records Administration in writing. Provide your name and mailing address and specify the number of forms you are requesting. There is a limit of five per request. Send requests to:

National Archives and Records Administration
Attn: NWCTB
700 Pennsylvania Avenue, NW
Washington, D.C. 20408-0001
inquire@nara.gov

Requests for Standard Form 180 should be sent to:

National Personnel Records Center
9700 Page Avenue
St. Louis, Missouri 63132
Available online at http://www.nara.gov/research/ordering/ordrfrms.html.

These forms may also be available at your local library and/or Department of Veterans Affairs office. Access to Military Service Records is limited. See Services for Veterans, Next-of-Kin, or the Veteran's Representative for more information at http://www.nara.gov/regional/mprpub1a.html. Individual states may also have additional access policies for veteran service records. Please consult the individual State Department of Veterans Affairs for those specific policies.

The National Personnel Records Center, Military Personnel Records [NPRC (MPR)] in St. Louis, Missouri, experienced a fire on July 12, 1973, that destroyed approximately 16–18 million Official Military Personnel Files. The affected record collections are described below.

Army Personnel discharged November 1, 1912, to
 January 1, 1960
Air Force Personnel discharged September 25, 1947,
 to January 1, 1964 (with names alphabetically
 after Hubbard, James E.)

There were no duplicate or microfilm copies of the destroyed records; nor were any indexes created prior to the fire. In addition, millions of documents had been in the possession of the Department of Veterans Affairs before the fire occurred. Therefore, a complete list of lost records is not available. Consequently, the NPRC (MPR) uses alternate sources in its efforts to reconstruct basic service information to respond to requests. Those alternate sources include personnel records such as final pay vouchers. These records provide name, service number, dates of service, and character of service. NPRC (MPR) personnel can usually verify military service and provide a Certification of Military Service. This Certification can be used for any purpose for which the original discharge document was used, including the application for veteran's benefits. Other alternate records consulted include medical records. More information is available at http://www.nara.gov/regional/mpralts.html.

The NPRC (MPR) is the repository of millions of military personnel, health, and medical records of discharged and deceased veterans of all services during the twentieth century. NPRC (MPR) also stores medical treatment records of retirees from all services and records for dependents and other persons treated at naval medical facilities. Access to these records is made available upon written request (with signature and date) to the extent allowed by law. This site is provided for those seeking information regarding military personnel, health, and medical records stored at NPRC (MPR). Requests are made using a Standard Form 180. It includes complete instructions for preparing and submitting requests. The link to these records is http://www.nara.gov/regional/mprmpm. html.

Requests utilizing NATF 85 and 86 generally take about 8 weeks; however, orders for the full pension files take 12 to 16 weeks. If you have not received your order in a reasonable response time, you can e-mail orderstatus@nara.gov or call NARA customer service at 1-800-234-8861.

Additional online information on the National Archives and military records are available at the following links.

http://www.archives.gov/publications/prologue/fall_
   2002_military_records_overview.html
http://www.archives.gov/research_room/genealogy/
   research_topics/military.html
http://www.archives.gov/research_room/research_
   topics/world_war_ii_records.html

ARCHIVAL COLLECTIONS FOR U.S. MILITARY BRANCHES

Air Force

Air Force Historical Research Agency
600 Chennault Circle
Maxwell AFB, AL 36112-6424
(334) 953-2396
http://www.au.af.mil/au/afhra/

Includes unit histories, history of the air force, Missing in Action reports, and individual air force service through various archival media, including oral histories.

United States Air Force Museum
1100 Spaatz St.
Wright-Patterson AFB, OH 45433
(937) 255-3286
http://www.wpafb.af.mil/museum/

Army

United States Army Military History Institute
http://carlisle-www.army.mil/usamhi/

Institute of Heraldry
http://www.perscom.army.mil/tagd/tioh/tioh.htm

United States Army Quartermaster Museum
http://www.qmmuseum.lee.army.mil/index.html

Coast Guard
http://www.uscg.mil/hq/g-cp/history/collect.html

Marines
http://www.usmc.mil/info.nsf/info

National Guard (various states)

Museum of the Kansas National Guard
http://skyways.lib.ks.us/museums/kng/

Massachusetts National Guard Museum
http://www.state.ma.us/guard/museum/museum.htm

Oklahoma National Guard
http://www.45thdivisionmuseum.com/

Wisconsin National Guard
http://www.volkfield.ang.af.mil/doc/museum1.htm

Navy

Department of the Navy
Naval Historical Center
http://www.history.navy.mil/

Naval Academy
http://www.nadn.navy.mil/Library/Spec_col.htm

OTHER U.S. MILITARY RESOURCES

Department of Defense
Directorate for Information Operations and Reports
Statistical Information Analysis Division-Personnel
http://web1.whs.osd.mil/mmid/mmidhome.htm

Statistical data related to military personnel and civilian work force information.

Selective Service Records
http://www.sss.gov/records.htm

The Selective Service System provides information from records kept on men currently registered with Selective Service, as well as on men who were registrants as far back as World War I. The agency follows the stipulations of the Privacy Act and will not release a registrant's home address, phone number, social security number, or any other protected information without the express consent of the registrant.

Military Awards Branch
http://www.perscom.army.mil/tagd/awards/index.htm

Federal Research Department
http://lcweb2.loc.gov/frd/tfrquery.html

The U.S.-Russia Joint Commission on POW/MIAs was established in March 1992 under the direction of the presidents of the United States and the Russian Federation. The Commission serves as a forum through which both nations seek to determine the fate of their missing servicemen.

http://lcweb2.loc.gov/pow/powhome.html

Database assists researchers interested in investigating government documents pertaining to U.S. military personnel listed as unaccounted for as of December 1991.

American Battle Monuments Commission
http://www.abmc.gov/

The American Battle Monuments Commission is an independent agency of the executive branch of the federal government. This commission is responsible for commemorating the service of the American armed forces where they have served since April 6, 1917 (the date of U.S. entry into World War I), through the establishment of suitable memorial shrines. The commission is also responsible for designing, constructing, operating, and maintaining permanent American military burial grounds in foreign countries. The commission also oversees the design and construction of U.S. military monuments and markers in foreign countries by U.S. citizens and organizations, both public and private, and encourages the maintenance of such monuments and markers by their sponsors.

Archdiocese of Military Services, USA
http://www.milarch.org/

Sacramental records for military service personnel.

INDIVIDUAL STATES

Military records at the state level vary with regard to content; however, by and large the records include those of the Adjutant General and the State Militia (National Guard), draft records, and records related to veteran organizations and the State Department of Veterans Affairs. In this part of the chapter, researchers will find individual state historical record repositories and specific resources related to the military history of the state. The resources vary in their depth of description and online access through finding aids. Usually records are arranged chronologically by war beginning with the Revolutionary War (where applicable) through the present.

Alabama

Alabama Department of Archives & History
624 Washington Avenue
Montgomery, Alabama 36130-0100
 (334) 242-4435
dpendlet@archives.state.al.us
http://www.archives.state.al.us/referenc/military.html

Alaska

Alaska State Archives
141 Willoughby Avenue
Juneau, Alaska 99801
http://www.archives.state.ak.us/

Arizona

Arizona Library, Archives and Public Records
1700 West Washington, Suite 200
Phoenix, Arizona 85007
(602) 542-4035
services@lib.az.us
http://www.dlapr.lib.az.us/

Arkansas

Arkansas History Commission
One Capitol Mall
Little Rock, Arkansas 72201
501-682-6900
http://www.ark-ives.com/selected_materials/index.php#mil/

California

California Military Museum
1119 Second Street
Sacramento, California 95814
(916) 442-2883
http://www.militarymuseum.org/History.html

Colorado

Colorado State Archives
1313 Sherman Street, Room 1B-20
Denver, Colorado 80203
(303) 866-2358 or (303) 866-2390
http://www.archives.state.co.us/military.html

Connecticut

Connecticut Historical Society
One Elizabeth Street at Asylum Avenue
Hartford, Connecticut 06105
(860) 236-5621
ask_us@chs.org
http://www.chs.org/

Connecticut State Library
231 Capitol Avenue

Hartford, Connecticut 06106
860-757-6500
http://www.cslib.org/collections.htm

Florida

http://dlis.dos.state.fl.us/barm/fsa.html
http://dlis.dos.state.fl.us/barm/PensionFiles.html
http://dlis.dos.state.fl.us/barm/fsa/civilwar.htm

Georgia

http://www.sos.state.ga.us/archives/

Georgia State Archives of Military Records

http://www.sos.state.ga.us/archives/rs/military.htm

Idaho

http://www.idahohistory.net/research.html

Illinois

http://www.sos.state.il.us/departments/archives/databases.html

Indiana

http://www.in.gov/icpr/archives/family/fam.html#MS/

Iowa

http://www.iowahistory.org/archives/research_collections/
state_gov_records/state_government_records.html#
Military/

Kentucky

http://www.kdla.state.ky.us/arch/civil.htm

Louisiana

http://www.sec.state.la.us/archives/archives/
archives-index.htm#research/

Tulane Military Archives
http://www.tulane.edu/~lmiller/Military.html#
TheWorldWars/

Maine

http://www.state.me.us/sos/arc/archives/military/
military.htm

Maine—Civil War

http://www.state.me.us/sos/arc/archives/military/civilwar/
civilwar.htm

Maine-Revolutionary War

http://www.state.me.us/sos/arc/archives/military/revlist.
htm

Maryland Archives

http://www.mdarchives.state.md.us/megafile/msa/speccol/
sc2900/sc2908/html/

Massachusetts

http://www.state.ma.us/sec/arc/arccol/colidx.htm

Minnesota

http://www.mnhs.org/library/Christie/intropage.html

Mississippi

http://www.mdah.state.ms.us/

Montana

http://www.his.state.mt.us/Default.asp/

Nebraska

http://www.nebraskahistory.org/index.htm

New Hampshire

http://www.state.nh.us/state/

New Jersey

http://www.state.nj.us/state/darm/index.html

New York Military Archives

http://www.nysl.nysed.gov/genealogy/miliante.htm

North Carolina

http://www.ah.dcr.state.nc.us/sections/archives/arch/
military.htm

North Dakota

http://www.state.nd.us/hist/sal/gen/infmilitary.htm

Ohio

http://www.ohiohistory.org/resource/archlib/index.html

Crile Archives
http://www.crile-archives.org/

The Crile Archives began as a student project in
1994 as part of the 50th commemoration of WW II.

Both the archive and the college were designated as a "Commemorative Community" by the Department of Defense in 1995. The Crile Archives is a repository of twentieth-century military history. It contains documents, artifacts, and oral histories of veterans of WW I, WW II, the Korean War, and the Vietnam War. The most recent additions are a POW archive, Nurses, and African American veterans. Crile Hospital was in continuous service from 1944 until 1964.

Oregon

http://arcweb.sos.state.or.us/milit.html
http://arcweb.sos.state.or.us/state/mil/milhome.htm

South Carolina

http://www.state.sc.us/scdah/homepage.htm

South Dakota

http://www.sdhistory.org/arc_gen.htm

Tennessee

http://www.state.tn.us/sos/statelib/techsvs/collections.htm
http://www.state.tn.us/sos/statelib/pubsvs/intro.htm#
military_records/
http://www.state.tn.us/sos/statelib/pubsvs/intro.htm#menu/

Utah State Archives

http://www.archives.state.ut.us/referenc/military.htm

Vermont

http://vermont-archives.org/genealogy/gene.html

Virginia Military Institute

http://www4.vmi.edu/museum/

Wisconsin

Wisconsin Historical Society
http://www.shsw.wisc.edu/

Wisconsin Veterans Museum
http://museum.dva.state.wi.us/

Wyoming

http://wyoarchives.state.wy.us/

CIVIL WAR RESOURCES

Civil War Military Records at the National Archives

http://www.misscivilwar.org/resources/bib-comp.html

Civil War Soldiers and Sailors System
http://www.itd.nps.gov/cwss/index.html

The Civil War Soldiers and Sailors System is a computerized database containing very basic facts about servicemen who served on both sides during the Civil War. The initial focus of the CWSS is the *Names Index Project,* a project to enter names and other basic information from 5.4 million soldier records in the National Archives. The facts about the soldiers are being entered from records that are indexed to many millions of other documents about Union and Confederate Civil War soldiers maintained by the National Archives and Records Administration.

Other information will include: histories of regiments in both the Union and Confederate armies, links to descriptions of 384 significant battles of the war, and other historical information. Additional information about soldiers, sailors, regiments, and battles, as well as prisoner-of-war records and cemetery records, will be added over time.

The Civil War Soldiers and Sailors System (CWSS) is a cooperative effort by the National Park Service (NPS) and several other public and private partners to computerize information about the Civil War. The goal of the CWSS is to increase the American people's understanding of this decisive era in American history by making information about it widely accessible. The CWSS will enable the public to make a personal link between themselves and history.

Confederate Army Records at South Carolina
http://www.state.sc.us/scdah/confedrc.htm

Duke Special Collections on the Civil War
http://scriptorium.lib.duke.edu/pathfinders/civil-war/

Confederate Pension Rolls, Veterans and Widows
http://image.vtls.com/collections/CW.html
http://www.lva.lib.va.us/whatwehave/index.htm

Pension acts were passed by the General Assembly in 1888, 1900, and between 1902 and 1934. The act of 1888 provided pensions to Confederate soldiers, sailors, and marines disabled in action and to the widows of those killed in action. Later acts broadened the coverage to include all veterans, their widows, and their unmarried or widowed daughters. Pension applications filed by sisters and daughters are not indexed. This collection consists of approved pension applications and amended applications filed by resident Virginia Confederate veterans and their widows. The applications contain statements pertaining to the service record of the applicants and may include medical evaluations, information about the income and property of the veterans or their widows, and, in the case of widows, the date and place of marriages.

Official Records of the Union and Confederate Armies
http://cdl.library.cornell.edu/moa/browse.monographs/waro.html

New York Historical Society—Civil War document
http://lcweb2.loc.gov/ammem/ndlpcoop/nhihtml/cwnyhshome.html

Papers of Jefferson Davis
http://www.ruf.rice.edu/~pjdavis/jdp.htm

The Papers of Jefferson Davis documentary editing project, based at Rice University in Houston, Texas, is publishing a multivolume edition of his letters and speeches, several of which can be found on this Web site. The page also has extensive information on Davis and his family and numerous photographs.

Civil War Maps
http://lcweb2.loc.gov/ammem/gmdhtml/cwmhtml/

Confederate Army Records
http://www.state.sc.us/scdah/confedrc.htm

WORLD WAR I

Doughboy Center
http://www.worldwar1.com/dbc/dbc2.htm

WORLD WAR II

National Archives and Records Administration
http://www.archives.gov/research_room/research_topics/world_war_ii_records.html

Southern Methodist University World War II Digital Collection
http://worldwar2.smu.edu/

Combat Artists of World War II
http://www.pbs.org/theydrewfire/index.html

Cold War Archives—Library of Congress
http://www.loc.gov/loc/lcib/0010/coldwar.html

KOREAN WAR

Truman Presidential Library and Museum
http://www.trumanlibrary.org/whistlestop/study_collections/korea/large/

State Casualty Lists
http://www.nara.gov/nara/electronic/kcasal.html

VIETNAM RESOURCES ONLINE

State Casualty Lists
http://www.nara.gov/nara/electronic/vcasal.html

The Virtual Wall
http://www.thevirtualwall.org/

PERSIAN GULF WAR

PBS-Oral History Project
http://www.pbs.org/wgbh/pages/frontline/gulf/

MAPS

United States Military Academy—Department of History
http://www.dean.usma.edu/history/dhistorymaps/MapsHome.htm

ORAL HISTORY COLLECTIONS

Naval Institute Oral History
http://www.usni.org/hrp/oralhist.html

Rutgers Oral History Archives of WW II Collection
http://fas-history.rutgers.edu/oralhistory/orlhom.htm

Vietnam Oral History
http://www.vietnam.ttu.edu/oralhistory/

An Oral History of Rhode Island Women during World War II
http://www.stg.brown.edu/projects/WWII_Women/tocCS.html

PHOTOGRAPHS

Civil War Photographs
http://memory.loc.gov/ammem/cwphtml/cwphome.html

Buffalo Soldiers
http://www.coax.net/people/lwf/portrait.htm

Dickey Chapelle
http://www.shsw.wisc.edu/archives/vismat/war.html

Edward Steichen—Naval photographs
http://www.nadn.navy.mil/Library/Spec_col.htm

VETERANS

Grand Army of the Republic
http://pages.prodigy.net/mistergar/garhp.htm

Veterans History Project
http://www.loc.gov/folklife/vets/

WAR POSTER COLLECTION

Washington
http://content.lib.washington.edu/warposters/

Northwestern University—World War II Poster Collection
http://www.library.northwestern.edu/govpub/collections/
wwii-posters/

OTHER MILITARY ONLINE ARCHIVES OF NOTE:

The War Times Journal
http://www.wtj.com/

Includes personal memoirs of General Ulysses S. Grant and General William Tecumseh Sherman.

MILITARY RESOURCES

MERLN
http://merln.ndu.edu/

Documents in Military History
http://www.hillsdale.edu/dept/History/Documents/War/
index.htm

Index

About the Contributors

Russell P. Baker, CA, is archival manager and deputy director of the Arkansas History Commission and State Archives in Little Rock, Arkansas. He has been a professional archivist since 1970 and a longtime member of the Society of American Archivists. He is widely known for his lectures on genealogy and family history research methods and problem solving. He is a life member of the Arkansas Genealogical Society and is immediate past president of that organization. He has been a certified archivist since 1989 and has taught U.S. and world history at the college level for several years. He is the author of a number of books, pamphlets, and articles on southern family and religious history. He conducted pre-conference workshops in genealogical research at Society of American Archivists sessions in 2001 and 2002.

Carrie Bohman is the Reference and Outreach Archivist at the Wisconsin Veterans Museum in Madison, Wisconsin, since December 2001. She holds a master's in library science from the University of Wisconsin–Madison, a master's in education and professional development from the University of Wisconsin–La Crosse, and a bachelor's degree from the University of Wisconsin–Madison, where her major was history and political science. Bohman was previously the Assistant Archivist for the Diocese of Madison from April 1997 to April 2001. During that time, she assisted with the editing of the Thesaurus for Catholic Diocesan Terms, published by the Association of Catholic Diocesan Archivists in August 2000.

Elisabeth Buehlman is a records manager with the biotech company Serono International S.A. and an associate professor in the information management department at the University of Geneva, Switzerland. She holds a master's degree in history of science and business history, as well as degrees in records management.

Wendy Chmielewski is the George R. Cooley Curator of the Swarthmore College Peace Collection, a position she has held since 1988. She holds a Ph.D. in women's history from the State University of New York at Binghamton. Dr. Chmielewski has published on the role of women in the peace movement and in utopian communities. She is currently the president of the Peace History Society.

Alan Delozier is an assistant professor, university archivist, and reference librarian at Seton Hall University in South Orange, New Jersey, a position he has held since 2000. He holds a B.A. in mass communication with a minor in theology from St. Bonaventure University, an M.A. in history from Villanova University, and a master of library science degree from Rutgers, The State University of New Jersey. He is currently chair of the New Jersey Caucus of the Mid-Atlantic Regional Archives Conference, vice president of the New Jersey Library Association History and Preservation Section, and member of the New Jersey Catholic Historical Records Commission.

Jackie R. Esposito is university archivist and associate librarian at Penn State University. She is currently working on a Ph.D. in higher education. She holds a master's degree from St. John's University and a bachelor's from St. Joseph's College. She joined the faculty of the University Libraries in July 1991 as assistant university archivist for records management/senior assistant librarian. Her appointment to the faculty followed five years of service with the University Archives in a variety of positions, including project archivist for the Pennsylvania Historical and Museum Commission re-grant that precipitated the creation of a records management program at Penn State. In addition to her duties as university archivist, Jackie Esposito is responsible for the development and day-to-day management of the Sports Archives and the Audio-Visual Archives collections. The Sports Archives, a joint project involving the University Libraries and Intercollegiate Athletics, encompasses more than 7,000 football and sport films and videotapes, as well as over 500 cubic feet (100,000 items) of biographical data on athletes, media guides, press kits, coaches' papers, photographs, and historical records for special events. Among her publications are *The Nittany Lion: An Il-*

lustrated Tale and *A Procedure Manual: A Guide to Managing an Institutional Archive Utilizing Process Flow Charts.*

Steven Fisher is an associate professor and curator of special collections at the University of Denver, a position he has held since 1981. He holds an M.A. in history and a master of library science degree, both from Case Western Reserve University. He is past president of the Society of Rocky Mountain Archivists and the Colorado Preservation Alliance. He currently teaches archival courses in the library and information services program at the University of Denver.

Gregory S. Hunter is a professor in the Palmer School of Library and Information Science, Long Island University. He also is president of his own consulting firm, Hunter Information Management Services, Inc. He earned a doctorate in American history at New York University and is both a certified archivist and a certified records manager. In 1989, Dr. Hunter was elected the first president of the Academy of Certified Archivists. He is the author of five books, including *Developing and Maintaining Practical Archives* (1997) and the award-winning *Preserving Digital Information* (2000). He is a frequent author and lecturer on archives, records management, electronic imaging systems, electronic records, and organizational change issues.

Tammi Moe has a bachelor of arts with an emphasis in art history from the University of Colorado at Denver and a master's in library science with an emphasis in archiving from the University of Denver. Tammi works as a contractor in the State of Colorado doing research for and about libraries. She co-authored "Colorado Public Libraries and the Digital Divide 2002" for the Colorado State Library and is involved in research for the Colorado Digitization Program concerning the use and impact of digital collections and the use of primary source materials in the classroom. Tammi is the current Webmaster for the Library Research Service http://www.lrs.org/ and author of

the Online Preservation Handbook http://www.re-evolve.net/. She belongs to the Society of American Archivists, Colorado Association of Libraries, Art Libraries Society of North America, and the Visual Resource Association.

Faye Phillips is associate dean of libraries for special collections at Louisiana State University, a position she has held since 1995. She has been with the LSU Libraries Special Collections since 1986. She holds B.A. and M.A. degrees in history from Georgia State University and an M.L.S. from the University of North Carolina at Chapel Hill. She is past president of the Society of Southwest Archivists, the Louisiana Archives and Manuscripts Association, and the Society of Georgia Archivists. She is the author of *Congressional Papers Management* (1996).

Willem Rodenhuis is the reference librarian for the performing arts (clustering musicology, film and television studies, and theatre studies) at the University of Amsterdam. He holds a B.A. in history from the University of Utrecht and an M.A. in theatre studies from the University of Amsterdam. From 1996 to 2000 he served two terms as secretary-general of SIBMAS, the International Association of Libraries and Museums of the Performing Arts. He teaches library courses on a regular basis at the University of Amsterdam.

Dwight Swanson is an archivist at Northeast Historic Film. He received a B.A. in history from the University of Colorado and an M.A. in American studies from the University of Maryland, with an emphasis on film and material culture. Following graduation from the L. Jeffrey Selznick School of Film Preservation at the George Eastman House, he served as archivist at the Alaska Moving Image Preservation Association. He is a co-author of a Web site on home film preservation and the creator and moderator of Smallgauge, the amateur film Listserv. His publications and research have focused primarily on early amateur film and itinerant filmmaking.